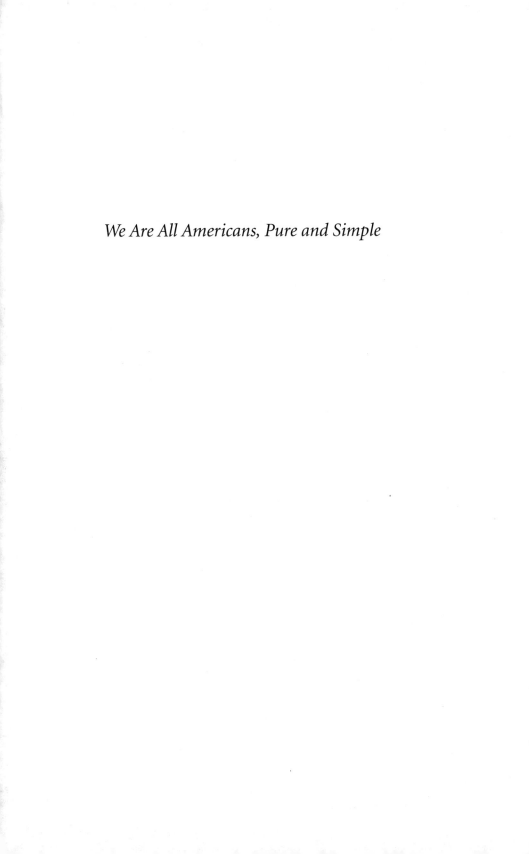

We Are All Americans, Pure and Simple

We Are All Americans, Pure and Simple

~

Theodore Roosevelt
and
the Myth of Americanism

Leroy G. Dorsey

THE UNIVERSITY OF ALABAMA PRESS
Tuscaloosa

Copyright © 2007
The University of Alabama Press
Tuscaloosa, Alabama 35487-0380
All rights reserved
Manufactured in the United States of America

Typeface: Minion

∞

The paper on which this book is printed meets the minimum requirements of
American National Standard for Information Sciences-Permanence of Paper for
Printed Library Materials, ANSI Z39.48-1984.

Library of Congress Cataloging-in-Publication Data

Dorsey, Leroy G., 1959–
We are all Americans, pure and simple : Theodore Roosevelt and the myth of
Americanism/ Leroy G. Dorsey.
p. cm.
Includes bibliographical references and index.
ISBN-13: 978-0-8173-1592-4 (cloth : alk. paper)
ISBN-10: 0-8173-1592-6 (cloth : alk. paper) 1. Roosevelt, Theodore, 1858–1919—Political
and social views. 2. Rhetoric—Political aspects—History—19th century. 3. Rhetoric—
Political aspects—History—20th century. 4. National characteristics, American.
5. Americanization—History. 6. Immigrants—United States—History. 7. Indians of
North America—Cultural assimilation—History. 8. African Americans—Cultural
assimilation—History. 9. United States—Race relations—Political aspects. 10. United
States—Ethnic relations—Political aspects. I. Title.
E757.D67 2007
973.91′1092—dc22
[B]

2007016102

For Alicia and Adam

Contents

~

Preface

My introduction to issues related to race, ethnicity, and identity occurred before I realized such things mattered. When I was eleven years old in 1970, and living in Berkeley, California, I knew a man named "Pop," an elderly Japanese American grocery store owner. I went to his corner store regularly to read the comic books and to visit with him. One day I noticed what seemed to be an official looking, weather-beaten sign partially hidden behind the counter. It said something about Japanese evacuation. I asked Pop what that meant and he explained that during World War II, he and thousands of other Japanese Americans lost their homes, businesses, and freedom when the government re-located them to internment camps. I asked him why that happened and he said that people did not think he was an American after the bombing at Pearl Harbor. I said, "But you were an American." Pop slowly shrugged his shoulders and said, "I guess I wasn't enough of one." Though we were of different races, it never occurred to me that others might not consider him an American. I thought we were all Americans. Pop was not the only one to tell me such things. My father also understood the burden American identity placed on some people.

From my youth, I can remember my father's daily advice. I can still hear him say, "You've got to work twice as hard as anyone else." For years, I just followed his advice, not really thinking about the underlying message in his mantra. Once I got to my rebellious teenage years, though, I asked him why I had to work twice as hard. He responded, "Because you're black and that's what you have to do to be considered just as good." He spoke as if he had just revealed an eternal truth. He spoke, not in anger, but in a matter-of-fact, resigned tone. It was then I realized my father had been working twice as hard as anyone else had. He had worked long shifts in a dangerous industrial job, and he was always painting houses, cutting lawns, and taking any odd jobs he could find. Years later at his funeral, my mother remarked, "He worked himself to death."

I did not realize it early on, but Pop and my father were teaching my first lessons in what it means to be an American. Both men were simply passing on the messages that permeate the culture, messages made explicit by one of the most controversial figures of the twentieth century, Theodore Roosevelt. In his own way, Roosevelt acted as a broker of national identity, one who used rhetoric to mediate the cultural, racial, and ethnic tensions of his day. For good and ill, his public discourse influenced the meaning of identity for those he and the nation considered outsiders. His rhetorical career on the public stage centered on the question asked often today about racial and ethnic "others," legal or otherwise: "What does it mean to be an American?"

Roosevelt answered that question by telling a story—a myth—that made American ideals appear timeless, natural, and available to anyone. He created a mythic reality in order to discuss the "real," contentious issues surrounding race relations, and to provide lessons for "outsiders" to understand the extent to which they could "fit into" the nation's identity. Paradoxically, he used a mythic rhetoric that was, much of the time, racist and xenophobic, to provide solace to nonwhites and immigrants in their struggle for identity, and to transport everyone to an idealized world where equality might be realized, in promise if not in practice.

This book, then, is an attempt to explain that paradox. It examines the mythic power of Roosevelt's public rhetoric, a rhetoric about race, ethnicity, and national identity that continues to influence the contemporary debates about such matters. For me, though, the motivation was more personal: I needed a way to understand why people like Pop and my father endured as much as they did to "become Americans."

Acknowledgments

～

I want to thank a legion of people for their assistance in the development of this project. Okay, maybe not a legion in the Spartacus sense of the word, but I would like to express my gratitude by mentioning some of the people and institutions that supported my work. The Department of Communication at Texas A&M University (TAMU) deserves mention for its steadfast encouragement as I labored over this project. I am particularly grateful to the following colleagues: Barbara Sharf for her insight on narratives and myths; Jim Aune and Eric Rothenbuhler for reading several early chapters and giving me the benefit of their wisdom; and special thanks to Randy Sumpter for his courage in reading the whole manuscript and for providing me with wonderful feedback. I also appreciate the departmental staff—Gilda John, Sandy Maldonado, Kristen Baker, and Katy Head—for their much-asked and well-meaning question, "When will the book be done so you can talk to us again?" I am thankful that Susan Dummer, a doctoral student in our program and now an assistant professor at Georgetown College, kept "her finger on the pulse of Hollywood" and kept me updated about pop culture. Special thanks go to Mary Haman, now at Penn State pursuing her doctorate, who was, by far, one of the best research assistants I have ever had. I would also like to thank the TAMU College of Liberal Arts for its financial support of my project, and I particularly appreciate the personal support of both Dean Charles Johnson and Associate Dean Larry Oliver. I also appreciate gaining insight on Theodore Roosevelt from H. W. Brands, now at the University of Texas, Austin. My warmest thanks go to Miriam Aune for her diligence in proofreading the manuscript; I am indebted to her.

As with most books, this one began years earlier while I was working on another project. Rachel L. Harlow and I wrote the article "'We Want Americans Pure and Simple': Theodore Roosevelt and the Myth of Americanism." This work originally appeared in *Rhetoric & Public Affairs,* Vol. 6, No. 1, 2003, published by Michigan State University Press. I am grateful to the editor of that journal, Martin J. Medhurst. That article serves as the basis for chapter 2, with parts of it also appearing in chapter 3. Some excerpts from Roosevelt's discourse come from the *Theodore Roosevelt Collection,* Harvard College Library; their use is by permission of the Houghton Library, Harvard University. Wallace F. Dailey, curator of the *Theodore Roosevelt Collection,* provided invaluable help. I would also like to thank J. Michael Hogan, now at Penn State University, who pointed me toward T. R. over fifteen years ago during my studies at Indiana University.

The staff at The University of Alabama Press provided me with calm assuredness and made the publishing process enjoyable. I also want to thank the anonymous reviewers that the press commissioned—their insights were both helpful and heartening. Of course, I take full responsibility for any errors contained in this work.

Finally, I want to thank friends and family for providing me the support to stay focused, and for ensuring that I still got a chance to play occasionally. In that regard, Bill and Tina Morelli are true friends and hard-fought "Scene It" competitors. My wife, Alicia, and my son, Adam, kept me going with their love and concern. And while my mother passed away while I was working on this project, I know what she would say if she were still here: "I don't really know what you do with that rhetoric stuff, but I know I'm proud you're doing it."

We Are All Americans, Pure and Simple

Introduction

Theodore Roosevelt and American Identity

Theodore Roosevelt was a larger-than-life character, a virtual Progressive Era action hero.[1] Throughout his life, his ultra-masculine public persona took on many forms. He was a cowboy who stalked horse thieves on the Bad Lands;[2] an "untouchable" and corruption-fighting New York City police commissioner;[3] a Rough Rider who charged into the Spanish-American War;[4] a "bully" chief executive who spoke softly, carried a "big stick," and swung it quite loudly on the national and international stages;[5] and a big gamesman who traveled the world looking for adventure.[6] His colorful feats, many of which he himself popularized, have made him into a veritable cottage industry for scholars, popular writers, and creative artists. Two new Hollywood films represent Roosevelt as character and as caricature: *The Rise of Theodore Roosevelt* (in development) is a serious biography to be directed by Martin Scorsese and to star Leonardo DiCaprio; *Night at the Museum* is an imaginative comedy during which exhibits in a museum come to life and unleash a Neanderthal, Attila the Hun, and Robin Williams as Roosevelt. Even Bugs Bunny was made to don the push-broom mustache and round pince-nez glasses as he campaigned for political office against Yosemite Sam.[7]

More than his cinematic representations, Roosevelt's popularity with contemporary politicos warrants attention to his discourse. Interestingly, both liberals and conservatives today find a use for Roosevelt. Pundits invoke Roosevelt's

"America first" rhetoric to justify George W. Bush's attempt to Americanize Iraq and reshape its national identity.[8] John Judis, senior editor for the *New Republic*, chastises President Bush for ignoring the lessons offered by the bully president on American idealism and identity in relation to the current war on terror.[9] The political theorist William Mansfield affirms Roosevelt's emphasis on masculinity, bemoaning the fact that liberals "have delivered themselves . . . to the feminists" and have thus diminished the Rooseveltian significance that manliness is a pragmatic necessity for national progress.[10] From left or right, Roosevelt's rhetoric provides vital and significant touchstones in contemporary political discourse as well as in historical scholarship.

American identity was of paramount importance in Roosevelt's worldview, and he seemed eager to prohibit anyone he considered unworthy from having that distinction. According to Edmund Morris, Roosevelt spent most of his time condemning racial and ethnic "others" as "un-Americans."[11] He made more than a few derogatory statements about nonwhites and immigrants whom he believed were not physically or morally capable of being Americans. Thomas Dyer's exploration of Roosevelt's racial education reveals that Roosevelt demonstrated an "utter contempt" for American Indians as a "racial type." Roosevelt believed that their traits consigned them to an "inferior station" in white society, and African Americans fared no better. Roosevelt articulated the notion that a black person was "largely incapable of assuming the role of citizen." Dyer also notes that Roosevelt cast a wary eye toward various immigrant groups, particularly those that seemingly split their allegiance to the United States by hyphenating their citizenship.[12] Sarah Watts's psychological examination of Roosevelt's manic obsession with masculinity and "white racial purity" locates him among those people who swore that immigrants, Native Americans, and blacks were nothing more than primitive, ape-like creatures.[13] H. W. Brands concludes that Roosevelt preached a message of "no patience [and] no tolerance . . . for what a later generation would call multiculturalism."[14] Among his personae, Roosevelt's most controversial image is that of a xenophobic racist.[15]

As contemporary politicians recognize Roosevelt's attempts to negotiate national identity, some echo his harsher messages regarding immigrants and nonwhites, promoting ideas that these "others" fail outright as citizens, or that they pose a threat to national culture.[16] Congressional representative Tom Tancredo declared recently that the millions of illegal aliens living in America are a "scourge that threatens the very future of our nation," lamenting generally the possibility of pro-immigration voices fostering a "cult of multiculturalism" and transforming America into a modern "Tower of Babel."[17] And with people like former education secretary William Bennett espousing the theory that aborting

African American babies can reduce crime, various ideas that Roosevelt popularized have lived well beyond his death in 1919.[18]

While contemporary politicians and public advocates have no excuse for using such discourse in the twenty-first century, similar statements by Roosevelt reflect his coming of age at the turn of the twentieth century, a historical period of high racism and xenophobia.[19] Offensive to a contemporary American ear, his bigoted dialogues and diatribes regarding immigrants and nonwhites may be reason enough for scholars to avoid their examination; Roosevelt's relations with immigrants and nonwhites have warranted little more than perfunctory coverage in his biographies.[20] When scholars do address such topics, they tend to mine Roosevelt's private writing rather than his public discourse, as his private musings leaned to the more insensitive racial epithets.[21] His public discourse, so full of discussion of American identity and the pretenders to it, can appear to be so obviously calculated that most dismiss it as disingenuous and signifying only "sound and fury."[22] While those private letters might reveal Roosevelt's true feelings, neglecting his public rhetoric for its purported self-serving nature denies its significance as evidence of his life-long public campaign to create a stable society among the citizenry. He recognized that nativists, those who believed only American-born whites were worthy of citizenship, unfairly targeted many nonwhite and immigrant groups, and that such divisiveness threatened the nation's stability.

Roosevelt was a product of his time, sometimes engaging in a form of virulent nativist discourse that people today might find distasteful. Any solution he offered to the identity crisis at the turn of the twentieth century maintained white privilege at the expense of true cultural diversity. However, he also believed in an orderly nation, and he possessed a near-legendary sense of right and wrong; these beliefs competed with, but did not conquer, his often mean-spirited attitude.[23] No public topic appeared to be more important to Roosevelt than national identity, as he believed too many different types of people were attempting to carve a distinctive place in the cultural hierarchy. He worried that the American identity might be lost amid a "tangle of squabbling nationalities, an intricate knot of German-Americans, Irish-Americans" and any other group of hyphenated Americans "each preserving its separate nationality."[24] To protect American identity and to prevent social chaos, Roosevelt took on a seemingly impossible task: he would bring race, ethnicity, and citizenship into the spotlight of public discourse, and he would offer all of these diverse groups the opportunity to see themselves and one another as "Americans pure and simple."[25] Dyer notes that "because of his enormous popularity [Roosevelt] became the most effective racial educator of all," helping to "set the tone for the American understanding" of race and national identity.[26] To that end, Roosevelt acted as a teacher helping his students answer what he considered to be the most pivotal question for the nation's destiny: "What does it mean to be an American?"

For Roosevelt, public rhetoric was an invaluable tool for the work he had selected for himself. He used words to create one American people out of many individuals. His public discourse, his speeches, published letters, books, and magazine articles communicated his philosophy of how immigrants and non-whites could become Americans. Roosevelt's reliance on both deed and word to shape the national community is evidence of what Donald Bryant calls "the rhetorical function." Discourse does not and cannot exist in a vacuum; public expression requires understanding of audience and adaptation of message to meet that audience. Thus, the function of rhetoric is that of "adjusting ideas to people and people to ideas."[27] Whatever the topic, Roosevelt's public rhetoric is replete with evidence that his messages were shaped by his knowledge of the audience he wanted to reach. Yet no one could accuse him of making his messages so palatable that they did consist only of "sound and fury." Roosevelt expressed acknowledgment of his audiences' demeanor as well as clarity in his message of how that demeanor must change.

This analysis of Roosevelt's public discourse falls within the tradition of rhetorical studies: it seeks to illuminate and to assess the argumentative and symbolic choices a speaker makes to persuade an audience about a particular topic within a particular context. Advocates, both public and private, attend to their situational opportunities and barriers, constantly forming and reforming rhetoric, hoping to find that combination of language and deeds to persuade others about matters great and small.[28] According to James White, understanding rhetoric means that we can understand the "ways in which character and community—and motive, value, reason, social structure, everything . . . that makes a culture—are defined and made real in performances of language." Far from the common conception that people use "mere rhetoric" to say meaningless things or to obfuscate the facts, rhetoric brings human ideals closer to reality. Or, as White reminds us, while the goal of "art is beauty," and the point of "philosophy truth," the "object of rhetoric is justice: the constitution of a social world."[29]

To Roosevelt, "real" citizens needed to embrace his concept of "Americanism," a belief that American identity revolved around a combination of physical strength, moral character, and the understanding that equality must be earned and not simply given. He promoted Americanism as the means to transform disparate groups of immigrants, nonwhites, and disgruntled nativists into "true" Americans. Given what he believed to be the real possibility of the nation descending into social chaos because of unresolved questions of American identity, he provided the national audience with a solution, an overarching vision of an America united within its borders and against its enemies.

To create his conception of a unified culture, Roosevelt discursively grounded Americanism and national identity in myth. Myth is a persistent story of extraordinary historical experiences and protagonists, real or fictive, which explain and empower a community's origin and sense of self.[30] A community's myth of origin promotes particular values—sacred principles—that distinguish it from other communities and justify its existence. Such dramatic stories and their protagonists provide historical lessons so that contemporary citizens can learn their proper roles in the community and prosper within it. When success is elusive, these mythic stories naturalize the contradictions of a community's practices, explaining the inequities and abuses by the community as part of the "natural" or inevitable flow of history. These dramatic interpretations of historical lessons, which rhetors use to explain the meaning of such things as politics, economic enterprise, civic responsibility, spirituality, war, ethics, and law, help to socialize the members of a society. They romanticize a community's values, philosophies, and sometimes drastic solutions to its fears, as they define individual and national identities. At the very least, myths become taken-for-granted, organizing narratives for why and how people should live their lives, revealing eternal truths for those who take them seriously.[31]

In his attempt to define American identity, Roosevelt focused on the Frontier Myth, a narrative that has informed America's beliefs and behaviors for over two centuries. This myth initially explained and justified the establishment of American colonies. As time passed, Richard Slotkin notes, the myth accounted for "our rapid economic growth, our emergence as a powerful nation-state, and our distinctively American approach to the socially and culturally disruptive processes of modernization."[32] The Frontier Myth framed frontier and Wild West protagonists as heroic archetypes who were responsible for the development of a democratic nation and who faced both human and environmental dangers in order to conquer the uncharted wilds of the North American continent. For example, the romanticized story of America's "conquest" of North America legitimized the abusive treatment of Native Americans. Although colonists were people of "the wilderness" too, they did not consider themselves "savages"; colonists evolved beyond their "savagery" through the establishment of their democratic institutions. American Indians, however, had not demonstrated a similar transformation despite centuries of contact with "civilized" immigrant settlers. Thus, new American citizens saw progress and civilization as the ends that justified the violent displacement and extinction of Native Americans.[33]

The nation's Frontier Myth, popularized in movies, television shows, speeches, artwork, and a host of other texts, has become a fundamental expression of what constitutes an American. It lauds the "rugged individualism" needed to survive on the frontier, but not at the expense of social order. For example, individualism, expressed in an immigrant's desire to keep his or her birth culture prominent, would have to give way, per the myth, to that person's new desire to identify with an American community that wanted to see itself as homogeneous.[34] In myth, Benedict Anderson observes, a community wants to imagine itself with a "deep, horizontal comradeship" regardless of the "actual inequality and exploitation" that certain groups suffer.[35] This mythic story provides guidelines for contemporary audiences to deal with their own crises in balancing individual identity and "comradeship." Rhetors offer a mythic story of America's historical origin, rife with conflicts against racial, ethnic, and indigenous others on an untamed frontier, as an inevitable and expected consequence of institutional democracy and freedom. These stories become what Lane Bruner would call a "strategy of remembrance." Such discourses not only help an audience to remember its origin as a community "based on rights, laws, and duties negotiated by a wide range of relatively well-informed citizens," but they also create a community "based on xenophobic patterns of identification," suppressing "important historical and political realities" in the process.[36] The grounding of contemporary behavior in a mythic retelling of history can create a compelling system of beliefs for listeners, as retelling often results in revision and reinterpretation of the familiar myth to suit the current crisis.

In constructing his version of events, Roosevelt revised America's mythic history from one in which white American-born characters strived and succeeded in spite of the efforts of expendable "others" to one that prominently featured immigrants and nonwhites in the title roles of heroes in America's archetypal narrative, giving them an exalted place heretofore unimagined. He constructed rhetorical opportunities for racial and ethnic others to prove the stability of American identity despite their "otherness." In doing so, he simultaneously promoted immigration and assimilation, and offered individual ability as a meaningful factor in national identity. Roosevelt's mythic treatment of Americanism provided opportunities for nonwhites and immigrants to strive for equality, refocused attention on the character traits of the individual, and gave everyone a foundational story that explained the fundamental requirements of becoming an American. While some believe that Roosevelt tossed only whites into the "melting pot," his mythic discourse promoted his version of a "rhetorical melting pot" that added immigrants, African Americans, and Native Americans to the national identity. His mythic rhetoric popularized "outsiders," identifying what these newly forged citizens brought to the nation's development, while assuring white audiences that they remained at the top of the social hierarchy. Roosevelt's retelling of the Frontier Myth does not go so far as to declare equality for all racial and ethnic groups; his rhetoric stands as a potent illustration of the necessary interaction between people and ideas.

Despite the seeming rehabilitation of his sometimes-racist demeanor, this study is no mere hagiographic portrait of Roosevelt. He was a product of his time, and he articulated as many or as few bigoted attitudes as did his contemporaries. Students of rhetoric should not dismiss his public discourse about race, ethnicity, and identity because he was not as enlightened as hindsight would ask him to be. His rhetorical solutions to the identity crisis in the nation undoubtedly maintained white privilege at the expense of a real conception of racial and ethnic diversity. His public rhetoric appeared odious and unnecessarily cruel at times, affirming the worst stereotypes of immigrants and nonwhites whose only sin was that Anglo-Saxon whites considered them different and inferior. As an African American myself, I have wondered on more than one occasion why I would subject myself or any student of rhetoric to his discourse. Despite the harshness of his rhetoric, his mythic framing of race and ethnicity did provide a critical element for the construction of American identity. Racial inequality and injustice are part of America's development; refusing to examine historical public discourse cannot lead to a better understanding of complex and difficult issues. This rhetorical analysis does not simplify Roosevelt, nor does it make Roosevelt a spokesperson for either a liberal or a conservative agenda, nor does it portray him as a one-dimensional thinker. It examines how he struck a rhetorical balance among the competing impulses of racism, nativism, assimilation, ethnic diversity, and group hopelessness by reworking a myth foundational to the nation's origin.

Roosevelt promoted his version of Americanism to create simultaneously a middle ground for culturally diverse groups to occupy as self-identified Americans, and for nativists to occupy while still considering themselves, as well as racial and ethnic "others," to be Americans, pure and simple. Considering the political and social anxieties that surround the crisis of American identity throughout the nation's history, Roosevelt's accomplishment was no small feat.

America's Identity Crisis

Matters of race, ethnicity, and identity in American society are often at the forefront of national and international discussions. The current "culture war" over illegal immigration is a prime example. With estimates of 11–12 million illegal immigrants in the United States, 70 percent of whom came from Mexico, the media in early 2006 reported a multitude of conflicting concerns about the meaning of national identity.[37] Part of the current public debate has focused on the economic and political aspects of illegal immigration. Columnists note that undocumented immigrants place an overwhelming burden on Medicare and other social services and take jobs away from "real" Americans.[38] Others observe that the nation benefits financially from immigrants' willingness to "do the jobs that Americans refuse to do."[39] Politically, this issue is troubling for both Republicans and Democrats. On the one hand, both parties recognize the need in a post 9/11 world to call for stringent immigration reform to safeguard the nation from possibly dangerous, undocumented strangers.[40] On the other hand, both parties also believe that finding a way to legalize these immigrants might win their allegiance as new, grateful voters.[41]

Grass-roots organizers staged numerous protests across the nation in April 2006 to illuminate the plight of illegal immigrants in America and to call for immigration reform that would grant millions of undocumented workers some opportunity for citizenship. These organizers' most ambitious strategy involved "A Day Without Immigrants." They designated May 1 as a day for nationwide protest, urging both legal and illegal immigrants to boycott businesses and to be absent from work. Hundreds of thousands of demonstrators marched in major American cities, held rallies and church services, and refused to shop on that day.[42] Reactions were mixed. Supporters of the event declared the day a success because it closed businesses and demonstrated the economic power of immigrants. Others argued that it served "notice . . . that the swelling Latino population has birthed a new political reality."[43] Some immigrants questioned the May 1 event, worried that they would lose their jobs, alienate business leaders, and create a political backlash.[44] Perhaps more telling were accusations that such events were not "homegrown, 'organic' demonstrations" by concerned citizens. Some media outlets claimed that immigration rallies were the products of agitators on Spanish-language radio, evidenced by protestors waving Mexican flags at these demonstrations.[45]

Despite the economic and political impact of illegal immigration, the subtext of the debate reflects the fear Americans have regarding immigrants who seemingly refuse to assimilate—to become Americans. For example, Mexican Americans, legal or not, have contended for centuries with the notion that they are unassimilated foreigners.[46] More important, the debate engaged the age-old fears about which race or ethnicity represented the standard for the nation's multicultural identity. As one reporter noted: "When someone complains that San Diego is 'becoming like Tijuana,' or when someone else says—as an Idaho woman recently told the *Los Angeles Times*—that her neighborhood has become a Spanish-speaking 'shanty town,' it's a dead giveaway that, for many Americans, the problem is not with people coming into the country illegally, but with the effect they have on their surroundings once here."[47] The controversy surrounding the Spanish version of the national anthem exemplified the racial and ethnic underpinnings of the current immigration debate.

Coinciding with "A Day Without Immigrants," British music producer Adam Kidron announced the release of "Neustro Himno" ("Our Anthem"), a Spanish-language version of the "Star-Spangled Banner" on the upcoming album, "Somos Americanos." Kidron noted that he intended this version to "honor" America's immigrants, not to discourage their embrace of national culture.[48] Overwhelming numbers of critics identified "Neustro Himno" as treasonous and divisive, and President George W. Bush stated bluntly that, "The national anthem ought to be sung in English, and I think people who want to be a citizen of this country ought to learn English and they ought to learn to sing the national anthem in English."[49] Although there are multiple, accepted versions of the national anthem, including Blues, and "soul and funk" interpretations, the controversy revealed "what many perceive as a threat to our country's customs and values," a "growing . . . fear that 'we' are being overrun," and that the "browning of America will mean its ruin."[50]

Not at all new, these fears reflect an American attitude that calls for foreign or indigenous "others" to discard their beliefs and languages, work hard at demonstrating their embrace of national ideals, and prove that they are ready for citizenship.[51] Despite the "no holds barred" appearance of the debate, the public conversation lacks depth. Former *U.S. News and World Report* editor and author Debra Dickerson noted the superficiality of public conversations about national identity. She argued that Americans today are reluctant to highlight differences in people beyond such stereotypic positions as "whites are all bad" or "minority cultures are all good"; as a result, substantive public conversations about race, ethnicity, and identity rarely occur.[52] Current debates about songs, peaceful demonstrations, and economics polarize the discussion and foster a reluctance to comment on the presumptions behind racial and ethnic distinctiveness in national identity, which in turn has created what some might consider a "politically correct" silence.[53] The current silence has made it difficult to address openly the tensions of culture, ethnicity, and race as they influence an individual's sense of belonging to or rejection from the national community.

From its earliest days, the silence about race and ethnicity was woven into the fabric of the emerging American republic. While the attack on slavery as an immoral and hypocritical institution had gained ground by 1776, earlier discussions of slavery depicted it in terms that were more benign. To early eighteenth-century colonists, the term slavery meant nothing more than a "specific political condition." According to Bernard Bailyn, white Americans believed that "black plantation laborers" were similar to "contemporary Frenchmen, Danes, and Swedes" who had simply "lost the power of self-determination."[54] The public debate avoided the question of African or native-born blacks' viability as citizens, instead depicting the degrading nature of their enslaved state as a form of political or civil economic imprisonment, one shared by white-skinned Danes and Swedes. Colonists took slavery "more or less for granted," Gordon S. Wood noted, as a required "hierarchy of dependencies" amid a "world of laborers."[55] Furthermore, early political leaders such as Thomas Jefferson avoided the debate about blacks ever attaining national identity by steering the conversation away from their assimilation once slavery ended; he proposed that their destiny lay in their colonization elsewhere, such as in the West Indies.[56] Although Bailyn noted that the "problem posed by the bondage tolerated in [America] became more and more difficult to evade," the Founders did just that.[57]

The foundational documents and celebrated articulations constructing the new American nation and its people's identity appear artfully ambiguous. The Declaration of Independence, the document that promoted the iconic ideas of freedom and democracy to nascent American citizens, asserted, "all men are created equal,"[58] as long as the unspoken adjective was "white." The Constitution made virtually no statement regarding race or ethnicity, and initial interpreters of it inferred that the document created a unique American identity that came from the purification of racial and ethnic outsiders via the legendary "melting pot."[59] While diversity of race and ethnicity were obviously a pressing concern even at the Republic's beginning, rhetors generally submerged such elements and treated them as secondary concerns.[60] Thus, early advocates of America as a nation proposed an uplifting but racially indistinct statement of who could be part of the national identity. Wood noted that the Founders understood their Republic to be a "beautiful but ambiguous ideal," hoping that such an ideal would lead to "harmony and public virtue" in the new land.[61] Proposing a system that called each person to sacrifice his or her individual interest to the public good would create a sense of natural equality, an almost idyllic state predicated on equal treatment among all people.

Unfortunately, the abstract equality and amorphous good will generated in the new national community seemed only to exist in regard to a specific group of people, that is, whites of northern European descent. Although Michel-Guillaume Jean de Crèvecoeur's 1782 classic, *Letters From an American Farmer,* highlighted the ethnic admixture of Americans, his work focused on what Americans would become, white citizens, rather than what they were, a racially and ethnically diverse population.[62] Crèvecoeur observed that "individuals of all nations are melted into a new race of men, whose labours and posterity will one day cause great changes in the world." In fact, such a new white man "who leaving behind him all his ancient prejudices and manners, receives new ones from the new mode of life he has embraced, the new government he obeys, and the new rank he holds."[63] More specifically, Alexis de Tocqueville's early nineteenth-century treatise, *Democracy in America,* pronounced a death sentence for non-whites in the new land. The "striking characteristic of the social condition of the Anglo-Saxon" was "its essential democracy," de Tocqueville wrote, and yet whites consigned blacks to an "abyss of evils" and condemned American Indians to a "wandering life, full of inexpressible sufferings." Social attitudes closed national identity to these groups. As a result, the "Negro, who earnestly desires to mingle his race with that of the European, cannot do so; while the Indian, who might succeed to a certain extent, disdains to make the attempt. The servility of the one dooms him to slavery, the pride of the other to death."[64] By the turn of the nineteenth century, whiteness became the default prerequisite for an American to assume national identity.[65]

The silence surrounding race, ethnicity, and democratic ideology was eventually broken. The paradox of slavery, along with bigoted practices against American Indians and certain immigrant groups, called for a public explanation, one that would maintain the integrity of the Founders' precepts. Toward that end, some Americans presented their arguments based in science, as disseminated in popular texts. Throughout the nineteenth century, ethnologists argued that environment made no difference in determining viability for citizenship; certain races had innate and "backward" traits that no amount of civilization could overcome.[66] Science thus consigned blacks to a permanent inferiority that prevented their consideration as Americans. Eugenicists confirmed the fears of native-born citizens that immigrants brought filth, disease, and other defective traits with them, and proposed that such unfit types stop procreating, especially with "normal" whites.[67] Legislators called on these "scientists" as experts in the immigration restriction debates.[68] Finally, Native Americans fared no better in becoming Americans. Phrenologists, "scientists" who studied the shape of the head as a means to determine intelligence and character, concluded that the shape of Native Americans' heads meant that they could never be anything but savages.[69]

The rejection of American Indians as worthy participants in national identity was particularly ironic. Early colonists had "played Indian" and adopted Native American dress and customs to articulate their own Revolutionary identity. According to Philip Deloria, whites believed Indian cultures symbolized a natural state of freedom on the untamed frontier, and so they used Indian imagery to "represent America as vulnerable, abused, and enslaved" when Great Britain intensified its conflict with the colonists. Once the war had ended, however, the indigenous Natives were again savages, a judgment affirmed by science, while new white Americans considered their "civilized" national identity distinct from that of Native Americans.[70]

Whites assumed their superiority in the early decades of the Republic; legal pronouncements made that assumption official. Legislative acts institutionally placed African Americans, Indians, and immigrants outside the confines of national identity.[71] Any legislative statute penned against African Americans, including laws against intermarriage, commingling and other forms of legal disenfranchisement condemned them not only to stand outside national identity, but also to be relegated to the status of nonhuman.[72] Governmental policies fulfilled the Frontier Myth's narrative and removed "savage" Indians from their land, and, as the number of Native Americans dramatically decreased, other institutional policies isolated them on reservations to protect and to "civilize" them.[73] Multiple Chinese Exclusion Acts in the early nineteenth century curtailed Chinese immigration to the United States and denied residing aliens access to citizenship.[74] Not even whites were equal under the law. For example, several Immigration Acts throughout the nineteenth century that barred "lunatics" and "criminals" coincided with increases in Irish and Italian immigrants, respectively portrayed as Celtic barbarians and villainous Mafiosi.[75]

In sum, race and ethnicity eventually became a prominent aspect of the public debate about national identity by the turn of the twentieth century. Although whites wanted to assume that democracy, liberty, and equality defined them as Americans, the existence of so many different races and ethnicities forced an explicit conversation as to how national identity also depended on a person's place of origin and skin color.

Despite these paradoxes and problems, Theodore Roosevelt possessed what Arthur M. Schlesinger Jr. called the American "genius . . . to forge a single nation from peoples of remarkably diverse racial, religious, and ethnic origins."[76] Roosevelt articulated the story of American identity in a way that all could feel better for believing it. This, perhaps more than anything else, represents Roosevelt's legacy: his ability to use his "genius" to help people consider one another in new ways—to help them feel better about themselves. As Patricia O'Toole confirmed, "ordinary people . . . loved [Roosevelt] for knowing the best that was in them and making them feel they could reach it."[77] Roosevelt's myth of Americanism allowed the modern age to create a "single nation from peoples of remarkably diverse racial, religious, and ethnic origins," one that guaranteed equality among those diverse groups, even when it was clearly not the case. His public discourse called a new community into existence, one that attempted to balance individualism and civic responsibility, one that still invoked "otherness" in stark terms, and one that resolved, albeit problematically, the contradictory notions surrounding the issues of ethnicity, race, and identity in modern America.

How Roosevelt achieved this bit of rhetorical legerdemain is the focus of this analysis, which will proceed as follows. In chapter 1 I provide a framework for the subsequent chapters, examining in detail what Roosevelt termed Americanism and illuminating the Frontier Myth as the means he used to popularize Americanism as an answer to the nation's identity crisis. I provide in chapter 2 a rhetorical analysis of Roosevelt's best-selling work, *The Winning of the West*. His multivolume history popularized simultaneously the idea of immigration and assimilation in American culture through a mythic narrative that grounded both the origins of American society and the future strength of its people in immigration and the frontier spirit of Americanism. Chapter 3 illuminates how Roosevelt recast mythically evil Native Americans into heroic individuals who embodied Americanism and who enhanced the national community. Specifically, he reconstructed their identity from that of "lazy savages" to hardworking people deserving of national identity, making them ready for their biological assimilation with Anglo-Saxon whites. In chapter 4 I examine how Roosevelt placed African Americans into the national myth. He moved them beyond their antebellum constraints by arguing that they demonstrated the mythic form of Americanism. Simultaneously, he appeased whites that freed slaves were not moving too far beyond their station by acknowledging the need for "frontier justice"—lynching—on occasion. In chapter 5 I demonstrate how Roosevelt heralded the success of German assimilation in America with the Frontier Myth. Yet, he also condemned German-Americans' use of the hyphen by including them as antagonists in a frontier-inspired "savage war" that linked them to their supposed demonic, war-obsessed homeland during World War I. In the final chapter I reflect on the nature of Roosevelt's Americanism with regard to contemporary perceptions of race, ethnicity, and identity. Specifically, I explore how his version of the Frontier Myth empowered the American Dream, a mythic interpretation of national destiny in its own right.

Roosevelt's public rhetoric, for all its faults, addressed a newly emerging multicultural society. By examining it, we can perhaps better illuminate the complexities in the frustrating and fascinating question still facing us today, "What does it mean to be an 'American, pure and simple?'"

1

Roosevelt's Americanism
and the Myth of Origin

~

One of the most persistent questions in U.S. history has been, "What does it mean to be an American?" The answer in the early days of the Republic appeared deceptively simple: Americans were people who believed in "Americanism." Americanism constituted the political and practical commitment an individual made to the moral values, democratic principles, and social norms identified with America.[1] Believers in Americanism were thought to embrace ideals such as freedom, liberty, rule of law, democracy, and love for their unique country.[2] The means white Americans employed to ensure that racial and ethnic "others" embraced those beliefs functionally excluded those others from participation.

To promote Americanism, politicians, educators, and nativists instituted the practices of "assimilation" and "Americanization." These advocates called for the assimilation of Native Americans, while excluding other nonwhite groups such as Asians and African Americans; likewise, whites wanted immigrants Americanized. Both terms would eventually become synonymous in the early 1900s since they both involved how to motivate "outsiders" to embrace the practices and institutions of white culture, becoming one people ideologically in the process.[3] Both terms, unfortunately, would also revolve around the notion of coercing a person, many times forcibly, to discard his or her birth culture. Thus, whites used the principles of Americanism to convince nonwhites and immigrants to believe in something greater than their supposed backward cultures, and employed the practices of assimilation and Americanization to control the outsiders' behavior within the nation.

Attempts at extermination and removal in the eighteenth and nineteenth centuries did not solve what many at the time considered "the Indian problem."[4] As a result, advocates such as Thomas Jefferson called for the assimilation of Native Americans by forcing them to reject their nomadic hunting culture and become farmers. Whites acquired Native Americans' land and then distributed it back to them in the form of small homesteading plots.[5] Along with compulsory education in agriculture, Christianity, and social studies, Americans waged a war in the classroom against Native Americans that was no less destructive than what they did on the battlefield.[6] According to Stephen Cornell, the program of civilization and assimilation downplayed the "disturbing specter of the United States, founded on principles of freedom and equality, setting out to destroy Indian nations for the sake of real estate."[7] Assimilation forced unwilling Native Americans to engage in an unwanted and bastardized version of Americanism's promise to life and liberty.

Many immigrants fared no better under Americanization. From the beginning of the Republic, political leaders spoke of the need for immigrants to discard their Old World clothing, religions, languages, ideologies, customs, and allegiances in order to become Americans.[8] While lawmakers controlled entrance to the country and citizenship through various acts, and some public organizations worked to Americanize immigrants through education, there was no systematic national mechanism to transform newcomers prior to the twentieth century.[9] Whites generally presumed the process of Americanization would occur on its own.

Israel Zangwill's *The Melting Pot* brought this presumption to the nation's attention. His play opened to enthusiastic reviews in Washington, D.C., in October 1908.[10] Theodore Roosevelt attended opening night and hailed Zangwill's message.[11] The play related the story of David, a Jewish immigrant who came to America to escape the Russian pogrom that had killed his family. Living in New York, David found the American Dream: opportunity, hard work, and success. More important, perhaps, David found a spirit of racial and ethnic equality forged in America, a point he stressed in the play's finale: "There she lies, the great Melting Pot.... There gapes her mouth—the harbour where a thousand mammoth feeders come from the ends of the world to pour in their human freight. Ah, what a stirring and a seething! Celt and Latin, Slav and Teuton, Greek and Syrian ... black and yellow ... how the great Alchemist melts and fuses them with his purging flame! Here shall they all unite to build the Republic of Man and the Kingdom of God.... What is the glory of Rome and Jerusalem where all nations and races come to worship and look back, compared with the glory of America, where all races and nations come to labour and look forward!"[12] For many people, the play affirmed the notion of automatic assimilation; no matter how it happened, immigrants would thankfully realize the benefit of being absorbed into the American body.[13] *The Melting Pot* symbolized the nation as a place where race or ethnicity did not matter in regard to acceptance, social mobility, and the realization of the American Dream.[14]

Yet, the play also troubled many people. The popularization of the "melting pot" idea dramatized a sense of confusion about its relationship to Americanism. Philip Gleason observed that after Zangwill's play, some Americans worried about the meaning of "melting together." Did the forging of America refer to the creation of an American/immigrant hybrid, or did the melting pot "strip [immigrants] of their cultural heritage, and make old-style, Anglo-Saxon Americans of them?" Concerned nativists worried if Americanization meant marriage between whites and "inferior" immigrant groups, or if the nature of Americanism itself changed with the addition of "foreign" ways of thinking.[15] These confusions pointed to a realization: whites, up until Zangwill's play, had presumed Americanization was a largely natural process, one that immigrants would gladly will for themselves. However, with increasing numbers of immigrants seemingly holding on to their Old World cultures, whites decided to take control of the process and systematically force aliens into conformance with American values. Just like assimilation, Americanization gave whites control of and access to the benefits of national identity.

With the fear of foreigners refusing to accept Americanism, the Americanization Movement was born. Businesses, private organizations, schools, and all levels of government participated in an organized crusade to Americanize immigrants. Political and public organizations instituted compulsory English education, established neighborhood counseling sessions to help foreigners understand the meaning of Americanism, and churches persuaded immigrants to reject their heritages.[16] Public schools in particular led the way in proselytizing Americanism. Educators redesigned curricula to socialize immigrant children, to instill loyalty for their new nation, and to inculcate in them Protestant beliefs.[17] The popularity of Americanization also led to a more consistent understanding of the "melting pot" symbol: by the end of World War One, Gleason concluded, the "melting pot came to be looked upon as almost exclusively a purger of 'foreign dross' and 'impurities.'"[18] This understanding would also lead many Anglo-Saxons to engage in wholesale outrages against those immigrants who seemed to resist the need to reject their "impurities."[19]

The assimilation and Americanization of immigrants and nonwhites contradicted the idyllic character of American identity. First, the philosophic appeal of Americanism—loving your country for allowing you to live a life of democratic harmony with all others—obscured the fact that whites acted as gatekeepers to limit access to this life based on erroneous beliefs about racial and ethnic inferiorities. Second, assimilation and Americanization acted as clubs to coerce cooperation in nonwhites and foreigners, ordering them to self-identify only with their new country by both legal and extralegal means. Third, assimilation and Americanization emphasized the stark differences between various groups without providing them a way to view their individuality within the larger community.

Roosevelt would generally agree with the goals promoted by advocates of Americanism, assimilation, and Americanization. He too believed in the necessity of new citizens loving their God-blessed, democratic nation, as well as the need for them to discard much of the trappings of their old lives. One of his first published utterances of the term "Americanism" appeared in the preface of his narrative history called *New York,* published in 1891. He asserted that New Yorkers of foreign descent represented prototypical Americans. Many of them had learned the lessons of Americanism: they had recognized that the person "who wishes to win honor" and to "play his part honestly and manfully, must be indeed an American in spirit and purpose, in heart and thought and deed." Such behavior, he offered, proved that these new Americans understood "the lesson of Americanism" by embracing a "devotion to the welfare of the commonwealth."[20]

Roosevelt's message stayed consistent throughout his life. Speaking before a St. Louis audience in 1916, he reiterated his egalitarian policy. He seemingly cared little about where someone originated. "If the American has the right stuff in him," he stated, "I care not a snap of my fingers whether he is Jew or Gentile. . . . I care not a snap of my fingers whether his ancestors came over in the Mayflower, or [born] in Germany, Ireland, France, England, Scandinavia, Russia or Italy or any other country." As long as each person proved "physically and intellectually fit, of sound character, and eager in good faith to become an American citizen," he declared, "I am for him."[21]

Roosevelt's articulation of Americanism appeared consistent with the common understanding of the belief. When he called on citizens to be "American in spirit and purpose," he affirmed Americanism as a belief in national ideals. He informed newcomers of their responsibilities to the nation and the benefits they derived from acceptance of those responsibilities. Roosevelt also reminded his audiences of the ideal notion that place of origin should not determine the validity for citizenship. Moreover, through some process, racial and ethnic others would assimilate and be Americanized. In many ways, his Americanism reflected and built on the familiar conception of the term.

Yet, Roosevelt actually recast the meaning of Americanism, narrowing it in the process to three essential elements. First, he deemed physical or martial hardiness integral to any understanding of American success. To "play" an American, to live the democratic ideals of the nation, one needed a manly vitality. Second, he offered moral character as a key ingredient for the American citizen; ideal virtue was needed to guide an individual's political, business, and social relationships with others. Finally, while the traditional perception of Americanism included equality, Roosevelt privileged it above all other values and reinterpreted its meaning. If racial and ethnic others aided the community with their strength and character, they deserved "some" level of equal respect from their white fellow countrymen. Immigrants and nonwhites could earn equality and find "some" room in the nation's identity. These three tenets of his Americanism—strength, integrity, and earned equality—became a staple in Roosevelt's rhetoric throughout his career.

Whereas nativists employed assimilation and Americanization to force immigrants and nonwhites to accept Americanism, a force many of those people resisted and rejected, Roosevelt offered a significant rhetorical alternative. By combining the philosophical appeal of national values with the practical tenets of strength, integrity, and earned equality, his Americanism contained the prescription for outsiders to bring about their own transformation into Americans. Roosevelt looked to the individual to change, to demonstrate his or her individual ability to succeed, which would then benefit the group. He affirmed on more than one occasion, "As it is with the individual, so it is with the nation."[22] If foreigners and nonwhites worked to make themselves both physically and morally strong, Roosevelt argued, and then turned such strength to aiding the community, they fulfilled their civic duty. As a result, they deserved some level of respect equal to whites. Through these processes, racial and ethnic outsiders could *seemingly* enter national identity unmolested, although whites would still be the judges of how well foreigners and nonwhites fulfilled those criteria.

So, on the one hand, racial and ethnic others could conceivably affect their own entrance into the nation's identity. On the other hand, whites could still work to deny access to anyone they deemed inferior. Roosevelt's rhetorical lessons acknowledged both ends of that continuum, but offered his Americanism as the moderate position between them.

Roosevelt and Modern America

Roosevelt's development of what he considered the foundation of national identity gave citizens an understanding of Americanism through which they could negotiate the extreme positions that divided the nation. Chief among those foundational elements was physical vigor.

Strength of the Body

Roosevelt's belief in bodily strength developed during his childhood, an inspiring tale now bordering on the legendary.[23] Born in 1858 with severe asthma, Roosevelt's resulting physical frailty made him a target as he grew into adolescence. As he wrote in his autobiography, "I was at first quite unable to hold my own when thrown into contact with other boys of rougher antecedents." He shared what he considered a pivotal moment that occurred when he was fourteen years old—a rough-housing encounter with two boys that demonstrated the indignity of weakness: "either one singly could not only handle me with easy contempt, but handle me so as not to hurt me much and yet to prevent my doing any damage whatever in return."[24] Spurred by the practical need to protect himself, as well as energized by the stories his mother told him about the southern traditions of manliness, young Roosevelt embarked upon a rigorous training regimen—including boxing, wrestling, horseback riding, and hunting. This training compensated for his lack of natural prowess.[25]

Throughout his life, Roosevelt gravitated to pursuits that tested his manliness. He served in the National Guard, established cattle ranches, served as the assistant secretary of the navy, fought in the Spanish-American War, and trekked the world over in search of adventure.[26] More important, he frequently used his positions to appear in public to promote Americanism and its link to physical vitality. For example, speaking as the police commissioner before the Liberal Club in 1895, Roosevelt delivered the speech "Americanism in Municipal Politics." He argued civic leaders needed a courage borne by strength of arms. "I can get along with him [the scoundrel]. He will hit me and I will hit him." But an honesty weakened by timidity served no one, and those men who demonstrated such a "delicate [touch]" were unworthy of their status as leaders or Americans.[27] For Roosevelt, politics appeared no different from any other physical struggle, and leaders unable to meet such a tangible challenge proved their weakness and brought into question their right to be called Americans. As the nineteenth century ended, two critical events help to explain Roosevelt's worry that a lack of manly vitality signaled America's decline.

The first event that interested Roosevelt involved a paper read at the American Historical Association in 1893. "The Significance of the Frontier in American History," written and presented by a young historian named Frederick Jackson Turner, challenged the prevailing historical thought. Turner did not affirm the conclusions of traditional historians who argued that the characteristics and institutions of America came unchanged from the Old World. Instead, he proposed that the frontier experiences of settlers in the wilderness of the North American continent had transformed them into something uniquely American.[28] In fact, Turner argued the frontier shaped the essence of the nation's identity: "That coarseness and strength combined with acuteness and inquisitiveness; that practical, inventive turn of mind, quick to find expedients; that masterful grasp of material things, lacking in the artistic but powerful to effect great ends; that restless, nervous energy; that dominant individualism, working for good and for evil, and withal that buoyancy and exuberance which comes with freedom-these are traits of the frontier, or traits called out elsewhere because of the existence of the frontier."[29] His thesis provided a fundamental and attractive explanation of America's origin. It provided citizens with an appealing image—that of dynamic, strong, reasoned, and uniquely capable people who had dominated their surroundings through their strength of body, mind, and character.

Turner's essay, however, ended on an ominous note. Three years earlier in 1890, he observed, the superintendent of the census declared the frontier officially closed. With this revelation, Turner implied that the forge used to make America was no more. "And now, four centuries from the discovery of America," he wrote, "at the end of a hundred years of life under the Constitution, the frontier has gone, and with its going has closed the first period of American history."[30] He posed a simple yet perplexing conundrum in the late 1800s: if America's material prosperity and democracy stemmed from its frontier experience, what would be the country's future without such experiences? Over the next few years, politicians and other public advocates predicted an end to American prosperity, citing the numerous economic depressions of the time as extensions of the frontier's end. Likewise, these doomsayers used the close of the frontier to call for an end to immigration. They argued that without the frontier to transform foreigners into Americans, the nation risked its resources on the worst elements from the Old World.[31]

Ironically, when Turner presented his theory to his fellow historians, they largely ignored it, making only perfunctory comments about it in the media.[32] Although Turner's peers largely ignored the significance of his Frontier Thesis immediately following his presentation, Roosevelt did not. He wrote a letter of congratulations to the young historian, telling Turner he had "struck some first class ideas" and had "put into definite shape a good deal of thought which [had] been floating around rather loosely." Roosevelt wrote Turner again after realizing Turner had reviewed several of his books on the narrative history of America, *The Winning of the West*. Roosevelt informed Turner that while their overall views did not differ widely, their points of concern did. While Turner's

Thesis focused on the development of institutions on the frontier, Roosevelt explained his works as more concerned with the hardy Americans who emerged from the "strife of races" on the frontier.[33] His focus on character development resulting from frontier experiences worked to create compelling archetypes in the public's mind. According to Richard Slotkin, Roosevelt's "hero centered narratives ... had far more appeal than the complexities, criticisms, and depersonalized sociology of Turner's histories."[34] Roosevelt wondered about the implications surrounding the close of the frontier and the end of the "strife of races." Without such an arena or its contestants, the potential for gaining manliness—a key requirement of Americanism—might be in jeopardy.

Later twentieth-century scholars would echo Roosevelt's acknowledgment of the importance of Turner's work. Many credited Turner with revolutionizing American thought. The historian Ray Billington noted that some scholars during Turner's time obviously recognized the importance of the frontier, but "no one of them demonstrated that significance as systematically and convincingly as Turner." It was Turner, Billington believed, who vividly reminded his audiences of their cherished agrarian past.[35] Ronald Carpenter would attribute Turner's impact to the young historian's ability to write like a "rhetorician." Turner's "evocative manipulations" and stylistic choices of metaphors and alliterations created compelling portraits of the early frontiersmen, Carpenter argued, creating a mythic frame for American development.[36] Mary Stuckey and John Murphy wrote that Turner's stylistic choices highlighted the symbolic nature of "rhetorical colonialism." They contended his paper constituted the identities of savages and settlers on the frontier, and depicted those combatants' respective roles in the colonization process as naturally occurring. Thus, America appeared as a foreordained conclusion when "savagery and civilization" met on the frontier.[37]

Turner's Frontier Thesis had a profound impact. It not only influenced the direction of his discipline for several decades, but politicians, economists, and other public advocates employed it to explain everything from commercial development to incursions in foreign lands.[38] As Turner formulated his theory, novelists and magazine writers had begun to write frontier stories populated with grittier characters and storylines revolving around the racial and economic conquest of the frontier. Such stories not only reawakened the public's imagination about the frontier, but they also reflected the growing interest of Americans in their storied agrarian past.[39] In a sense, Turner brought a scholarly credibility to the frontier imaginings of popular storytellers such as Roosevelt.

The second event shaping Roosevelt's discourse involved his friend and confidant, Brooks Adams. Adams published *The Law of Civilization and Decay* in 1895. In his book, Adams continued the argument he and Roosevelt enjoyed debating when they had attended Harvard together. Adams contended America would collapse like every other powerful nation from what he called the "law of history." Civilizations flourished, he observed, when cultures employed their martial strength in service to the imagination—to explore the natural and supernatural world to understand better their place in it. Unfortunately, the "law of history" dictated a culture would eventually turn away from such manly and lofty pursuits and instead would engage the world simply to attain material riches. Thus, concepts such as bravery and honor ceased to be important; and the moneyed class dismissed true warriors, employing simple "paid police" to protect their interests. With economic concerns trumping martial strength and moral integrity, Adams reasoned, whole civilizations, such as the Roman Empire, collapsed.[40]

While H. W. Brands noted that Roosevelt perhaps thought friend Adams was not "quite straight in the head,"[41] Roosevelt accepted the seriousness of his friend's claims. Roosevelt reviewed Adams's book in an 1897 issue of *The Forum*, and initially judged Adams's conclusions about America's fate as false. Yet, upon closer inspection, Roosevelt actually endorsed Adams's basic theory about the "law of history." Proclaiming Adams's perceptions "brilliant," Roosevelt lauded his friend's ability to single out the "vital factors in the growth and evolution" of civilizations during the last several centuries and his celebration of the martial man. He admitted that if the nation could not repeal the "law of history," it would collapse: "If we lose the virile, manly qualities . . . and subordinate everything to mere life of ease, then we shall indeed reach a condition worse than that of the ancient civilizations in the years of their decay."[42] Roosevelt denied America had reached the point of no return, yet he believed America suffered from a "growing concern for security and comfort."[43] America was losing its manliness just as Adams had predicted.

Roosevelt identified with the larger debate on the nature of manliness occurring at the turn of the twentieth century. In the early nineteenth century, as the agrarian way of life gave way to city life, and men distinguished themselves as professionals, managers, and entrepreneurs, middle-class men reoriented manliness away from brute strength. Instead, manhood meant being the master of your own destiny in the workplace. Yet, by the end of the 1800s, many men realized that forces beyond their control stripped away their manliness in the workplace. Due to changing economic conditions such as depressions and bankruptcies, Gail Bederman noted, men learned the "reality that even a successful . . . small businessman might lose everything, unexpectedly and through no fault of his own." As a result, the "sons of the middle class faced the real possibility that traditional sources of male power and status would remain closed to them." Coupled with the popular notions of the middle class appearing over-civilized and effeminate, the world of business no longer offered men their haven of masculinity. Even Roosevelt himself needed to masculinize his middle-class image because the public saw him as effeminate when he first entered politics.[44]

Although born of the patrician class, Roosevelt reacted against the genteel culture of middle-class life and its enervating effect on American prowess. He became "obsessed" with physical power and wanted the nation to become preoccupied with it too.[45] He actively trumpeted the need for a virile type of Americanism in much of his rhetoric. He took aim at anyone who overemphasized the "life of the mind" and a "life of ease" instead of the development of a rough-and-tumble grit. In particular, he rhetorically targeted those refined intellectuals who he believed advocated anti-American sentiment in their scholarship. Writing in 1896 about the dangers of too much college education, he warned that it could drain the "feeling of a robust Americanism" and minimize the feeling of patriotism for the country. "It is an admirable thing," Roosevelt wrote, "to possess refinement and cultivation, but the price is too dear if they must be paid for at the cost of the rugged fighting qualities which make a man able to do a man's work in the world, and which make his heart beat with that kind of love of country." Commenting about America's manly responsibility in the world, he chastised the "anemic man of refinement and cultivation" whose intellect considered "any expression of the Monroe Doctrine as truculent and ill advised." According to him, such men undervalued the "great fighting qualities" necessary for survival in the world.[46] For Roosevelt, being educated was fine as long as such an education did not transform the man into an effeminate prig.

One of Roosevelt's most recognized speeches, "The Strenuous Life," captured his mantra of physical might. Less than two years after America's war with Spain, he appeared before a Chicago audience to urge it to accept the "doctrine of the strenuous life," a life filled with "toil and effort [and] of labor and strife." For him, modern America could only thrive in the world if it remembered "the iron in the blood of our fathers" and the men who "bore sword or rifle." Metaphorically, Roosevelt transformed the nation into an armed warrior, proving its worth by its ability to police the world. "The army and navy are the sword and the shield," he argued, "which this nation must carry if she is to do her duty among the nations of the earth." He approved of a Darwinian contest between the martial practicality of Americanism and any foreign powers. "If we stand idly by, if we seek merely swollen, slothful ease and ignoble peace," he warned, "if we shrink from the hard contests where men must win at hazard of their lives and at the risk of all they hold dear, then the bolder and stronger peoples will pass us by."[47] He offered "The Strenuous Life" as the antidote to both Turner's and Adams's conclusions. With the close of the frontier, Roosevelt would look to foreign lands for Americans to challenge their hardihood. America would need to prepare itself through force of arms and the reawakening of a fighting spirit last seen on the frontier. Such messages he took with him to the presidency and to his post-presidential advocacy.

Consistent with the advice offered early in his presidency that America should "speak softly and carry a big stick," Roosevelt urged the nation to continue developing its martial might.[48] Far from speaking softly, Roosevelt went to great lengths to demonstrate such might via his rhetorical presidency.

In the germinal article "The Rise of the Rhetorical Presidency," James Ceaser, Glen Thurow, Jeffrey Tulis, and Joseph Bessette argued that early presidents traditionally limited the use of popular rhetoric to address national audiences.[49] Following the wishes of the Founders, chief executives instead directed their "reasoned and deliberative" discourse toward Congress; the public might read those addresses, but such speeches would only acquaint audiences with the nature of deliberative discourse, not exhort them "in the name of a . . . spirit of idealism." According to the authors, rhetorical presidents such as Woodrow Wilson and later presidents used the media to help them carry their inspirational messages, engaging in a form of moral leadership. The authors identified this leadership by a rhetoric articulating the "unspoken desires of the people," one which depicted for them a grand vision of the nation's sacred destiny. No longer would the president content himself with addressing only Congress—now he would mobilize a national audience as a warrant for his agenda. Ironically, the article's authors judged disapprovingly those presidents who attempted to inspire the public through moral rhetoric. According to Ceaser and colleagues, too much inspirational rhetoric creates unrealistic expectations in the audience, widens the gulf between what is promised and the means to fulfill those promises, and ultimately makes the job of national governance that much more difficult.[50]

Despite the admonition of a rhetorical presidency, the authors reified a key concept: presidents morally lead through symbolic acts such as speeches. Chief executives can speak to the nation, inspire it to look beyond itself, cajole it to accept unwanted responsibilities, and can warn it of the dangers that come from a weak body and spirit like no other public advocate.

Considered the "father of the rhetorical presidency," President Roosevelt exemplified the notion with various symbolic acts.[51] For instance, after wrangling with Congress about the need for a new battleship navy, he sent the nation's battle fleet—painted white for the occasion instead of the traditional gunmetal gray—on an unprecedented world tour. Roosevelt framed the event in a number of speeches as the realization of America's martial destiny. As a rhetorical president, he handpicked journalists to accompany the tour who would continue his themes and tell rousing stories of the fleet's adventures as a way to inspire the populace. Contrary to the predictions of disaster about leaving the navy exposed to foreign machinations, countries all over the world welcomed the fleet with something akin to awe.[52] Roosevelt pointed to the world's reaction as corroborating his belief in the need for martial strength in the modern world: when foreign nations recognized and celebrated America's fleet as a symbol of power, they granted the country a measure of respect only the martially fit could earn.

While Roosevelt's arguments about establishing America's presence abroad undoubtedly heartened entrepreneurs who needed untapped resources and new markets, his concern was not solely economic. Roosevelt recognized the need for a firm financial base, but he also supported what one writer termed an "internationalist vision" of American destiny. Internationalists such as Roosevelt saw the close of the frontier as being responsible for the economic and social chaos of the time. To counteract this, the internationalists championed the idea of strategic superiority as the means for the spiritual health of the nation. Thus, Roosevelt's fight to secure the area for the Panama Canal involved more than an economic avenue for transoceanic travel. He saw it as an opportunity to go over the heads of Congress and promote its martial meaning for the public. By employing the rhetorical presidency, he brought the media spotlight to the back-breaking work accomplished on the isthmus by being the first American president to visit a foreign country. The nationally distributed picture of Roosevelt sitting atop one of the giant earthmovers akin to a cowboy riding a wild horse displayed the rhetorical nature of his presidency. He portrayed himself as an embodiment of strength, and he called on the media to record his larger-than-life activities. Roosevelt's tour of the canal workers in the driving rain and knee-deep mud fostered the "image of a commander visiting his troops at the front," with military metaphors acting as staples in the president's rhetoric about the canal. Furthermore, through a "Special Message" to Congress that included pictures of this incredible feat of excavation, Roosevelt gave credence to the relationship between physical might and the essence of America.[53]

However, Roosevelt's notion of Americanism perhaps got its most thorough treatment during World War I. As martial fitness was a central American characteristic, a just war would present American citizens with the kind of dramatic confrontation the Frontier Myth required, and Roosevelt relished the opportunity. Discouraged by the country's nonparticipation early in the war, aghast at the lack of preparation as the conflict continued, and incensed by President Wilson's refusal to allow him to raise a regiment and go fight, Roosevelt became one of the most vocal advocates for participation in the Great War.[54]

As the issue of loyalty among immigrants with ties to the warring nations took center stage, Roosevelt seized the opportunity to press his case for hardy

Americanism. Speaking before the Knights of Columbus in late 1915, Roosevelt invoked the need "not to make life easy and soft," but to "fit us in virile fashion to do a great work for all mankind" by holding our "own against aggression by any other nation." He reminded his audience about an American past rife with icons of martial hardihood who defended the nation. More important, these icons had descended from European stock. Strategically, Roosevelt linked immigration to Americanism: "Among the generals of Washington in the Revolutionary war were Greene, Putman, and Lee, who were of English descent; Wayne and Sullivan, who were of Irish descent. . . . So it was in the Civil War. Farragut's father was born in Spain and Sheridan's father in Ireland . . . and Grant came of a long line of American ancestors whose original home had been Scotland."[55] The lesson of history seemed clear: Roosevelt believed past American honor and fortitude rested largely with immigrants. When whites looked back at their past, they would see the immigrants who helped to initiate America's development.

The European war gave Roosevelt the opportunity to call for institutionalizing his childhood quest for physical development. According to him, countries such as Belgium would not have suffered the indignities they had if they had been "wise in time": "Let us inaugurate a system of obligatory universal military training. . . . Let ours be true Americanism. . . . Let us prepare ourselves for justice and efficiency within our own border during peace, for justice in international relations, and for efficiency in war. . . . Let [us] furthermore remember that the only way in which successfully to oppose wrong which is backed by might is to put over against it right which is backed by might."[56] For him, a culture obviously needed the physical might to defend itself at home and abroad. Newcomers to the nation would need to demonstrate this crucial aspect of Americanism to prove them worthy of American identity. Yet, strength of sinew alone did not completely define the essence of the nation.

Virtuous Character

Roosevelt also believed moral character reflected the individual's embrace of Americanism. Again, his childhood proved crucial by providing him constant lessons in moral reform. Roosevelt's father embodied what one biographer called a "muscular Christianity," demonstrating, like Christ, a "moral purity" in thought and action for dedicated humanitarian efforts in the community.[57] Young Roosevelt learned that people in a position to help should aid those who most needed it; later, Roosevelt would revise the idea of service to mean helping those who could first help themselves. Likewise, the older Roosevelt taught his son the need for moral vigor in everyday life.[58] For Roosevelt, the concepts of good and evil became clear and indisputable, and each individual needed to recognize that clarity. As a result, much of his rhetoric took on a reformist tone.

Much has been made of Roosevelt's supposed reformist or progressive impulse. For some, his lectures on moral behavior proved disingenuous since he did not compile a consistent record of accomplishment regarding reform. For instance, corporate institutions he threatened to "bust" actually flourished in number while he was president. Others complained Roosevelt lambasted true reformers—such as the Muck-Rakers—who sought to bring political corruption to public attention. Still others noted Roosevelt simply jumped on the reformist bandwagon when it served to enhance his own political career.[59] As I have argued elsewhere, there seems little doubt Roosevelt demonstrated his *rhetorical* commitment to reform during most of his public career. He confronted the nation's social ills with a discourse of practical reform that called for a system of institutional changes implemented in a measured fashion to help only those deemed worthy of such help. His rhetoric probably seemed harsh to those advocates asking for help for the most downtrodden of society. Furthermore, his practical rhetoric undoubtedly appeared contrary to those progressives who called for wholesale institutional changes, but Roosevelt believed laws alone could not create a humanitarian spirit in modern America.[60] Thus, his rhetoric focused on reforming the character of the citizenry.

Roosevelt thought he had good reason to call for the uplifting of the nation's character. He feared turn-of-the-century America was unraveling at the seams, evidenced by the abuses suffered by laborers in the workplace and the social vices rife in cities.[61] Coupled with the admonitions of Frederick Jackson Turner and Brooks Adams, the seeming disintegration of America's agrarian lifestyle also signaled the decline of homely qualities—virtues which had distinguished early citizens.

To address this decline, Roosevelt utilized a type of sermon known as a "jeremiad." The jeremiad is a rhetorical genre that distinguishes the audience as a Chosen people, threatens that status by condemning the audience for sinful behavior, and finally offers the means of salvation to restore the audience to its preeminent place above all others.[62] Puritan ministers in the New World employed the jeremiad to remind listeners of their faith and their mission in the new land. These sermons identified the challenges of the New World as a rite only the most ethical people could endure, and distinguished the vast wilderness as a sacred bounty only the most principled of communities deserved. Jeremiads awakened audiences to their responsibility for rejecting evil and embracing good. Rather than meeting the challenges of the uncharted wilderness with depravity and wickedness, early Puritan settlers could find redemption by recognizing the "good" such trials provided—recognizing those challenges as the means to develop a noble spirit and to affirm their "unique covenant with God."[63]

Used in a political context, jeremiads promise citizens an American nation blessed by God. They emphasize the glorious nature of a bold experiment in democracy, freedom, and liberty that was unrivaled anywhere else. This discourse also compels behavior by prophesying doom for those people who violated God's will, such as through some form of anti-Americanism. By conforming to the political agenda espoused, communities would once again find greatness as a Chosen people. In other words, political jeremiads call for individuals to demonstrate the requisite character necessary to affirm sacred virtues and national values; otherwise, they risk separation from the glory of God and America. Perhaps even more important to the development of Americanism, such rhetoric fuses notions of otherworldly mandates and national principles.[64]

"Pastor" Roosevelt spent a great deal of time on issues of character. He, like Puritan minister Jonathan Edwards, blasted his congregations by cataloguing their respective sins and the consequences of their immoral behavior.[65] For Roosevelt, modern America suffered from too much greed and self-interest. Thus, he demonized rampant materialism—and the resulting "life of ease"—as a threat to the spiritual fortitude of the nation. However, similar to early American ministers, he offered absolution. He offered Americanism as both the promise and the realization of the nation's salvation.

According to Roosevelt, greed constituted a major character flaw. He particularly rebuked those who put making money above serving the public interest. Writing for *The Century* in 1886, Roosevelt chastised the "pompous, self-important" merchant who appeared "unused to any life outside of the counting-room." Too often such people regarded "everything merely from the standpoint of 'Does it pay'?" Just as he disdained the physical weakling, Roosevelt likewise denounced those with a cowardly spirit. "Many cultured men neglect their political duties simply because they are too delicate to have the element of 'strike back' in their natures, and because they have an unmanly fear of being forced to stand up for their own rights when threatened with abuse or insult."[66] This greedy and timid behavior violated the Rooseveltian sense of service to the community. His speeches highlighted what he considered a covenant forgotten in the modern era—people needed to work toward one another's benefit, not actively against it. While small business people shirked their duty at the local level, galling Roosevelt in the process, he saved some of his most vituperative condemnations for his favorite target at the national level. For him, the weak character of corporate owners threatened the moral integrity of the entire nation.

With the burgeoning of technology, increases in immigrant workers, and the availability of natural resources, industrial production increased exponentially by the end of the nineteenth century. Many industries turned to a corporate form of control to manage the evolutionary changes taking place. Typical commercial organizations, such as the family business or simple partnership, found themselves overshadowed by corporate bodies controlling nearly all aspects of production, distribution, purchasing, and raw materials.[67] Despite the advantages to corporate ownership, there existed pernicious problems. Roosevelt's friend, Brooks Adams, warned that the consolidation of wealth led to a state where the society's leaders "ceased to be chosen because they were valiant or eloquent, artistic, learned, or devout." Instead, society came to name leaders who were greedy people who excelled at the "faculty of acquiring and keeping wealth."[68] To that end, corporations became a "legally sanctioned fiction" whose arcane practices separated the owners' interests, workers' compensation, and the public's welfare from one another.[69] These corporate institutions embodied one of Roosevelt's worst fears—an entity consumed with an unbridled materialism and a greed that led to malicious behavior. Corporate owners obsessed with materialism at the expense of their workers and the buying public exhibited a meanness of character.

The rise of corporate America coincided with the Progressive impulse to safeguard the public from such malevolent forces. This synergy actually reflected attempts by capitalists to increase their power by linking themselves to the state. "The dominant fact of American political life," Gabriel Kolko observed about Roosevelt's era, "was that big business led the struggle for the federal regulation of the economy." If business owners could not ensure their material success through cooperation on their own, the government might be able to bring order to the economic arena.[70] Kolko noted the "most important business constituencies . . . had attained the essential legislation they sought from the federal government. There were undesired aspects to their triumphs, but . . . above all they had virtually complete mastery over the implementation of the laws they advocated and the personnel of the [regulatory] commissions they created."[71] As a result, the social good became associated with burgeoning corporate interests, although those interests came at the expense of the consumer. Roosevelt stood against private greed by condemning the will of corporate America.

Roosevelt easily acknowledged the benefit of corporate institutions. They were an inevitable part of American progress. However, he also recognized in them a potential for great sin. "Evils are real and some of them are menacing," the president observed in a 1902 speech, "but they are the outgrowth, not of misery or decadence, but of prosperity—of the progress of our gigantic industrial development."[72] As chief executive, he turned a baleful eye toward corporate titans, and like a minister, he smote them.

For Roosevelt, the corporate owners' quest for wealth spurred them into all manner of illegal and immoral behaviors that abused the public good. For example, Roosevelt pointed to the railroad titans as the chief culprits. When

J. P. Morgan and James Hill joined with one-time competitor Edward Harriman to form the Northern Securities trust, a company seeking to dominate the railroad business in the West, critics believed that it was not only possible, but such a combination could eventually control all transportation in the United States.[73] As president, Roosevelt ordered the attorney general's office to investigate Northern Securities for possible violation of the Sherman Antitrust Act. Roosevelt publicly chastised the men behind this trust, and others like it, who fixed prices, drove smaller merchants out of business, bribed legislators, and disobeyed laws.[74] In what the biographer William Harbaugh called his "most bitter" Message to Congress in 1908, Roosevelt cast such men as having no better morals than a parasite. "Just as the black-mailer and the bribe-giver stand on the same evil eminence of infamy," Roosevelt blasted, "so the man who makes an enormous fortune by corrupting legislatures . . . and fleecing his stockholder and the public, stands on the same moral level with the creature who fattens on the blood money of the gambling-house and the saloon."[75]

Perhaps the greatest crime of corporate leaders involved the example they presented to those who were not wealthy. According to President Roosevelt in 1905, success through immoral means created a "false standard" by which to live life. "Venomous envy of wealth [and] cringing servility toward wealth," he warned, came "from a fantastically twisted . . . idea of the importance of wealth as compared to other things."[76] Unchecked, such feelings would lead to a disastrous weakening of the national character, demonstrated by a "carelessness toward the rights of others," and the "awakening in our breasts [the] mean vice of viewing with rancorous envy and hatred the men of wealth merely because they are men of wealth."[77]

Roosevelt's crusade against what he considered corporate greed clearly appeared hyperbolic. Depicting business leaders as parasites and deliberate promoters of sin cast them in extreme terms, yet his exaggerated castigations cemented his image as a "trust buster." Roosevelt had initiated investigations on a number of industries he deemed "evil." However, his outrageous accusations affirmed to corporate titans their belief that he posed a real threat to them if their more sordid abuses did not stop.[78] In other words, his rhetorical show of excessive condemnations convinced corporate owners that they should exhibit moral character or suffer the consequences.

More important, Roosevelt feared the cries from political and public quarters to cripple the trusts because of their abusive acts, a move he believed would impede the financial progress of the nation. "Hasty legislation of a violent type," he explained during William McKinley's campaign for the presidency in 1900, would likely crush "the evil at the expense of crushing even more of good."[79] Legally overreacting to corporate entities would cause more harm than good since "much of the legislation" proposed against them, Roosevelt claimed, was ill conceived.[80] During his presidency, Roosevelt chastised those journalists he believed were partly responsible for the unreasoning attack on the trusts. According to him, these "muck-rakers" did not necessarily serve the public good if they exposed crooked politicians and business executives by attacking them in a "sensational, lurid, and untruthful fashion." He feared that too many "yellow journalists" made "crude and sweeping generalizations as to include decent men in the general condemnation, [creating] a general attitude either of cynical belief in and indifference to public corruption or else of a distrustful inability to discriminate between the good and the bad."[81] Such stories, he believed, generated an irrational hatred of all trusts, or a costly indifference to their actions.

Roosevelt fought these journalistic excesses with his own exaggerated rhetoric about an anxious public violently rendering the trusts impotent, which worked in tandem with his and the media's pronouncements about demonic corporate owners who malevolently abused the public trust. In emphasizing these extremes, Roosevelt placed audiences in an uncomfortable position from which to decide the common good. To alleviate their anxiety in wrestling with either radical position, he proposed a middle ground.

As Roosevelt would do repeatedly during his attempt to make "Americans, pure and simple," he proposed Americanism as the remedy for greed, immorality, selfishness, and the inequities in public life. Writing for an 1894 periodical, he defined Americanism as the ideal expression of character, a sort of homely spirit needed to suffuse the very being of citizens and provide them the needed solace in their modern lives. "One quality which we must bring to the solution of every problem," he remarked, was an "intense and fervid Americanism." When that happened, success followed. Conversely, without that fortitude of "heart and soul [and] spirit and purpose," a person failed to live up to the title of "American." In particular, Roosevelt's essay concerned those "silly" Americans who seemed willing to "throw away" their birthright by seeking to "model themselves on the lines of other citizens." Too many Americans saw themselves as "second-rate" Europeans: "over-civilized, over-sensitive [and] over-refined." Such people, Roosevelt claimed, undoubtedly suffered from "some organic weakness in their moral" character. He reminded his audiences that "it remains true that no one of our people can do any work really worth doing unless he does it primarily as [a virtuous] American."[82] If citizens attempted to idolize what he considered effeminate foreigners, they would not have the strength of will to stand against sordid corporate titans. When citizens respected the homely virtues instead, Americanism appeared the key to attaining national identity.

Both policy makers and business people needed to understand the practicality of Americanism. Speaking about corruption in government and business, Roosevelt explained Americanism as a "perfectly simple" concept. It involved "common honesty, common sense, and that reasonable amount of courage, of willingness to accept responsibility and to stand punishment." For him, this constituted nothing more than a respect for the Ten Commandments and the Golden Rule, an understanding of "decency and righteousness" that would lead to an existence worth living.[83] In the tradition of a jeremiad, he fused sacred principles with political ends. The revitalization of these Christian tenets in everyday life could slow both the excesses of corporate machination as well as dampen the anxiety audiences had about such machinations. At the very least, his rhetoric put audiences on notice that their selfish behaviors risked their relationship with God.

Roosevelt strategically defined Americanism as strength of character in which anyone strong enough to embrace the nationalist belief demonstrated his or her worth as an American. As president, he spoke directly to this issue regarding foreigners. "Let us remember that the question of being a good American," he offered in one Annual Message, "has nothing whatever to do with a man's birthplace." Simply put, "good Americanism is a matter of heart, of conscience, of lofty aspiration, [and] of sound common sense." He also displayed his disdain for nativist critics who believed foreigners polluted the national character: "If they [foreigners] are sound in body and in mind, and above all, if they are of good character," they deserved their place.[84] The president offered a blunt observation about demonstrating the requisite character: "We should keep steadily before our minds the fact that Americanism is a question of principle, of purpose, of idealism, of character; that it is not a matter of birthplace, or creed, or line of descent. . . . Representatives of many [races] . . . will be combined in one; and of this new type those men will best represent what is loftiest in the nation's past . . . who stand each solely on his worth as a man; who scorn to do evil to others, and who refuse to submit to wrongdoing themselves; who have in them no taint of weakness, who never fear to fight when fighting is demanded by a sound and high morality."[85] Roosevelt's pronouncements seemingly placed the responsibility for American identity on the individual. Thus, broadly conceived, Americanism was open to anyone willing and capable of exercising it.

Whereas whites forced assimilation and Americanization on ethnic and racial "others," Americanism seemingly allowed individuals to affect their own change in identity. Roosevelt held out the promise of national salvation to immigrants and nonwhites if they coupled both physical hardihood and strength of will to benefit the community. By doing this, they had the opportunity to earn equality and become a "true" American.

Earning Equality

The third theme of Roosevelt's Americanism involved the embracing of national spirit—those underlying ideals such as democracy, freedom, rule of law, and liberty. Specifically, though, he featured equality as the essential trait of Americanism. Citizens needed to discharge two simple duties: earn their equality and, in turn, treat others as equals. In that way, the nation would realize its destiny. Understandably, he wondered about equal treatment for all given the increasingly diverse nature of the population, and the popular and legislative reactions to that diversity.[86]

America had begun as a multi-ethnic nation. Crèvecoeur noted as such in 1792 in his *Letters From an American Farmer*. He recognized the "strange mixture of blood" found in the people of the North American continent (excluding Native Americans and African Americans). After asking, "What then is the American," Crèvecoeur offered this answer: the European who sheds his old life like dead skin would then embrace the democracy of the new world.[87] This answer undoubtedly reassured the dominant culture. Whites could believe foreigners ceased to be foreigners and became Americans upon arrival, especially since the former had welcomed immigrants before the middle nineteenth century to expand the labor force in the new country.[88]

Yet, this welcome came in grudging form. White Americans had felt uneasy at permitting large numbers of foreigners into the country. Some people particularly opposed this in the latter part of the nineteenth century when immigration rates spiked. During this time, nativists used political and public forums to speak against and to legislate against immigrants of all kinds, casting them as terrorists, subversives, and other unseemly types whose presence threatened the welfare of the nation.[89] Moreover, with the realization that many foreigners were not becoming Americans, public disputes about immigration and Americanization dominated the culture at the time. Such disputes pondered Crèvecoeur's question, but in a slightly different form. The question of "what then is an American" prompted the query: "who deserved to be an American?"

Roosevelt responded to the virulent nativist rhetoric, casting it as the opposite of his Americanism. According to him, such discourse epitomized "un-Americanism" with its "boasting and vainglorious ignorance of everything, good and bad, in this country."[90] Native-born citizens needed to cast off their unthinking prejudices and extend to immigrants, in particular, some sense of equal belonging. "If you don't act on the theory that every man who in good faith assumes the duties and responsibilities of an American citizen in a spirit of true Americanism is an American," Roosevelt chastised an 1895 New York audience, then native-born white citizens proved "unfit" to be Americans.[91] Presumably, those immigrants who demonstrated they had assumed their "duties and responsibilities" would have earned the right to equality. In a clever rhetorical maneuver, Roosevelt turned nativists' argument against them: he accused nativists of being un-American for espousing nativism. In doing so, Roosevelt highlighted the inanity of the nativist argument of foreigners being un-American because of their foreign origins.

Policy makers argued over the means to Americanize immigrants and to assimilate Native Americans. Some of these groups would achieve some level of equality in the national identity, albeit within proscribed limits. Unlike the Americanization attempts for immigrants, and the assimilation indoctrination for Native Americans, many whites never really considered African Americans as viable entrants to American culture. After centuries of soul-crushing slavery, blacks continued to endure physical, legal, and social atrocities. The Black Codes, a series of laws instituted following the Civil War, kept African Americans and white Americans "separate but equal."[92] Roosevelt himself, as president, closed off legal avenues by refusing to support anti-lynching legislation, and summarily judged African American soldiers guilty of attacking the Texas town of Brownsville without clear and unbiased evidence of their participation.[93] Reconstruction offered blacks some small advances in the political realm, but age-old prejudices, realized in the emerging power of the Ku Klux Klan, along with the incompetence and greed of government officials, largely derailed the program's goals.[94]

As a child, Roosevelt read what other upper-middle-class families had their children read, books and periodicals that highlighted white superiority and nonwhite inferiority. These ideas also appeared in the scholarly literature in university classrooms.[95] Roosevelt too shared in the national prejudice against foreigners and people of color. Yet, in response to such intellectual and popular impulses, he offered *his* version of equality. Being true to Americanism, Roosevelt argued, meant, "We Americans give to men of all races equal and exact justice," regardless of "foreign origin" or "native-born Americans of a different creed."[96] Of course, Roosevelt usually qualified his unequivocal statements about equality by informing audiences that true equality would never be "perfectly attained."[97] Rather, nonwhites and foreigners would have the opportunity to participate in the drive toward "perfect attainment," while, for all practical purposes, whites would determine when such attainment would be realized. "True" equality in Roosevelt's Americanism, then, became a moderate option between the problematic positions of full equality and the total exclusion of racial and ethnic "others" from national identity.

Of particular concern to Roosevelt was the treatment of African Americans. In too many places across the country, he stated, African Americans found any form of equality too distant. According to him in an 1897 article, some advocates used legislation to put "negroes . . . on an intellectual, social, and business equality with the whites. The effort has failed completely." His explanation for the failure affirmed unthinking racism as the culprit: whites erred by attempting to elevate blacks too quickly. Yet, Roosevelt blamed "large sections of the country" where the "negroes are not treated as they should be treated, and politically in particular the frauds upon them have been so gross and shameful as to awaken not merely indignation but bitter wrath." He called for everyone to recognize that hope for the African American "lies, not in legislation, but in the constant working of those often unseen forces of national life which are greater than all legislation."[98] Those "unseen forces" represented an individual's strength and character. In other words, he argued that blacks could effect their own change in status by demonstrating those tenets of Americanism. If they worked hard enough for it, they could move from the extreme of "no equality" to something akin to "full equality." People who had suffered the indignities of slavery for centuries would not likely be able to do that any time soon. Thus, Roosevelt gained the support of blacks by offering them the opportunity to gain a more favored place in national identity, while at the same time whites could feel assured that most blacks would not be able to meet that challenge.

Roosevelt would take his rhetoric of equality for blacks into the White House. Addressing attendees at the Republican Club in New York in 1905, for example, the president called for the "white men of the south" to give "hearty and respectful consideration to the exceptional men of the negro race." Those "exceptional men" deserved to have "liberty [and] equal opportunity," political recognition, the ability to earn a living, build a home, and have "protection before the law."[99] Roosevelt's unequivocal rhetoric of equality appeased two audiences. On the one hand, a handful of blacks who might achieve some limited aspects of the American Dream would not threaten white superiority. Furthermore, Roosevelt's separation of those few "exceptional" African Americans who might distinguish themselves from their group consequently affirmed whites' belief in that group's inferiority. On the other hand, southern blacks were important not only to the Republican Party, but to Roosevelt's reelection bid in 1905. Thus, he appealed to African Americans with his unequivocal statements regarding their right to equality. His frequent "equality for all" mantra heralded him as racially sensitive and a friend of blacks. In practical terms, at no time was Roosevelt asking for an equality that extended beyond certain proscribed limits. However, he argued for blacks to have at least the opportunity to acquire *some* basic rights due them as American citizens. The extent of those rights would still fall under the discretion of whites. According to Joel Williamson, "black leadership was slow to realize that Roosevelt's affection was barely skin deep," and even when the president's statements were unequivocally "pro-black," whites still believed Roosevelt's allegiances rested with them.[100]

Leaving the presidency did not deter Roosevelt's promotion of Americanism and equality. His first trip abroad after leaving the White House garnered as much media attention as he did when he left for Panama. This attention allowed Roosevelt a national outlet for his discourse while striding the international stage as if he were still a head of state. "To travel with Theodore Roosevelt," one biographer observed about the ex-president's trek, "was to travel in a carnival led by a conjurer and trailed by an idolatrous throng."[101] Lecturing at Oxford University in 1910, Roosevelt offered the key to any nation's success. "As regards every race, everywhere, at home or abroad, we cannot afford to deviate from the great rule of righteousness which bids us treat each man on his worth as a man." He addressed the fears of whites back home about nonwhites by acknowledging that this equality "has nothing to do with social intermingling." Rather, "it has to do merely with the question of doing to each man and each woman that elementary justice which will permit him or her to gain from life the reward which should always accompany . . . respect for the rights for others."[102]

Such idealistic pronouncements by Roosevelt served pragmatic ends. He believed and felt some of the same prejudices many white people of the time did. Yet, he also believed a disorderly nation—one trapped in a divisive debate about who could be an American—fueled explosive tensions and threatened the social stability of the country. Social order, for Roosevelt, was paramount.[103] Thus, he highlighted these absolute positions in the public debate, trapping audiences between choices of social disorder and unequivocal equality. Again, Roosevelt's Americanism became the reasonable option, pulling white audiences away from their extreme denunciation of granting any form of equality and moving immigrants and nonwhites away from calling for too much equality or independence from American ideals. Earning Rooseveltian equality was the key: whites would still have control of deciding when and if "inferior" people met their obligation to the community, and foreigners and nonwhites would believe they were responsible for shaping their own American identity.

With war beginning in Europe, and nativist rhetoric becoming more frequent and violent, Roosevelt focused on immigrants. Speaking in 1915, he warned audiences it was a "wicked thing" to discriminate against someone solely based on creed, place of origin, or race. Some of the country's greatest military men proved birthplace or creed did not determine how well someone served the nation. Individuals in ethnic groups had demonstrated their worthiness for equal respect in the nation. Generals such as Farragut and Lee, Roosevelt believed, showed that they were not "Scotch-Americans or Irish-Americans or English-Americans or German-Americans. They were all Americans and nothing else." Roosevelt concluded that the nation could ill afford to "continue to use hundreds of thousands of immigrants merely as industrial assets while they remain social outcasts and menaces any more than fifty years ago we could afford to keep the black man merely as an industrial asset and not as a human being." However, foreigners in particular needed to embrace the spirit of Americanism by recognizing that American culture had no equal. In other words, they needed to discard the significance they attributed to their culture of origin. Only then would they have the opportunity to realize true American equality and identity. "What is true of creed is no less true of nationality," Roosevelt asserted. "There is no room in this country for hyphenated Americanism. . . . Americanism is a matter of the spirit and of the soul. Our allegiance must be purely to the United States." For him, the hyphen symbolized a rejection by immigrants to embrace fully their belief in and loyalty to Americanism. Newcomers to the nation earned equality by casting off their origins, and Roosevelt called "good" Americans to "condemn any man who holds any other allegiance."[104]

Immigrants who used the hyphen exacerbated the hostility between themselves and nativists during World War One. Roosevelt's attacks on hyphenated Americans being un-American would make him even more famous during that time.[105] His was not the only national voice promoting a rabid nationalism, however. His rhetoric echoed that of President Woodrow Wilson. According to Stuckey, Wilson considered "unassimilated immigrants" as "dangerous." The president argued repeatedly that such foreigners "offered a potential national identity that was an amalgam of various loyalties and identities."[106] Between the two of them, a Roosevelt biographer concluded, Wilson and Roosevelt "unleashed an anti-hyphen movement."[107]

For Roosevelt, though, foreigners could earn their opportunity for "true" equality by discarding their hyphen. "For any man who tried to combine loyalty to this country with loyalty to some other country," he warned in 1917, there would be tension, and tension indicated treachery. However, "Americanism has two sides," Roosevelt assured. If the immigrant "in good faith, in soul and in body" embraced the nation, he would stand "on a full and entire equality with everybody else, and must be so treated, without any mental reservation, without any regard to his creed, or birthplace, or descent."[108] Ultimately, he concluded, if all outsiders proved their loyalty by dropping the hyphen, learning the "language of Washington and Lincoln," and strengthening their body and mind through universal training, the country could achieve an "absolute and undivided Americanism."[109] Otherwise, he pronounced grimly, immigrants who refused to demonstrate their loyalty "should be interned at hard labor" and, if their disloyalty was of an active type, they "should be buried."[110] At one end, Roosevelt placed the national ideal of an unequivocal equality. At the other end, he offered foreigners prison or death for their unwillingness to let go of their old culture. Only by dropping the hyphen could individual immigrants reap the benefits of American identity.

Roosevelt's Americanism responded to the differing prejudices of his day. He offered its elements as an antidote to the nation's ills, including immigration and Americanization concerns, assimilation problems, and issues of national integrity. Indeed, Americanism affirmed the intellectual and political impulses that he championed and responded to the social policies he criticized in the modern nation. For him, the public needed to understand the fundamental elements of national existence: martial vigor, strength of will, and the sense that equality was earned by virtue of vigor and will.

How did Roosevelt promote his version of Americanism to whites, immigrants, and nonwhites? How did he popularize the idea that the means to acquire national identity was open to any, that it constituted a natural process of self-transformation rather than of artificial forcing, and blur the fact that it still separated the nation along racial, ethnic, and class lines? The next section will elaborate how Roosevelt contextualized his version of Americanism within mythic themes. Specifically, he invoked elements of what some consider the foundational story that Americans have been telling themselves about their origin and destiny since the beginning of the Republic—the Frontier Myth. However, as was Roosevelt's penchant, he co-opted the story's elements to serve his own ends.

Mythologizing America

As mentioned previously, a myth is a narrative that articulates a community's origin and sense of identity. According to Richard Slotkin, myths are stories that "define the total world-picture of a human culture," and articulate a "scenario or prescription for action."[111] These narratives, of a factual or fictional nature, ground modern ideologies and practices in historical experiences. In doing so, they articulate the values upon which a community rests, celebrate those values as sacred and necessary for someone's success, and resolve any contradictions for "outsiders" to the community who embrace the sacred values but do not find success. Simply put, myths are the building blocks of a society because they convincingly popularize and affirm the moral truths of that society. While a culture's storytellers reveal any number of myths to educate its members, the myth of origin represents the most compelling narrative.[112] These stories reveal a fantastic realm and a particular group of beings who enter that realm and emerge with discovered insights of their potential. As a result, the "chosen" people become so significant that they affect the world around them. For Americans, one such group is the Puritans.

The Puritans constructed America's symbolic origin with their rhetoric of a divine "errand" into the New World. Just as the Bible recounted the Israelites' struggles to reach their promised land, seventeenth- and eighteenth-century Puritans on the North American continent spoke of a similar destiny. Ministers repeatedly told their flocks that their earthly mission reflected a Godly mandate. Leaving their known, yet problematic existence in Europe and braving the unknown in a new land would bring them success heretofore unknown to them. "It was not a matter of attaining innocence, more land and wealth," Sacvan Bercovitch explained, but that those narratives provided the "equation of progress with biblical prophecy as *American* millennialism."[113] He noted that the "fantasy of Puritan origins had worked," because the Puritans "represented . . . the movement toward modernity, because they associated that movement with their prospects in the New World." Puritan rhetoric gave early settlers a means to reconcile the modern prospects of agrarianism, industrialization, religious freedom, and a host of differing customs. Their narratives about their mission in the New Israel provided them a "set of metaphysically (as well as naturally) self-evident truths; a moral framework within which a certain complex of attitudes, assumptions, and beliefs can be taken for granted as being not only proper but right; [and] a superempirical authority to sustain the norms of personal and social selfhood."[114] The Puritan narrative consecrated the settlers' journey into the wilderness, having left their familiar world to prosper in the unknown vastness of North America. Their story distinguished America as a chosen nation with a divine purpose. It was their myth of origin.

The Puritan's myth of origin laid the groundwork for people to envision their "New" England as a "United States of America."[115] Yet, the hallowed nature of the Puritans' adventure had perhaps grown distant as new groups of people entered the nation with varying religions and attitudes, as well as the dominant culture itself seeming to discard its pastoral history to embrace an urban future, one that carried a number of modern evils. Standing in the way, however, was Roosevelt. He essentially called for a retelling of the Puritans' mission into the wilderness and the application of the lessons they learned to the modern era. He would link that mythic history to the more modern notion of Western expansion, and as a means to explain and to popularize immigration, assimilation, race, ethnicity, and national identity. The Puritans' narrative would manifest in Roosevelt's era as the Frontier Myth, a story he told repeatedly during his public career.

The Frontier Myth has been a commonplace in American politics, history, and social culture for the last few centuries.[116] According to the myth, as European settlers migrated across the North American continent, they encountered evermore dangerous circumstances. The frontier acted as a scene that called forth viciousness in the story's protagonists. This wild frontier hosted a violent battleground where settlers regressed into a state of savagery to survive against Native "savages," but who redeemed themselves by struggling for the greater democratic good of the new nation. As Slotkin explained, "The compleat 'American' of the myth was one who had defeated and freed himself from both the 'savage' of the western wilderness and the metropolitan regime of authoritarian politics and class privilege." The myth of rugged individuals who settled the unexplored universe of the North American continent articulated an ideology for national identity, a narrative that accounted for the democratic government, economic growth, progressive policies, and international exploits of the American nation.[117]

Slotkin too recognized the rhetorical power of this myth. The symbols of the frontier, he explained, have become common, appearing in all manner of media; they need no real explanation. The myth "does not argue its ideology," he observed, "it projects models of good or heroic behavior that reinforce the values of ideology, and affirm as good the distribution of authority and power that ideology rationalizes."[118] Consider the Puritans who braved the new frontier to escape religious persecution, and the virtues they exhibited during their trials, to become the "models of good or heroic behavior" that contemporary culture reveres. Yet, consider also that the narrative contextualizes the Puritans' intolerance and vaunted self-righteousness as "good behavior" warranted by the frontier scene that led to the forging of a nation.[119] Furthermore, the Frontier Myth derives much of its rhetorical power from the fact that it appears as a repetition of "ageless and transcendent traditions and principles." Each succeeding generation points to its frontier-inspired predecessors to rationalize current acts, both good and bad. Thus, America appears timeless and part of the predictable course of history. Through such taken-for-granted, identity-shaping myths, human behavior, no matter the motivation or consequence, can simply feel a part of the natural and Godly state of things.[120]

In fact, the Frontier Myth provides a number of compelling icons and themes that seemingly speak only to the American nation. Through the myth, rhetors provide audiences with three important themes: a chaotic universe, a heroic protagonist, and an account of the lessons learned by the protagonist in the universe, the "moral" of the story. The unknown universe depicted in the Frontier Myth provides the scenic backdrop for the protagonist's evolution. The frontier scene reveals a fantastic place of unknown challenges and life-altering opportunities. Jenni Calder noted that the frontier forests and the mountains each have "an individual brand of beauty," a beauty that is also "ominous."[121] Janice Rushing echoed that notion about the frontier narrative, observing the North American continent as a "promised land" containing "dark forests" and "bleak prairies."[122] Dime novels made the West appear as an extremely violent realm, giving refuge to desperadoes, vigilantes, horse thieves, and other malcontents.[123] Such descriptions provide the scene with an alluring yet dangerous aura, delighting the audience with an impression of peace and beauty while gratifying its appetite for the thrill of violence and change. Perhaps more important, the violence and chaos of the frontier demanded martial strength to conquer it and called for the right character to civilize it.

The valiant protagonist of the Frontier Myth has become a staple in popular culture.[124] Various media have told the story of settlers who, because of the frontier, represent the prototypical American icon—a unique entity with rugged, virtuous, progressive, and democratic traits. Novels, such as the still popular *Leatherstocking Tales* of the mid-nineteenth century, affixed the Daniel Boone persona in the public's mind, the rugged huntsman who braved the chaotic frontier to help civilization flourish. Other frontier warriors, such as gallant Davy Crockett, epitomized the "frontier superman" who wore a "coonskin cap [and] buckskin shirt," doled out generous helpings of "homespun wisdom," and demonstrated "awe-inspiring bravery" against savage forces.[125] These individuals, and others like them, represented what can only be termed "heroes," those transcendent supermen from a historically wondrous time. Such individuals personify mythic warriors who braved the "harsh frontier," Rushing noted, stalwart outdoorsmen "who fought to conquer the land and its endemic inhabitants" for the good of the American community. In the best tradition of virtuous heroics, these people sacrificed themselves for the greater good.[126] Magazine articles, dime novels, movies, and speeches trumpeted the fact that the frontier wilderness was where anything could happen, and which consequently called for a superhuman, righteous protagonist who could meet the waiting challenges. This image continues today in countless media.[127]

The moral of the Frontier Myth identified how the nation would achieve its distinctiveness as a "chosen" culture. "At the core of the Myth," Slotkin noted, "is the belief that economic, moral, and spiritual progress are achieved by the heroic forays of civilized society into the virgin wilderness, and by the conquest and subjugations of wild nature and savage mankind." According to the narrative, early Americans learned the lesson that strength and character were necessary for the establishment of a democratic and equal community. Unfortunately, they also learned that the safety of their community rested on the taming of the wilderness. As a result, the community could brook no interference from inferior peoples living in the scene; the Frontier Myth had set the stage for racial violence. Slotkin argued that this mythic narrative was synonymous with "savage war," making "coexistence between primitive natives and civilized Europeans impossible on any basis other than that of subjugation."[128] The savage, or alien, would not be allowed to interfere with the sacred destiny of the nation. "Behind the mystique of the Indian war," Slotkin asserted, "lay a concept of social relations that insisted on the racial basis of class difference, and insisted that in a society so divided, strife was unavoidable until the more savage race was wholly exterminated or subjugated."[129] America's myth of origin taught a fundamental lesson: "civilized" folk would eliminate "savage" others, and the elimination was simply a natural consequence of the story. Any idea of equality between these groups was out of the question.

That moral of the Frontier Myth had driven white Americans to war on Native Americans, first to gain their land and then to eradicate their presence. While the myth employed Native Americans in the role of savages, nativist rhetors in Roosevelt's era easily replaced iconic natives with other savage groups, such as immigrants and African Americans. Instances of lynching and race riots reflected mythic underpinnings, and wars against the "other" routinely invoked the mythic language of Armageddon.[130]

It should come as no surprise that Roosevelt embraced the Frontier Myth. He voraciously read historians, such as Francis Parkman and James Fenimore Cooper, who wrote of a romanticized past with upright characters who demonstrated the requisite strength to stand against antagonistic forces. His own life on the frontier and in the wilds hunting big game undoubtedly allowed him to identify with the rugged heroes of another time. He even cofounded the Boone and Crockett Club, an organization for social elites, which revolved around hunting and other rigorous, outdoor activities. It gave these adults the opportunity to play "Cowboys and Indians," not so much as a game, but as a testament of American progress and virtue. Many of the histories, novels, and short stories that Roosevelt wrote featured civilized warriors crushing native savages. It seems natural that a myth he himself so fervently believed would become the framework for much of his public advocacy. Specifically, to promote his idea of Americanism, Roosevelt grounded his concept in the story he loved best, the Frontier Myth. Most noticeable, according to Slotkin, was Roosevelt's insistence that this frontier drama revealed the requisite type of person whose exploits acted as the basis for American life.[131]

Roosevelt would write about the exotic nature of the frontier, romanticizing the dangers and rewards in any number of narrative histories. For him, however, the importance of the frontier also came from its potential to transform character. The hardships of the frontier exacerbated traits, both good and bad. "A man who in civilization would be merely a backbiter," he wrote in *Ranch Life and the Hunting Trail*, "becomes a murderer on the frontier." Likewise, he noted an individual who might greet you with a "cheery good morning" in the city would likely be "full of chivalric and tender loyalty" in the wilderness. The frontier was not completely determinative, as it did not guarantee successful transformations. As Roosevelt remarked, "foolish people . . . will probably fail anywhere."[132] Instead, the frontier scene of challenges and dangers provided opportunities for protagonists to develop virtuous character, the hallmark of Americanism. Like everything else with Roosevelt, an individual seemingly had a choice between virtue and villainy. And in the case of national identity regarding foreigners and nonwhites, they seemingly had a choice between being accepted or staying independent based on their own will.

In his narrative histories, such as *The Winning of the West*, Roosevelt's protagonists exhibited a martial ability that distinguished them as superhuman progenitors of the American nation. An individual, who left the known world and faced the dangers of the unknown world with strength of arm, transcended a "savage" existence and evolved into a being who understood the sacred principles of Americanism. "See what the things are that you are proudest of as you look back," Roosevelt stated in 1905, "and you will in almost every case find that those memories of pride are associated not with days of ease but with days of effort, with the day when you had to do all that was in you for some worthy end." For Roosevelt, strength would always be a necessary component to reach worthwhile goals. With no frontier savages to fight in the modern age, however, manly strength was still necessary for less martial ends. According to him, a person needed strength to bring about the "worthiest of all worthy ends," and that involved making "those that are closest and nearest to you . . . happy and not sorry that you are alive."[133] Roosevelt would develop his own version of frontier supermen in his myth of Americanism. However, even without the opportunity of a wild frontier scene during the turn of the twentieth century, such strength would still be important in the social chaos of the modern universe.

With the wild frontier declared closed in his era, Roosevelt would use the complexity of modern life as the catalyst for change. American culture appeared to be disintegrating into extreme positions of corporate power versus small business viability, private influence versus public welfare, and national culture versus hyphenated identity. Hyphenated identity troubled him most: an increasingly diverse and disorderly population was losing its knowledge of and connection to the nations' sacred origin. By reawakening his audiences to their frontier memories, Roosevelt would demonstrate how strength and virtue could lead to the realization of equality.

Roosevelt's strategy was simple. Although the Frontier Myth pit civilized whites against all other cultures, he would use its thematic elements to elevate "others," making them appear equal to that of whites. He employed the Frontier Myth, replete with his reorientation of it for the modern era, to give Native Americans, blacks, and immigrants a preeminent place in the story, a place usually reserved for whites. In other words, he featured some of the nation's immigrants and nonwhites as the heroic protagonists in America's mythic origin. Furthermore, he demonstrated how these racial and ethnic outsiders continued demonstrating the Frontier Myth in modern America. The moral of his story, then, demonstrated that these outsiders proved ready for some level of equal consideration within the national identity.

Roosevelt's persistent "equality for all" pronouncements about American identity countered the notion of citizens choosing hyphenated and other racial and ethnic identifications. Mythic Americanism, then, became the more moderate position: it privileged an earned equality that offered some opportunity for basic rights. The only thing a person had to do was simply swear allegiance to the nation. For immigrants, that meant dropping the hyphen. For others, it meant staying within certain proscribed boundaries, restrictions reinforced through frontier-inspired, mythic themes. Of course, constructing a unified and equal identity from a diverse group of people would work only to the extent that inferior groups could meet the challenge set by the rhetoric of the dominant group, while retaining their position of inferiority.[134]

Roosevelt resolved issues of identity, assimilation, Americanization, ethnicity, race, and equality by complicating them—through myth—keeping similarities and differences between the varying groups in tension. By offering mythic portraits of whites, immigrants, blacks, and Native Americans within his concept of Americanism, highlighting their commonalities as well as their diversities, he kept the debate about identity ongoing, preventing it from polarizing one way or the other. Consequently, Roosevelt offered Americanism as the resolution to the social contradictions of the day. For example, Americanism worked to pull nativists from their destructive position of hatred and lawlessness, just as it educated immigrants away from the unrealistic position of privileging their old culture in modern America. He kept the tensions of national identity in play, not allowing either side to dominate. The myth of Americanism became the uneasy middle ground for the modern citizen.

At some level, Roosevelt may have understood that a culture's tensions keep it moving forward and its complacencies keep it stifled. To address that tension, his mythic rhetoric provided possibilities for new identities and roles to emerge in the modern era. At the very least, he promoted the notion of racial and ethnic others having a status heretofore unknown to them, even while the racist mindset of twentieth-century white America continued.

The next chapter begins the examination of Roosevelt's synthesis of Americanism and myth. Specifically, it reviews *The Winning of the West,* Roosevelt's retelling of America's frontier history. His multivolume work privileged immigrants by maintaining the focus on the foreign nature of those frontier protagonists. It kept the sense of national identity in tension, highlighting the idea that immigrants were not socially worthless to American society as many nativists believed. His rhetoric transformed early immigrant settlers into true mythic heroes. Not only could native-born whites see an immigrant as a frontier icon, but it also provided foreigners with a story they could embrace on their way to becoming "real" Americans. As will be demonstrated later, Roosevelt employed the mythic themes from *The Winning of the West* to contextualize Americanism for other groups not usually considered a part of the frontier experience. Of course, Roosevelt's stories may have transformed immigrants and other non-whites into frontier heroes, but it also limited their choices in the modern era. As a public rhetor, Roosevelt sought to adjust the idea of Americanism to his listeners while simultaneously adjusting them to the significance of what it meant to be an American. This he accomplished with his retelling of the nation's mythic origin.

2

Forging Americanism on the Frontier

~

Immigrants and *The Winning of the West*

Theodore Roosevelt was not alone in discussing matters of race and ethnicity at the turn of the twentieth century. Other political leaders also voiced their concerns. According to several rhetorical scholars, presidents, in particular, articulated the growing tensions regarding American identity and immigration. Vanessa Beasley noted that chief executives such as William Henry Harrison, William McKinley, and Grover Cleveland failed to reconcile this tension and heightened xenophobic fears in the process.[1] Their inaugural addresses and state-of-the-union messages made no room in the national identity for immigrants, excluding them based on their supposed "weakness of mind and character as proof" of their inability to share in the ideological and spiritual foundations of the nation. Their unwillingness to grant some benefit of the doubt to newcomers, Beasley observed, "sanctioned more general anti-immigrant feelings among the American people."[2] Mary Stuckey likewise found Woodrow Wilson unwilling to "espouse inclusion for [any] group that the mass of general opinion did not support."[3] Despite his attempt to depict the nation as grounded in a shared belief of universal and democratic principles that extended to all citizens, Wilson seemingly went out of his way to highlight and to reaffirm the racist stereotypes of his day. The preponderance of his exclusionary rhetoric concerning anyone he deemed too different coincided with the fact that "immigration became more restricted on his watch."[4]

Chief executives seemed adept at excluding nonwhite and immigrant groups from the nation's identity, and for exacerbating those newcomers' ethnic and racial differences in the process. At first glance, Roosevelt appeared no different. According to Edmund Morris, while President Roosevelt "welcomed the clash of alien cultures, as long as it did not denigrate into mass collision," he also felt that America's "first responsibility was to its literate, native-born working poor." Yet, Roosevelt also worked to mediate the tensions surrounding who could be included within the national identity. To that end, he backed legislation that limited the immigration of poverty and disease-stricken persons from various ethnic groups, but in no way called for immigration to end.[5]

The concern here, though, is Roosevelt's pre-presidential career, one in which he wrote and spoke extensively on immigration. He considered immigration necessary, but not simply for altruistic reasons. He wanted a nation that embodied his mythic conception of Americanism—a nation able to fight, with the will to fight, for democratic virtue. Immigrants, in that regard, represented a potential means to revitalize the nation. Therefore, unlike political contemporaries Harrison, Cleveland, McKinley, and Wilson, Roosevelt welcomed immigration and the infusion of "new blood." He believed that anyone who looked suspiciously at immigrants simply because they were immigrants was foolish. "I have no sympathy with mere dislike of immigrants," Roosevelt observed in the late 1890s, "there are classes and even nationalities of them which stand at least on an equality with the citizens of native birth." Although his comment may speak to his belief about a fundamental difference in the racial or ethnic humanity of immigrants and Anglo-Saxons, he still offered those "classes" and "nationalities" the means to find some access to American identity. "The mighty tide of immigration to our shores has brought in its train much of good and much of evil," he declared, "and whether the good or the evil shall predominate depends mainly on whether these newcomers do or do not throw themselves heartily into our national life."[6] Roosevelt wanted to ensure that the newcomers would in fact leave their old cultures behind and become what he considered to be "true" Americans. Moreover, he recognized the need to assuage fears about newcomers.

To that end, Roosevelt took on the role of educator of both immigrants and native-born whites in *The Winning of the West,* his set of narrative histories published in several best-selling volumes between 1885 and 1894. These narratives recounted the struggle for westward exploration and settlement on the North American continent from 1763 to 1803.[7] Through his histories, he addressed the tension between whites who feared foreigners and those immigrants who stubbornly held on to their old customs. To move both parties away from their unproductive positions, he offered a revised version of American history.

He featured immigrants as the lead protagonists who embraced his notion of Americanism, discarded their Old World, and forged the American nation. In a sense, Roosevelt "proved" that immigrants could become "real" citizens because they had done so in America's storied past. Roosevelt's stories identified immigrants as the stuff of national myth, settlers who embodied Americanism with their combination of strength and morality. As a result, they earned their equal status in the new nation they had created. Thus, Roosevelt challenged modern whites' assumption that foreigners were inferior and not qualified to become Americans, as well as immigrants' belief that they could hold on to their Old World heritage in the modern universe.

Roosevelt popularized the idea of immigration and assimilation in American culture through a mythic narrative that grounded both the origins of American society and the future strength of its people in immigration. His stories identified the moral and social lessons that early immigrant heroes had learned, that immigrants of his era would have to understand to become wholly American, and that nativists would have to recognize as the standard by which they should assess their own identity. His mythic stories offered a taken-for-granted view of American culture, one seemingly founded on timeless values and that explained the nation's historical development as naturally inevitable.

Roosevelt responded to the nation's legal, political, and social condemnation of immigrants in *The Winning of the West*. His version of the Frontier Myth heralded immigrants as the archetypal heroes of American history, one whom many of his contemporaries seem to have overlooked.[8] Immigrant explorers represented the true heroes of American history, arriving in an unknown land, exhibiting the physical strength and high character to contend with an untamed wilderness. Furthermore, the moral of his story addressed the nature of foreign "blood inferiority" and Anglo-Saxon "blood superiority." For Roosevelt, bloodlines and places of origin did matter, but not exclusively; the knowledge of Americanism was fundamentally more important. Archetypal immigrant heroes, regardless of birthplace or bloodline, demonstrated the knowledge that strength, character, and the need to earn their equality spoke directly to citizenship. Richard Slotkin noted that Roosevelt's heroes, and the myths about them, "became one of the major constituents of cultural and political discourse" in the twentieth century.[9] Roosevelt's heroes and storylines promoted the development of the national community. By celebrating a heroic individualism in service to a greater good, Roosevelt illustrated how immigrants had become American citizens during the founding of the nation. Late-nineteenth- and early-twentieth-century immigrants benefited from their ancestors' heralded portrayal in the nation's frontier history. Furthermore, in assuaging the fears of Anglo-Saxon whites that immigration proved detrimental to America, Roosevelt rhetorically maneuvered whites to accept the immigrants' mythic legacy as their own.

American Immigration in the Modern Era

The Constitution of the United States makes little mention of immigration, save prohibiting immigration restrictions until 1808. In fact, Marion T. Bennett observed that immigration was not regularly monitored until 1820. Between 1820 and 1880 only a few major ethnic groups, mostly from northern Europe, emigrated from their homelands to the United States. As most American citizens of that time claimed an ethnic heritage from the same European region, opposition to these immigrants appeared relatively minimal. According to Bennett, "In general, Americans tended to welcome the foreigner. Their main objection to him revolved around his attempt to perpetuate foreign languages and customs as a part of American life." As the ethnic composition of immigrants changed, this sense of separatism contributed to a growing presence of ethnic and racial antipathy. Irish immigrants, for instance, met with considerable antagonism in the cities of the eastern United States. Some of the antagonism stemmed from the sheer number of poverty-stricken individuals and families who landed in American ports after the potato famine of the 1840s.[10] Between 1845 and 1855, two million Irish left their country for England and the United States, a number that remained high through the next generation.[11]

Legal restrictions of immigration reflected American attitudes; immigration law varied by state and locality, and the severity of the restrictions generally followed local immigration rates. Legal restrictions intensified throughout the 1840s and 1850s as political and economic upheaval spread across Europe, prompting an ever-greater flow of foreigners to American shores. As immigration rates climbed and the demographic profile of immigrants shifted between 1880 and 1920, Congress passed various acts and bills by which the federal government claimed the power to regulate both the number of immigrants and their countries of origin.[12]

New distinctions between "old" and "new" immigrants indicated the degree to which certain groups had assimilated into a distinctively American culture. Whereas "old" immigrants generally came from northern and western Europe, spoke English or a language from which English derives, and had begun to assimilate into mainstream American society, many people considered the "new" immigrants from southern and eastern Europe (Slavs, Russians, Eastern European Jews, Italians, Turks, Spaniards, etc.) less desirable. These new groups tended to be poor and uneducated, bringing unfamiliar languages and customs to the United States, largely settling in urban groups that were not readily assimilated into mainstream American culture, and differing physically from the tall, fair Europeans of the north.[13] Propelled by the upsurge of nativism that resisted these groups, the federal government's laissez-faire attitude toward immigration gave way to centralized control and increasingly restrictive policies.

To defend these positions, immigration restrictionists generally relied on arguments based on one of two premises: one emphasized economic objections to unrestricted immigration, and the other focused on the racial inferiority of newcomers. The economic argument advocated closing American borders, at least partially, to the "new" immigrant. Until the mid-twentieth century, most Americans lived outside urban areas and were highly suspicious of urban areas and urban problems. According to Keith Fitzgerald, "Those who saw themselves as American natives identified new immigrants with loose morals, social unrest, labor radicalism, racial inferiority, and the boss system" associated with urban areas.[14] Furthermore, between 1880 and 1920 periods of economic recession were commonly attributed to the influx of unskilled, uneducated "new" immigrant laborers accused of stealing American jobs. Most of the 25 million immigrants who had entered the country by 1880 settled in urban areas and entered the work force as industrial laborers.[15]

The economic argument identified immigrants as a dangerous source of cheap labor: men, women, and children who flooded the unskilled labor market, displacing American workers, depressing wages, and who depended on state and private charity to support them in times of recession and economic instability. "The net result of the whole process," William Bernard concluded, "was that the economic problems of our agricultural society were translated into terms of cultural differences" in the cities.[16] While Roosevelt did not directly engage this line of reasoning in *The Winning of the West,* he extolled the independent pioneer spirit that distinguished Americans from their metropolitan European forebears, and he continually decried the materialism endemic in cities as a weakness that would destroy that spirit.[17]

American policy toward Asian immigration, in particular, was shaped primarily through state labor and immigration laws until 1882, with the important exception of the 1868 Burlingame Treaty between the United States and China, which specifically provided for free mutual migration and citizenship. By 1882, however, the constitutionality of state laws regarding labor and immigration came under scrutiny for restricting interstate commerce. As a result, federal laws took over the regulation of immigration. By 1882, trade unions, "the American Legion, the American Federation of Labor, the National Grange, and other powerful opinion-molding groups in the United States" favored restricting immigration in general and Asian immigration in particular, a position "based both on economic competition and racist resentment of nonwhites."[18]

This racial aspect to immigration proved critical. The most provocative of the restrictionists' arguments was patently racist, claiming that assimilating "new" immigrants proved dangerous to American civilization. This argument grew out of Social Darwinism, the popular social philosophy that had gained widespread acceptance during this time.[19] According to Kitty Calavita, "[t]his distortion of the Darwinian theory of evolution and its application to the social world announced that the fittest survived and, therefore, that the polarization of social classes was merely a reflection of inherent abilities."[20] That the "new" immigrants also entered the United States at the bottom of the economic scale only affirmed nativists' conceptions of foreigners' inferiority.

Social arguments against immigration in the 1880s and 1890s clearly identified the "new" immigrants—Hungarians, Slavs, Poles, Italians, Russians, Jews, Spaniards, and Portuguese—as well as more recent Irish immigrants, as racially inferior. Proponents of immigration restriction, led by such intellectuals of the day as Henry Cabot Lodge, claimed the "Nordic" Caucasian nationalities to be superior because of their highly developed civilizations, rather than any inherent racial characteristics. Many believed that the "new" immigrants could not, in one generation, become equal to their more civilized neighbors. Rhetors argued that the "new" immigrants did not and would not assimilate culturally; even if they could assimilate, doing so would be deleterious to the quality of American citizenship, to its racial composition.[21] H. W. Brands acknowledged that Roosevelt had "little use for the anti-immigrant ravings" of nativist groups, but that Roosevelt was willing to be associated with such groups, given his own campaign against those "hyphenated Americans" he considered inferior and disloyal.[22]

Put more simply, "new" immigrants challenged the notion of Anglo-Saxon whiteness. From the nation's start, "white" had represented a singular, privileged term and the key to citizenship. The problem, however, emerged when nativist whites realized their initial conception of whiteness did not automatically exclude new influxes of white-skinned immigrants.

A "white" citizen is largely a political fiction, one that had its roots in the nation's first Congress. In 1790, America's first congressional representatives passed legislation allowing "all free white persons" the opportunity to gain citizenship. Their debate raged over how long foreigners would have to be in America before acquiring citizenship, whether Catholics would be eligible, and if immigrants should endure a probationary period after citizenship before they could hold political office. The one taken-for-granted element was that citizenship was limited to white people.[23] "White" acted as a unifying term for early Americans, a way to distinguish them from what they considered the inferiority of nonwhite races, such as African Americans, Asians, and American Indians.[24] Whiteness offered Anglo-Saxon citizens an inclusive place in the national hierarchy.

Yet, the inclusiveness of "white" in that congressional act backfired when it set the stage for a staggering change in the new country's demographics. The founders had not foreseen the influx of eastern European Jews, Poles, Lithuanians, and others who would attempt to claim "whiteness."[25] Anglo-Saxon citizens were hesitant to include other "whites" in the national identity. To that end, they found ways to differentiate themselves from "other" whites. The easiest way to do that was to link "new" immigrants to blacks.

Many whites considered Irish and Italian people equally inferior to African Americans. When the Irish first arrived in large numbers during the mid to late nineteenth century, they lived alongside African Americans. "In the early years," Noel Ignatiev wrote, "Irish were frequently referred to as 'niggers turned inside out,'" while "Negroes . . . were sometimes called 'smoked Irish.'" Ignatiev argued that the Irish moved closer to whiteness once they learned racism and rejected any relationship with blacks.[26] Thomas Guglielmo reached similar conclusions regarding Italian immigrants. Although native-born whites considered Italians "white on arrival," Italians' status was tenuous given their southern European origin, and the fact that they "treated African-Americans . . . no differently than anyone else." Because of the resulting social and sexual relationships between Italians and blacks, the former were often victims of lynching.[27] Once they began leaving African American neighborhoods in great numbers in the mid-twentieth century, Guglielmo concluded that Italians were "openly identifying and making demands as whites."[28] While the Italians and the Irish eventually distanced themselves from blacks, other foreigners would look to the legal system to attain greater inroads to whiteness and national identity.[29]

Unfortunately, the courts provided no real relief to anyone deemed "too different." For instance, the courts prevented the naturalization of anyone from countries such as Japan, China, and Hawaii. For the most part, they utilized whiteness in two problematic ways. First, the legal system generally offered no criteria of whiteness; they simply decided who was "not White." For example, the "one drop" rule—that no one with "one drop" of black blood could be white— defined whiteness through negation. In addition, the courts did not so much define whiteness as they simply ruled that nonwhites were inferior. Second, courts at the turn of the twentieth century relied on the "common knowledge" doctrine to determine inferiority. For instance, the Supreme Court ruled that immigrants from South Asia were inferior and thus not eligible for citizenship because the "great body of our people recognize" their inadequacy. In other words, white

Americans could clearly see the inferiority of nonwhites, allowing the court to conclude likewise based on this common-sense observation. Obviously, the courts ruled using fallacious and circular arguments. Yet, their legal pronouncements did designate whiteness as the "superior opposite" to nonwhiteness.[30]

The courts would also look to scientific evidence to support their "common knowledge" dictates. During an 1894 federal court ruling that denied citizenship to a Japanese immigrant, the judge not only argued that clear differences exist between people of varied skin colors, but that the "popular discernment of racial differences also served as the basis for the scientific categorization of human races." Research in the nineteenth century had focused on ranking types of people based on skin color. Any number of pseudo-scientific measurements designated whites as superior. Scientific tracts of this era merely celebrated the intellectual, spiritual, and physical beauty of whites.[31] However, they carried enough scientific weight for a public already willing to believe such conclusions. Science thus validated the common-sense notion that darker skin was inferior.[32]

The political, legal, and scientific impulses of the modern era propagated a xenophobic mindset in modern audiences, Roosevelt included. Some scholars have identified what they believe to be a racist tone in Roosevelt's discourse about immigration. For instance, Thomas Dyer concluded in his book, *Theodore Roosevelt and the Idea of Race,* that Roosevelt obsessed over the dangers of "race suicide." According to Dyer, Roosevelt believed that unless the white "American race stock" was preserved through increased procreation, unregulated immigration would lead to the demise of the white race.[33]

Roosevelt was a product of his time and he undoubtedly believed in the sacrosanct nature of whiteness. However, dismissing his rhetoric as racist is unproductive. The point here involves illuminating the rhetorical dynamics of his public discourse, not a simple condemnation of it. Publicly, he negotiated the anxiety between the native-born and immigrants, recognizing that a divided society would collapse or, at the very least, fail to reach its potential. Thus, he found a way to promote Americanism for the sake of both nativists and immigrants. Irrespective of his private thoughts (to which he gave voice from time to time), his public rhetoric on immigration articulated a consistent message, one he must have hoped would become affixed in the public's mind. Roosevelt's story envisioned a new America filled with possibilities and active roles for virtually anyone deemed worthy. Herein lies the power of myth in general and the Frontier Myth in particular.

The Winning of the West expressed Roosevelt's pragmatic, perhaps harsh philosophy, in novelized terms. It also provided the underpinnings for a popular myth of American culture that continues to resonate today. Before Israel Zangwill's invocation of America as a "melting pot" in his 1908 play, Roosevelt popularized the idea in his narrative histories. "Under the hard conditions of life in the wilderness," Roosevelt noted, the frontier crucible "was enough to weld together into one people the representatives of these numerous and different races."[34] Like the "melting pot," the frontier involved the destruction of differences and a melding of many types into one. What distinguished the urban symbol from the frontier story, however, rested in how those differences disappeared. For immigrants to become Americans in the urban jungle, whites forced them to undergo artificial therapies in the guise of assimilation and Americanization. Roosevelt's narratives demonstrated that this process—the harsh process of fusing a set of common American traits in immigrant settlers—occurred as a natural course of history. On the frontier, immigrants seemingly had a choice: by demonstrating their own individual strength and virtue, they would be welcomed into the nation they themselves created. Retelling the frontier story in the modern era not only informed immigrants of their historical responsibility to prove themselves, but it also assured whites by offering historical evidence that immigrants could indeed become Americans.

Now, Roosevelt's "strenuous life" philosophy did play on class biases. He used his own experiences—that of a prominent, white, upper-middle-class man—to establish criteria for groups of people far removed from such experiences. His life-threatening adventures notwithstanding, weekend jaunts with his fellow aristocrats in the Boone and Crockett Club fell within the province of aristocratic white men only.[35]

More important, Roosevelt's mythic storyline provided hope to immigrants and solace to whites. Regardless of where people originated, it seemed, the frontier forge purified them into citizens. His message was simple: remember the lessons of the frontier experience that shaped immigrant settlers of early America. Immigrants thus represented the necessary counterpart to Anglo-Saxon whites. In adopting personal qualities and moral values in service to the larger community, both native and foreign-born melded into a singular, equal group of people with the capacity to fulfill America's destiny as a thriving and powerful nation.

The Immigrant Hero on the Frontier

Audiences typically consider heroes the most influential elements of a myth.[36] Striving alone while fighting impossible odds, achieving a level of material and spiritual success theretofore unseen, the early American pioneers represented a model for citizens of Roosevelt's era to emulate.[37]

Like most mythic heroes, frontier immigrants undertook quests that tested their moral and physical mettle. Such rites of passage characterized heroic adventures in many traditional myths.[38] The travails of protagonists, resolutely undertaking something of transcendent importance, served as the catalyst that initiates the mythic cycle through which they and the people they represent recognize their greatness. Joseph Campbell noted that when heroes leave the comfort of familiar surroundings to enter a "region of supernatural wonder," they encounter "fabulous forces" against which they strive to win a decisive victory. Afterward, they returned home from their "mysterious adventures," empowered by the experience and ready to pass their knowledge to those whom they had initially left behind. This "cosmogonic cycle is presented with astonishing consistency in the sacred writings of all the continents," Campbell wrote.[39] This supernatural underpinning played out pragmatically in the Frontier Myth.

As that myth of origin states, heroes initially separated themselves from the known world. Early in *The Winning of the West*, Roosevelt stressed the importance of immigrants' separation from the Old World and their eagerness to explore the New. "Among the lands beyond the ocean America was the first reached . . . conquered by different European races, and shoals of European settlers were thrust forth upon its shores." In fact, he believed that the "vast movement by which this continent was . . . peopled cannot be rightly understood if considered solely by itself," and that the true significance would be lost "unless we grasp . . . the past race-history of the nations who took part therein." Roosevelt outlined in good detail early German, English, Spanish, and French histories of European conquest, lauding those peoples who had ventured outside their spheres of influence to establish themselves in foreign places such as the North American continent. "Each intruding European power," he observed, "had to wage a twofold war, overcoming the original inhabitants with one hand, and with the other warding off the assaults of the kindred nations that were bent on the same schemes."[40] By focusing on European history, and how various people of those cultures separated themselves from their known world, Roosevelt highlighted for readers the distinctive European origin in the unknown universe of North America.

Having left the comfort of their foreign homes, immigrants faced the challenges of the unknown universe. This trial by fire revealed the nature of the protagonist; it foreshadowed his or her potential to transform into a hero.[41] In Rooseveltian terms, the results revealed immigrants' willingness to demonstrate the taken-for-granted traits of American culture, strength, and character. Their survival meant they had achieved Americanism and had "soon became indistinguishable from the people among whom they settled."[42] In some respects, the potential hero's rite of passage began with his or her struggle with the world-scene itself. In the case of immigrant settlers, their struggle against the very environment of their new home proved to be a rite of passage; from metropolitan European cities, the immigrants struggled to survive in the primeval universe of Kentucky or the Old Northwest. Thus, Roosevelt's story painted the unexplored North American continent as a mythical place of rebirth for those strong enough to survive this rite of passage. Immigrants, then, fundamentally earned their American heritage.

For Roosevelt, the constant act of taking and holding the land distinguished early settlers from the hunters who preceded them and the merchants who succeeded them. These immigrant pioneers pushed civilization westward, where "every acre, every rood of ground which they claimed had to be cleared by the axe and held with the rifle."[43] It was these brave "frontier folk," Roosevelt identified, who individually "pushed westward [with] warlike skill and adventurous personal prowess."[44] His vivid anecdotes of the harsh conditions of life on the frontier invoked for his readers the pleasure and the brutality that immigrants faced in the mythic realm of the American wilderness.

The description of a mythical universe—the scene in which the hero must struggle—provides an emotional link for audiences to enter the narrative. According to Campbell, the audience's interest in unknown regions comes from its psychological need to project its own unconscious feelings of violence and delight.[45] The mythical universe, then, reflects the audience's psyche; it exists as a site wherein both aggression and amusement can be experienced, and where these experiences can potentially transform men and women into heroic legends or abject cowards.

The universe of the Frontier Myth reveals a place of success and savagery. In his depiction of the frontier, Roosevelt blended its majesty and its menace in a romanticized description of the environment. "Here and there copses of woodland lay like islands in the sunny seas of tall, waving grass," he wrote, while "stretches of grass land seemed limitless." Yet, so extensive were the forests, he observed, that a "man might travel for weeks as if in a perpetual twilight, never once able to see the sun" because of the trees. Everywhere, game abounded. Hunters followed trails through forests made by generations of buffalo and elk. Settlers feasted regularly on swarms of turkey, geese, ducks, and deer.[46] The game provided not just sustenance, but the reason for the immigrant settler's existence: "[he] enjoyed to the full his wild, lonely life," passing "his days hunting and exploring, wandering hither and thither over the country."[47]

But along with the benefits of seemingly unlimited land and plentiful game came the cost of surviving in that universe. Roosevelt highlighted the fierce conditions of day-to-day life for early immigrant heroes. Strength of body and of will was paramount for survival. Death became a constant companion of settlers, taking any one of numerous forms including hypothermia, starvation, disease, and drowning. In his mythic history, the majesty of the environment inevitably gave way to the forces of nature: "Swarms of deer-flies, mosquitoes, and midges rendered life a torment in the weeks of hot weather. Rattlesnakes and copperheads were very plentiful, and, the former especially, constant sources of danger and death. Wolves and bears were incessant and inveterate foes of the livestock, and the cougar or panther occasionally attacked man as well. More terrible still, the wolves sometimes went mad, and the men who then encountered them were almost certain to be bitten and to die of hydrophobia."[48] Immigrants demonstrated their resilient strength and spirit by contending with these unrelenting forces every day. But the environmental dangers proved to be the least of the settlers' worries. More ominous than death or disease were other wild "creatures," perhaps the most terrifying entities on the frontier scene—Indians.

The Frontier Myth features heroes routinely struggling against the unknown universe's forces of evil.[49] Roosevelt so characterized Native Americans, writing of their malevolent acts. He noted that they preyed on those powerless to resist; it was the newly arrived "immigrants coming in by pack train or flat-boat . . . with their wives and little ones who had most to fear" in the New World. On regular occasions, he continued, parties of "immigrants . . . were set upon by Indians," and thankfully, sometimes, the "children were tomahawked at once." This proved merciful, "for the hideous, unnamable, unthinkable tortures practised [sic] by the red men on their captured foes," Roosevelt noted, "were such as we read of in no other struggle, hardly even in the revolting pages that tell the deeds of the Holy Inquisition."[50] Immigrants knowingly set themselves against such forces, demonstrating an unflinching courage that marked them as heroes to the nation.

Overcoming the trials of this hostile environment required a fundamental element of the traditional mythic hero: physical prowess. Roosevelt's Americanism similarly lauded immigrant backwoodsmen, revealing numerous anecdotes of their incredible struggles with their savage foe: "In 1784, a family of "poor white" immigrants . . . were attacked . . . while in the immediate neighborhood of their squalid cabin. The father was shot, and one Indian was in the act of tomahawking the six-year-old son, when an elder brother, from the doorway of the cabin, shot the savage. The Indians then fled. The boy thus rescued grew up to become the father of Abraham Lincoln."[51] Roosevelt further demonized Native Americans by making them responsible for nearly causing America's hero, Abraham Lincoln, to have never been born. Yet, and perhaps more important, he affirmed his fundamental point about the potential that immigrants brought to national culture. Without giving them the opportunity for citizenship, the nation could not have benefited from Lincoln's presence, the man Roosevelt proclaimed as the "greatest man of the nineteenth century."[52]

Alongside tales of Daniel Boone, whose ancestors, Roosevelt noted, were English immigrants, the writer appointed other immigrant characters to the pantheon of frontier heroes. For example, Roosevelt's anecdotes of John Sevier, the "son of a Huguenot," who was "the most renowned Indian fighter of the Southwest," and German-born Kasper Mansker, an "expert" Indian fighter, marked them as legendary heroes of the frontier. Repeatedly, immigrant heroes demonstrated strength of sinew and of will, fighting off scores of Native Americans single-handedly, running gauntlets of club- and knife-wielding foes, facing antagonists unarmed, and making incredible escapes.[53] Clearly, these immigrants embodied Americanism.

Even the female characters of Roosevelt's frontier myth were larger than life. Now, Roosevelt's story identified frontier women in their traditional role—that of the "housewife and child-bearer."[54] Yet, he also recognized that women "fearlessly fronted every danger the men did, and they worked quite as hard."[55] He frequently featured immigrant females contending against formidable opponents. In a typical anecdote, he described how a "brawny frontierswoman" repelled an attack against her home. As Roosevelt related the tale, Indians had attacked a cabin inhabited by two men, a woman, and several children. As one of the men grappled with an intruder, he called out for the woman to hand him a knife: "Instead, she snatched up an axe and killed the savage on the spot. But that instant another [Indian] leaped into the doorway . . . the woman instantly turned on him, as he stood with his smoking gun, and ripped open his body with a stroke of her axe. Yelling for help, he sank on the threshold, and his comrades rushed to his rescue; the woman . . . cleft open the skull of the first, and the others fell back, so that she was able to shut and bar the door."[56] Like their male counterparts, Roosevelt demonstrated that immigrant women heroically met the harsh trials of the frontier. They routinely engaged in extraordinary feats that spoke not only of physical strength, such as giving birth while escaping from Native Americans, but of their moral character as well, such as when they ignored their own wounds to aid others, and risked their lives to bring needed supplies to settlements.[57]

Of course, Roosevelt's mythologized version of early immigrants' struggles against Indians justified their displacement as a former enemy.[58] "The ground had to be not only settled," he believed, "but conquered" since the "Indians themselves formed one of the main factors in deciding the fate of the continent."[59] Roosevelt considered it "foolish" to be sentimental about the fate of Indians.[60] Immigrant settlers had to fight and displace Native Americans because of the Indians' anti-progressive tendencies with the land. Roosevelt explained that "Indians had no ownership of the land in the way in which we understand the term," and that this "great continent could not have been kept as nothing but a game-preserve for squalid savages."[61] The movement west by settlers realized the sacred ideal of progress. Slotkin concluded that the "lesson Roosevelt draws from his historical fable is that no class or race can stay the march of history, and that those who seek to do so are the foes of progress."[62] Roosevelt's story naturalized the historical violence against Native Americans by casting them as the immigrant settlers' evil opponent. His mythic retelling of history not only explained genocide as a pragmatic process of progressive ideology, but it also lauded those immigrants who survived as progenitors of American culture. Moreover, he implicitly argued that immigrants had taken part in the "march of history" that resulted in the United States. Whites, now, could not refuse all newcomers lest they be judged "foes of progress."

As the countless anecdotes of immigrant heroes and their mythic struggles reflected, physical hardihood equaled success. Immigrant Americans possessed great strength, similar to that of other mythical heroes. Roosevelt's "strenuous life" philosophy permeated much of his writing, and *The Winning of the West* represented a testament to that philosophy. He wrote that "each group of rough settlers and rough soldiers" did their part "in the great epic of wilderness conquest." According to him, without that effort by the Irish, the Scots, the English, and the Germans, America would not exist. "Success is for a mighty race," he observed, and if "a race is weak, if it is lacking in the physical and moral traits which go to the make-up of a conquering people, it cannot succeed." The immigrants' struggles with American Indians supported Roosevelt's point: history showed that those immigrant settlers who were frail were "harried without ruth, and the vanquished maltreated with merciless ferocity."[63] Using strength as a marker in his mythic narrative, modern Americans should welcome strong immigrants into the American body. Conversely, the narrative also lent credence to increasing restrictions in immigration policy. Those immigrants from southern European regions considered "weak" might prove incapable and unworthy to become Americans.

Beyond physical strength, though, Roosevelt called also for moral character as a sign of citizenship. Of all the virtues, justice and honesty appeared frequently in *The Winning of the West*. One anecdote in particular emphasized the distinctive sense of justice "good" frontier folk displayed. Roosevelt recited an incident where three brothers of Scottish descent caught a slave trying to rob their cache of supplies. Initially, the brothers were so angry they threatened to kill the thief. Instead, they formed themselves into a court to try the case. Although they found the man guilty and sentenced him to be hanged, neither of them could carry out the sentence, so they took the prisoner back to his owner. The incident, Roosevelt noted, was typical: "the prompt desire of the backwoodsman to avenge his own wrong; his momentary furious anger, speedily quelled and replaced by a dogged determination to be fair ... spoke well for the doer's determination to uphold the essential that make honest men law-abiding."[64] In other words, immigrant protagonists on the frontier demonstrated a morally uplifting character.

As he typically did, Roosevelt highlighted virtuous conduct by identifying those values he considered morally inappropriate—in this case, dishonesty. He pointed an accusatory finger at those he considered one of the greatest evils on the frontier: that class of white men who followed frontier immigrants once they had already tamed the environment. Invoking Brooks Adams's "law of history," Roosevelt decried the men animated by an economic spirit, condemning their dishonest practices as representing the "vilest poltroonery." He pronounced the moneymen—the merchants and the land speculators—as the real "scum of the frontier."[65] Greedy merchants seemingly eschewed the lessons of his frontier Americanism.

Roosevelt revealed the insidious machinations of the merchant class. He noted that, like some of the wealthy industry owners of his own time, the average trader on the frontier increased his wealth at the expense of immigrant pioneers. Merchants, unmindful of the general poverty of frontier families, dishonestly charged whatever they could get for items necessary for survival. Roosevelt wrote that the "pioneer, in his constant struggle with poverty, was prone to look with puzzled anger at those who made more money than he did, and whose lives were easier." In fact, the hardworking immigrant "did not quite understand how it was that the merchant, who seemed to work less hard than he did, should make more money."[66] Such anecdotes proved that not all native-born Americans proved worthy to be Americans themselves. The burden, though, rested with immigrant settlers who needed to learn that virtuous conduct was necessary for "real" citizenship.

In *The Winning of the West*, immigrant men and women represented the archetypal heroes in America's mythic origins. Per the ideology of the Frontier Myth, these European settlers left familiar homes to chart new territory and to establish their dominance over environmental and human enemies in an unknown universe. The mythic story came full circle when the heroes returned from their adventures and revealed their knowledge to those left behind. While the immigrants Roosevelt lauded did not physically return to Europe, they returned in a mythic sense to American civilization, sharing their hard-won knowledge of strength and character with their compatriots. This knowledge renewed and strengthened the community.[67] Roosevelt's moral was simple: the nation's early success came from immigrants' individual vigor and spirit, traits that they would have to manifest in some form in the modern era.

Just as the mythical Prometheus delivered fire to humankind, immigrant heroes provided valuable instruction regarding the nature of community to settlers who followed them. Roosevelt's multivolume history illuminated the lessons of strength and character from these heroes. Moreover, he used those historical lessons not only to promote Americanism, but also to clarify which immigrants warranted an opportunity for citizenship.

Blood and Destiny in the Frontier Narrative

Restrictions on immigration had increased by the early 1880s. This stemmed, in part, from the perception that all immigrants were not "created equal." In the early 1800s, over 70 percent of "old" immigrants came primarily from northern and western European countries; yet, by the late 1870s, census data revealed that the numbers of "new" immigrants coming from the southern and eastern European regions (i.e., Italy, Portugal, and Spain) were increasing. With that change, perceptions about the "new" immigrants being less desirable intensified. The "restrictionist turn in American immigration policy," Desmond King argued, "rested on assumptions about the types of immigrants and their suitability for citizenship." Public advocates argued that "new" immigrants were more commonly illiterate, less skillful, and generally of low class. While Roger Daniels denied the "polar differences" between the "old" and the "new" immigrants, he recognized that the negative perceptions of the latter constituted "one of the great shibboleths of American immigration history."[68]

As mentioned earlier, part of the negative perception of "new" immigrants stemmed from white Americans troubled by the influx of white-skinned newcomers. Given the perceived strangeness of southern European cultures, native whites found any number of legal, political, and scientific means to draw finer distinctions in the culture's perception of whiteness. Modern audiences could look at Roosevelt's narrative history, one in which he valorized the first wave of immigrants, as proof that the second wave of pseudo-white foreigners was indeed inferior. He too recreated the "old" versus "new" immigrant blood distinction. His retelling of world history demonstrated that success depended, at least in some part, on having the right bloodline, and, by extension, the right skin color. At some level, having the right blood and skin color appeared to be the prerequisite to developing the right character.

While not completely determinative, one's birth nation might have some significance on his or her ability to succeed. Roosevelt admitted this in his narrative, undoubtedly appeasing nativists who embraced such notions. Likewise, it offered a guideline by which the nation could regulate immigration. However, the larger story in *The Winning of the West* revolved around how some immigrants transcended their bloodline.

To some extent, Roosevelt affirmed what Daniels termed the "great shibboleth." Early in his narrative, only "old" immigrants of certain bloodlines appeared either capable of or necessary for American development. "Among the foreign-born immigrants," Roosevelt observed, "success depended in part upon race."[69] One of the most successful backwoodsmen in his narrative possessed Irish blood. In fact, the Irish "formed the kernel of the distinctively and intensely American stock who were the pioneers of our people . . . the vanguard of the army of fighting settlers." It was a "bold and hardy race," Roosevelt observed, that had "plunged into the wilderness as the leaders of the white advance." Even with successful settlements by the English, Germans, and Swedes, it was the Irish settlers he praised for being "the first and last set of immigrants to do this; all others have merely followed in the wake of their predecessors."[70] Roosevelt's mythic story called into question modern audiences' perceptions of Irish immigrants. According to him, they represented a fundamental component of American identity.

However, the Irish were not the only immigrant group he lauded. Scotch and German families proved their heroic mettle as well. On the one hand, their physical hardihood allowed them to adapt to the harshness of the frontier. On the other hand, their high character gave them the determination to adjust the frontier to a more civilized state. "The Scotch were frugal and industrious," he wrote, and when engaged in trade, faced "danger at every moment" when dealing with the Natives. Germans, who came to the wilderness as missionaries to administer to Indians, earned Roosevelt's congratulations. For him, these missionaries had accomplished the impossible. Working with the Moravian Indians, whom Roosevelt considered a "restless, idle, bloodthirsty people," the Germans successfully transformed their charges in "one generation . . . into an orderly, thrifty, industrious folk."[71] Although Roosevelt's anecdotes privileged white immigrant settlers and their ability to civilize "red savages," they also argued that some of the "red" race could rise above their supposed "bloodthirsty" natures and perhaps warrant some consideration by whites.

While Roosevelt praised the "old" German, Irish, Scotch, and English settlers, he criticized the bloodlines of those "new" immigrants from the more southern region of Europe. Many times he portrayed the Spanish as deceitful, citing incidents when Spanish agents fomented discontent in the Cherokee tribes against western settlers.[72] In a chapter titled "Separatist Movements and Spanish Intrigues," Roosevelt denounced the treacherous nature of the Spanish officials and settlers. When realizing that Americans were a "real menace to their power," the Spanish attempted to destroy the newly formed Union "by every species of bribery and corrupt diplomacy," trusting to "fraud rather than force."[73] He castigated the Spanish, not so much for their insidious behavior, but because they privileged such unmanly machinations over the "strenuous life."

The French represented another bloodline that appeared problematic in character. "Many a [French] trader perished in the wilderness," Roosevelt wrote, "by cold or starvation, by an upset where the icy current ran down the rapids like a mill-race, by the attack of a hostile tribe." While he noted that they blazed numerous trails in North America as they sought out areas conducive to their livelihood, he also revealed that these traders had failed to rise above their base natures. "Hospitable," he wrote of the French, "but bigoted to their old customs, ignorant, indolent, and given to drunkenness." In fact, Roosevelt noted that the French were so lazy that they let themselves nearly starve on more than one occasion: "They were not very industrious," he indicted, lolling "in the sunshine smoking their pipes" while "their fields often lay untilled."[74] Again, he made the message of Americanism clear: without both strength and character, immigrants would not realize success on the frontier or, by extension, citizenship in the modern era.

Roosevelt's attention to "old" and "new" blood leads to three critical observations. First, just as his contemporaries differentiated between northern and southern-born European immigrants, Roosevelt's mythic history seemed to validate that point, appeasing the nativist mindset with such a distinction. However, implicitly, he still promoted one of his primary arguments: no matter from which country someone originated, immigration constituted a fact of American life. Arbitrary biases against newcomers did not serve the nation— they penalized "good" immigrants along with the "bad" ones. Thus, he pushed the notion that the country would only realize its destiny by remembering its history; Anglo-Saxon whites might then see the citizenship of some immigrants as essential or, at the very least, unavoidable. Second, Roosevelt largely eschewed the debate over whiteness and immigrants in *The Winning of the West*. For him, there were only three "races" on the frontier, "white, red, and black," and all immigrant settlers were simply white.[75] For him, it was not important to discriminate between people based on skin color when the people concerned all had white skin. Finally, Roosevelt kept the notion of immigrants' inferiority in tension with those foreigners who had excelled on the frontier. In emphasizing extremes, he provided Americanism as a middle ground. Americanism had the potential to mute the call for too stringent of immigration restrictions, yet it could also promote the profound obligation that any immigrant needed to understand about citizenship. Regardless of blood, skin color, or place of origin, he offered "some" room in the national identity for almost any individual who worked for it.

Roosevelt made his point simple. The issues of immigration, race, ethnicity, and identity did not revolve around what separated immigrants from Anglo-Saxon whites. Rather, he focused on what brought them together. His mythic narratives naturalized the fusion of immigrants and whites into one American entity.

While the frontier differentiated immigrants by their worth as settlers, Roosevelt also argued that it assimilated foreigners at a fundamental level. In biological terms, he assured his readers that the bloodline of foreigners was simply being absorbed into the American body, fusing Americans into one pure people. "Some latter-day writers deplore the enormous immigration to our shores as making us a heterogeneous instead of a homogeneous people," he noted, "but as a matter of fact we are less heterogeneous at the present day than we were at the outbreak of the Revolution." In fact, despite the mixture of English, German, French, and Dutch blood, Roosevelt declared, "all were rapidly fused into one people" in the crucible of the frontier.[76]

Consider that many believed at the time, and probably still do, that an immigrant's place of origin determined his or her relative success in the United States. Even though Roosevelt believed that to a certain extent, he publicly offered other factors that, arguably, he considered more important in determining immigrants' success. He advanced the notion that the equality of stress caused by the frontier environment, and immigrants' willing rendezvous with it, compensated for the inequality of blood. Their frontier-derived strength and will determined their ability to balance their sense of independence with their sense of community. While blood may tell to some extent, success appeared open to whichever individual could win it, from whatever foreign region a person may have come.

Therefore, purity of blood was not the only salient issue for Roosevelt. It was important, as many nativists believed, but not the only factor. For him, America's identity reflected some notions about blood, but not the counterproductive, racist ideas that many Anglo-Saxon whites held. Roosevelt wrote, "It is well always to remember that at the day when we began our career as a nation we already differed from our kinsmen of Britain in blood as well as in name."[77] By keeping the idea of Anglo-Saxon blood in tension with southern European blood, Roosevelt complicated matters, but opened the possibility of finding a workable resolution to immigration concerns. Those differences between white nativists and everyone else reflected two ideas that "real" Americans had learned on the frontier: first, that the need for "rugged individualism" must not outweigh the need to develop a thriving community; and second, immigrants would balance that tension by discarding completely Old World ways of thinking. Americanism, then, promoted the worth of this knowledge over place of origin as the crucial determinant of national identity.

Roosevelt framed that timeless knowledge within a vital tension of the Frontier Myth. Janice Rushing outlined this dialectical strain: in order to be a frontier hero (i.e., American), a person demonstrated the qualities of a "rugged individualist" and was someone of high moral character who recognized that "he must continually face the demands of the community for cooperation and conformity." To emphasize one value over the other interfered with the audience's fascination and acceptance of the main protagonist's cultural identity. Thus, how the hero managed this paradoxical state of individuality and community "provides much of the poignancy, mystery, and perennial appeal" of the Frontier Myth.[78] While Roosevelt heralded the value of individualism in immigrant heroes, he also showed them to possess a strong sense of community. They had learned to band together as equals to win success. The lesson was clear. "Old" immigrants had foresworn their foreign culture on the frontier, and, given the opportunity, "new" immigrants could follow suit. Modern nativists, then, could find "some" room in the national identity for those immigrants who likewise proved themselves as individuals and as members of the American community.

Repeatedly, Roosevelt declared the individual immigrant responsible for the conquest of North America. "On the border each man was a law unto himself," Roosevelt explained, "and good and bad alike were left in perfect freedom to follow out to the uttermost limits their own desires."[79] He credited the development of the North American continent solely to those who possessed the trait of rugged individualism. "So far the work of the backwoodsmen in exploring, conquering, and holding the West," he observed, "had been work undertaken solely on individual initiative. . . . The frontiersmen who chopped the first trails across the Alleghanies, who earliest wandered through the lonely Western lands . . . acted each in consequence of his own restless eagerness for adventure and possible gain." In fact, states such as Kentucky and Tennessee, founded by German, Scotch, and English immigrants, existed because of the "individual initiative of the backwoodsmen."[80]

Though individual initiative may have started the process, Roosevelt's narrative illustrated that an individualist, or foreign mindset, could not lead to greatness. Balancing the tension inherent in the Frontier Myth, Roosevelt described the pioneer hero's penchant for individualism "tempered by a sound common sense." This character trait led immigrant settlers to throw off ancient ways, to see others as equals, to combine with them, and to determine that their first duty "was to institute civil government." Their "efforts to overcome and beat back the Indians went hand in hand with their efforts to introduce law and order in the primitive communities they founded."[81] Roosevelt highlighted that something more than survival drove the immigrants to form associations with one another. Early settlers' forted communities, even before the Revolution and the drafting of the Constitution, seemingly resembled a fully realized Americanism. For instance, Roosevelt wrote that the German and Irish settlers' "self-government" in the Watauga Commonwealth of Tennessee represented a typical model of American political thought: "[The] dwellers, in this little outlying frontier commonwealth, exercised the rights of full statehood for a number of years; establishing in true American style a purely democratic government with representative institutions . . . the will of the majority was supreme, while, nevertheless, the largest individual freedom and the utmost liberty of individual initiative was retained."[82] Early American immigrants had balanced their individual desires by recognizing the importance of the community.

Roosevelt's moral was that immigrants had embraced their destiny in the frontier universe. Specifically, they had realized the democratic ideal of community and equality. Given the "great equality of conditions" on the frontier, Roosevelt observed that it made life simple: "duties and rights" were evident, and the traits of "courage, thrift, and industry" were known to bring the attending benefits with them. The frontier equalized everyone, ridding people of any notions of social distinction. "The poorest and the richest met on terms of perfect equality," Roosevelt wrote, "slept in one another's houses and dined at one another's tables." Although he chastised the French on more than one occasion, Roosevelt also used them to prove his point about the nature of learning equality, and the transformative power of embracing Americanism. In one anecdote, he noted that "real" Americans had a simple duty to inculcate "in the minds of the French the value of liberty," given that the group was "utterly unsuited" for it. As soon as the French learned about and embraced the democratic ideals of the nation, "they were received by Americans on terms of perfect and cordial equality."[83] This homely bit of wisdom spoke to the need for modern readers to treat immigrants of their day in a similar fashion. It demonstrated that even the most maligned of immigrants, such as the French and the Spanish in Roosevelt's tales, had the potential to become worthy participants in the American nation. As a result, nativist whites needed to give some level of consideration for individual immigrants to gain entrance to the national identity.

Roosevelt's historical narratives proved that immigrant heroes had formed the American community because these heroes were no longer European. These individuals had demonstrated the necessary strength and character to earn them equal status with all others. The lessons of Americanism had transformed those settlers into more than immigrants; it transformed them into Americans, pure and simple. By divorcing themselves from their European origins, Roosevelt noted that many immigrants readily Americanized their names or dressed in ways that were atypical for Europeans. At a pragmatic level, he claimed that because of their frontier experiences, many immigrants "had lost all remembrance of Europe and all sympathy with things European." In fact, so powerful was this mythical experience of the frontier crucible, he believed that the spirit of the American nation actually predated the first Continental Congress and remained even after the closing of the frontier in 1890.[84] Obviously, modern-day immigrants did not have access to a frontier transformation, but by making the idea of Americanism seem timeless, Roosevelt offered its protection to newcomers in the twentieth century. Americans, immigrant or not, were born through no document or prejudiced thought, but were transformed by an enduring knowledge that served as a remedy for the racial and ethnic tensions of the modern age.

Conclusion

Theodore Roosevelt's version of the Frontier Myth complicated the debate on American identity by distinguishing immigrants as the archetypal heroes of the nation's history. Roosevelt asserted that early immigrants endured a rite of passage on the frontier that shaped them into paragons of Americanism. According to his mythic story, that rite of passage centered around the acts of claiming and holding land, developing it into something greater than it had been, and defending it against the forces of nature and of evil. His immigrant heroes had proven worthy of an American identity through that mythic rite of passage: by facing the unknown and learning to renounce their old ways and old lives, they could acknowledge their inherent strength and individualism and develop a democratic community of equals, thereby becoming fully and utterly American.

Not all scholars accept this view of the Frontier Myth. Paul W. McBride, for one, argued that "the advent of the environmentalist historians led by Frederick Jackson Turner [did not] reverse the anti-immigrant outlook of the historian." Instead, "Turner's challenge to the theory of Teutonic origins and his emphasis on the environment as a molder of American character and institutions actually worked in just the opposite way. Not only were the new immigrant groups not of the right pedigree, but they settled in the city where they could not benefit from the rigor of the frontier process. . . . Thus, the frontier hypothesis with its emphasis on environmentalism rather than racial origins helped to degrade rather than exalt the new immigrant."[85]

Given the psychological climate of the time, McBride may have a point. Anti-immigrationists held that certain races could not or would not assimilate into American life, and were "undesirable" additions even if they did assimilate. Roosevelt's version of the Frontier Myth addressed that. While he leaned on the environment as an important factor, he kept the confluence of environment and race actively in tension. Neither was solely responsible to determine who was worthy to become an American. However, without the transformative power of the frontier, Roosevelt still resolved the modern dilemma caused by whites' fears about where newcomers originated.

The Winning of the West offered Americanism as a critical idea to be learned, even if newcomers no longer had access to the frontier crucible. It emphasized an individual's embrace of physical strength, principled behavior, and sense of equality as the most important factors in citizenship. While Roosevelt based some of his predictions on generalizations about ethnicity, individual will and individual struggle were simply more important. His narrative histories offered a moderating view for the time: immigrant heroes and their frontier-proven traits were melded into an American whole that idealized the uniqueness of national identity. Consequently, Anglo-Saxon whites should have nothing to fear. Moreover, Roosevelt's myth offered immigrants the possibility that they could gain access to American identity, despite the modern-day cost. Immigrants needed to embrace the idea of Americanism now, as had their mythical ancestors then, and become Americans in thought and deed; otherwise, they would suffer the indignities of non-identity. Roosevelt's mythic treatment of Americanism promoted the values considered important to the nation, offered foreigners the means to achieve success in relation to those values, and explained away the loss of their Old World culture as a manifestation of equality in the New World.

Although the U.S. Census declared an end to the frontier, Roosevelt still offered it as a means to frame modern life. He engaged aspects of the frontier to frame all outsiders' potential, to show them and native-born whites that outsiders could realize Americanism and enhance the nation. He kept the tensions of immigration, race, ethnicity, assimilation, and identity alive—as well as his attempts to find a middle ground for those contradictions—through his lessons from American history. As would be the case in propagating such tensions, the mythic themes used to frame them would be rich with potential and problematic in practice: Roosevelt's mythic conception of Indians in America's history and their controversial future in the modern nation.

3

Red into White

Native Americans and Americanism

Native Americans represented one of the more troublesome groups for Anglo-Americans to consider as Americans. The racism of white Europeans identified "red" Indians as inferior.[1] In fact, many arriving settlers considered Indians inhuman.[2] Moreover, Indians' long-established economic systems, religions, and customs contrasted starkly with the emerging culture of immigrants.[3] Colin Calloway noted, for example, that eighteenth-century Native Americans in the eastern region of North America "pursued diversified economies" to provide for their needs "while imposing minimal demands on the ecosystem." They satisfied the necessities of life with "relatively light expenditures of time and labor." Settlers, on the other hand, believed such "nonuse" of the environment was "wasteful" and "barbaric," and developed colonial governments and businesses to use the land, as they believed God wanted.[4] As Europeans slowly dominated the land, and turned away from the Old World to develop their American identity, Indians worried about their identity. Although Native Americans had borrowed ideas and items from white culture, and vice versa, many questioned giving up their centuries old societies.[5]

Whites argued that Indians hesitated or outright resisted wholesale changes to their cultures. As a result, for at least a century and a half, Native Americans found themselves under fire from both the government and popular media. Government policies targeted the indigenous people with military force, fraudulent treaties, disease, addiction, constant displacement, and "rehabilitation."[6] Popular media demonized American Indians as the chief antagonists in tales of the frontier. Mythically, they were malevolent counterparts to heroic immigrant settlers, providing whites a needed "evil" against which to define Americans as "good." The image of bloodthirsty "savages," consequently, justified whites' cruel and inhumane treatment of Native Americans.[7] Virtually no Indian—whether "barbarian," ally, or "noble savage"—could escape the psychologically destructive and paternalistic policies of government-run reservations.[8]

Theodore Roosevelt echoed these beliefs and endorsed such anti-Indian policies. Even without his infamous 1886 statement, "I don't go so far as to think that the only good Indians are dead Indians, but I believe nine out of every ten are, and I shouldn't like to inquire too closely in the case of the tenth," many scholars have noted Roosevelt's racist sentiment.[9] Gary Gerstle observed that even though Roosevelt admired Indians' martial ability, he also loathed them and cared little for their continued existence: "Roosevelt did not worry much about the proper place of Indians in the nation, for the savage wars with the Americans had culminated in their expulsion or extermination." According to Gerstle, Roosevelt saw Native Americans as an inferior race that, when mixed with some European races on the frontier, resulted in even weaker races.[10] Accordingly, they would never be fit to be Americans. Thomas Dyer likewise observed that Roosevelt considered Indians as barbarians needing extermination. Even if he softened in his feelings toward them as he matured, Dyer noted, Roosevelt still stressed the "red man's savagery" as an obstacle to Indians becoming accepted in America.[11]

As president, Roosevelt seemed less harsh toward Indians but was still guided by his racist mindset. According to Lewis Gould, President Roosevelt attempted to make assimilation practices less exploitative, but he still endorsed policies that were "debilitating and demoralizing" to Indians.[12] Following such "demoralizing" policies appeared consistent, Frederick Hoxie observed, since the president "maintained a pessimistic view of Native American abilities."[13] Brian Dippie argued that Roosevelt did not "subscribe to exterminationist doctrine," but he "operated on a simple premise: the Indian was a savage" who needed civilizing. To that end, the Roosevelt administration's policies "prepared" Indians to exist in the modern world, casting them as unruly children being prepared for adulthood.[14]

Clearly, America worked to crush Indians out of existence, through genocide if possible, or by psychologically and physically abusive methods of assimilation. When both policies were not completely successful, much of the nation refused to consider Indians as Americans, labeling them as social misfits undeserving of any access to national identity.[15] Given some of his private and public statements, as well as some of the policies he endorsed, Roosevelt appeared to dismiss Indians with the same contempt as most other white Americans.

The scholarly assessment that Roosevelt treated Native Americans despicably—in both deed and word—is not in doubt. Yet, Roosevelt also wanted to *include* Indians in the national identity and to promote them as a fundamental part of America's destiny. Roosevelt acted not altruistically, but pragmatically. He was driven by his need to oversee a martially fit nation, comprised of people with moral character who could work together respectfully for the betterment of the country. He saw some Indians, like some immigrant groups, as the additional elements needed to empower the nation, revitalizing its body and spirit in the process. Far from dismissing Native Americans because of their supposed racial inferiority and barbarity, he offered them a place in the nation, albeit problematic, that most other whites had refused them.

To that end, Roosevelt included Native Americans in his myth of Americanism. For him, Americanism called for individuals to possess martial vigor and strong will in order to earn equal respect. Thus, his mythic treatment of American Indians positioned them, not as unredeemable "savages" nor as helpless children, but as exemplars of those traits that marked anyone for a respected place in American identity. First, Roosevelt offered alternatives to the media portrayals of Indians as fearsome barbarians roving the mythic frontier maliciously killing settlers. To counter such imagery, imagery he himself used in *The Winning of the West,* he also celebrated Indians as consummate mythical adversaries, providing explanations which submerged the more malicious aspects of their martial actions, and which rationalized Indian "ferocity" as a response to weak-willed whites. Likewise, Roosevelt reinterpreted the idea of the "noble savage" to grant nobility based on physical vigor, and not the traditional assumption that such Indians were martially weak and overly "civilized." Second, since whites considered Native Americans inferior, *as a group,* Roosevelt established the idea of Indian *individuality.* According to him, *some* of them proved their "rugged individuality" while enduring the difficult conditions on reservations. Because of that, he argued that those Indians had earned an equal place in the nation—signified by allowing them to intermarry with whites. Life on the frontier, he argued, had proven the success of mixed blood for both Indians and immigrants. American Indian "blood" added to the national body in the same way that immigrant "blood" did—it rejuvenated the nation.

Obviously, Roosevelt's discourse affirmed many of the stereotypic biases against Native Americans. His rhetoric, like much of the rhetoric of the time, left no room for Indians to act on their own; instead, they were acted upon. His racist thinking, though, should not preclude an examination of the critical role he played in constructing national identity. Tapping into the Frontier Myth, he balanced Indians between two extreme social tensions. For both good and ill, Roosevelt rhetorically maneuvered Native Americans between the country's hatred and its cynicism of them. He took the complexity and anxiety surrounding the national identity of both "red" Indians and white nativists and moderated those tensions so that everyone could become Americans, pure and simple.

The "Indian Problem" in the New World

Since first arriving in North America, several Europeans powers considered Indians a "problem." Spanish explorers in the sixteenth century, for instance, found it difficult to reconcile their Christian orthodoxy with the indigenous people they "discovered." Given that they believed biblical scriptures failed to mention Native Americans, the Spanish considered them worthless and subject to slavery and casual extermination.[16] Indian tribes fought back, sometimes burning their own villages and supplies rather than letting them fall into enemy hands, and startled Spanish soldiers with a battlefield coordination they did not expect. Of course, pitched battles in the open against Spanish guns taught Native Americans to assume guerilla tactics in most subsequent engagements. "Europeans looked with contempt on the Indians 'skulking way of war,'" Calloway noted, "but they soon learned to fear it" and eventually adopted it as their own.[17] Not all confrontations between Indians and Europeans involved violence, however.

Other European nations in the mid-sixteenth through the late-eighteenth centuries saw Native Americans as an economic problem—as a trading competitor. With fur demand increasing in Europe, England and France struggled to dominate the fur trade in North America, and both quickly realized that Indian nations were pivotal to that trade.[18] Rather than simply fight Indians for the fur, both countries sometimes engaged in diplomacy with native tribes, treating the latter as sovereign nations and as respected trading partners.[19] Native Americans, in return, became consumers of European goods. By the late 1700s, however, this capitalist relationship had resulted in problematic consequences for Indians. To ensure a steady flow of European luxuries, more and more tribes focused on procuring furs, depleting game to the point that they relied on European nations for much of their food and materials for clothing. Furthermore, tribes moved around more to find the best trapping areas, and fighting increased among various native groups trying to secure fur for their European partners. The nomadic nature of such Indian trappers also allowed European traders to make claims for the abandoned land and to establish outposts deeper in the continent, outposts that evolved into settlements and eventually into towns. According to Stephen Cornell, the fur trade "marked the beginning of a long decline in Indian political autonomy and economic self-sufficiency."[20]

As the power of the new American nation grew, Indians suffered. Militarily, Indians lost their British allies with their joint defeat by the American colonists in the War for Independence and again in the War of 1812. Economically, fur trading decreased in importance by the late nineteenth century, and along with it the negotiating power of Indian tribes. Land now trumped fur as a commodity, with land seen by Americans as the means to power and wealth.[21] As Henry Fritz remarked, "no habitable plot of ground was so insignificant that white men did not want it."[22] Racially, Indians' "red" skin marked them as different from Anglo-Saxon "whites," eventually becoming a "single, despised non-white group."[23]

Broadly speaking, there were two major responses by white Americans to Native Americans. The first response involved the federal government's attempt to "acquire" Indian resources.[24] Treaties and other governmental policies stripped them of their land. Whether or not Indians rebelled against these dicta, they became the targets in a campaign of violence. The second response manifested through whites confining Indians on reservations and, more important, working to "rehabilitate" them.[25] These two responses were not mutually exclusive; they overlapped each other repeatedly during the first century and a half of the nation's existence. Each response buoyed the other and facilitated the economic and social superiority of whites.

America's first response to its perceived "Indian problem" involved acquiring Indian lands and quashing any resistance.[26] Native Americans appeared to be an obstacle to the nation's Manifest Destiny, and several early presidents worked to remove that obstacle. President Thomas Jefferson frequently met with Indian delegations and assured them that the United States would only buy land that they freely offered to sell. However, Jefferson initiated a number of subversive policies. According to Richard Drinnon, Jefferson launched a "systematic campaign of psychological warfare" against Indian tribes, cajoling them to run up debt at government trading posts "so they would have to sell their lands to pay." Jefferson saw Indians as unruly children and thus tried to deal with them more benignly, believing he could coerce and, if necessary, chastise them rather than outright destroy them to acquire their land.[27] For example, the national government, pressuring tribes through diplomacy and strategic shows of force, coerced the Cherokees, the Chickasaws, and the Creeks in the late 1790s to cede land in Georgia and Tennessee.[28] Similar agreements continued through the early part of the nineteenth century, such as the Treaty of Dancing Rabbit Creek of 1830. This treaty between the government and the Choctaw nation ostensibly reflected the Choctaws' consent in being removed from their land, accepting the promise of "peace, friendship, and land" in return for their ceding territory that would become Alabama and Mississippi. In reality, the political and material assistance promised never materialized.[29] Such broken pledges occurred repeatedly in the nineteenth century and robbed Indians of their economic power.[30]

Government actions also took a more violent and deadly course to secure land. Dippie noted that when Indian forces sided with Great Britain in 1812, and Tecumseh "conspired" to unite several tribes to stand against American expansion, the "ungrateful Indians had forfeited any claim to sympathy."[31] As a result, some chief executives had little patience in dealing with Native Americans. For instance, President Madison ordered then-general Andrew Jackson to destroy Seminole villages and farms in Florida after Indians retaliated against settlers who had attacked them.[32] Federal and local policies covertly worked to exterminate tribes. President Jackson's Indian Removal Act of 1830 resulted in the Cherokee nation's disastrous trek on the "Trail of Tears," where approximately four thousand members of that tribe died en route from their Georgia homeland to the earmarked Indian Territory in the western United States.[33] According to Calloway, Colorado's territorial governor, John Evans, believed the "best way of clearing the territory for development and securing statehood with himself as senator" was to destroy Indians. In 1863, Evans proclaimed any Indian activity as a sign of a "major uprising," and in 1864 convinced Arapahos that if they were not a part of the uprising, to seek protection from a nearby military fort. Once there, troops from the fort butchered them.[34] Similar government-sanctioned police actions against peaceful Indians occurred repeatedly, including the Sand Creek slaughter of defenseless Cheyennes in 1864 and the deadly mistreatment of the Nez Percé after their escape attempt to reach Canada in 1877.[35]

Indian reactions to white encroachment varied. Some tribes, such as the Delaware Indians, sought to live in peace with whites, even entering into military alliances with the new government to prove their good will.[36] Other tribes, such as the Navajo, attempted to end the bloodshed and sought to establish themselves as a trading partner with the United States, similar to what some tribes had negotiated decades earlier with Great Britain and France. Still other American Indian tribes violently resisted immigrants' march across the continent. For example, the Sioux nations engaged in a forty-year war against America during the latter half of the nineteenth century.[37] But whether natives met whites on the battlefield or at the peace table, any opposition given to white expansion was deemed the predictable response of inferior savages.

The image of Indians as barbaric fiends has been a crucial part of frontier mythology from the beginning. This imagery offered evidence that *white*-skinned Anglo-Americans were superior to the *red*-skinned Native Americans. "The Indians were savages," James Robertson noted about natives' role in

American myth, "they were colored, they were on the wrong side of the frontier, and they were uncivilized, un-Christian."[38] Thus, Indians were cast as savage villains in the nation's myths. To reconcile the conflict between embracing ideals such as "all men are created equal" and the need to advance materially in the New World, whites needed Indians to be scapegoats. As a result, the Frontier Myth made peaceful coexistence impossible between white Anglo-Americans and "primitive" natives.[39] Many immigrants, believing in their God-given right to possess the resources of the new continent, looked at the indigenous peoples' way of life as uncivilized. The depiction of Indians as evil brutes thus justified and encouraged the dismissive and inhuman treatment of them by their civilized Christian superiors.[40]

The narrative sequence of Indian violence became a staple in newspapers and novels: wild natives dragging fearful settlers from their homes, flaming arrows destroying crops and buildings, men mercilessly killed, and women and children forced to watch these abuses.[41] Media in the late eighteenth century, particularly, focused on lurid tales of white women in Indian clutches. Drinnon noted, "Countless crude illustrations in the captivity narratives . . . depicted a dusky but never completely nude figure always lifting his trade hatchet to commit 'Horrible and Unparalleled Massacre!' "[42] In these early stories, the female captive has her innocence threatened, escaping before actually succumbing to native advances; such myths goaded readers' puritanical fears of the supposed lascivious appetites of nonwhites. Later stories of Indian captivity included illustrations that focused on supposed Indians' fantasies of violently subjugating white women.[43] Philip Deloria noted that "gory tales of white women murdered, raped, and scalped by Indian people" transformed all natives into a "generic, inhuman, savage Other."[44]

Despite the supposed willful maliciousness of Indians, some whites wanted to help "rehabilitate" them. To that end, America's second response to its "Indian problem" involved assisting the indigenous people in becoming "civilized." Assimilation, like military conquest, served to rationalize the taking of Indian land; helping natives become civilized meant they no longer needed that resource.[45] More important, assimilation provided a morally comfortable reason for Indian subjugation—whites were "helping" Indians, not harming them.[46] Thus, along with deceiving them, brutalizing them, and dispossessing them of their land, whites provided Indians the opportunity to assimilate into the dominant culture. Of course, whites believed that Indians would assimilate successfully when all vestiges of their old life were destroyed. As a result, attempts at assimilation resulted in Native Americans suffering through innumerable outrages, which included forced pedagogical and religious training, and prescribed career paths in which they could not succeed.

When the government initially displaced Indians from their homeland, it moved them to a different region of the country, with no concern of environmental similarity or of preparation of the group for the changes. "Removal was a solution geared to the Jacksonian predilection," Dippie wrote, "for isolating society's misfits—the poor, the criminal, [and] the insane." If they could not survive in their new, isolated, and harsher environment, then so be it.[47] Eventually, the growing cries of concern by those sympathetic to this mistreatment of Indians initiated a change in national policy. Generally, starting in the mid-nineteenth century, the U.S. Government systematically took a paternalistic approach to Indians and established reservations for them.[48] Reservations acted as indoctrination sites in which Native Americans could learn the ways of "civilized" society. These ways could not exist in tandem with long-held cultural, social, or religious mores, so the job of rehabilitation was to crush any connection between their native charges and tribal life. For the rehabilitation to be successful, the government would have to replace the internal workings of Native American societies with imposed total control of everything that touched the natives' lives. For this, each reservation had a strong governmental presence with ultimate power over day-to-day life.

The U.S. Government agency charged with the control and assimilation of natives was the newly created Bureau of Indian Affairs (BIA). Where before natives' societies had tribal councils made up of an internal hierarchy of self-governance, the BIA agents, with the full force of governmental bureaucracy, acted as dictators, controlling everything from the local police force to the distribution of food.[49] Indians on reservations were stripped of any outward manifestation of their former tribal life. To effect such wholesale change, the BIA regulated the schooling of native children, the enforcement of religious conversion and the proscription of natives' former nomadic hunting.

As the instrument of the BIA, the reservation schools tried to "strip away all outward signs of the children's identification with tribal life," and inculcate the "ideas, values, and behaviors of white civilization."[50] Officials cut off the long hair of Indian boys, gave all children standard school uniforms, only spoke in English, showed little patience for learning Indian names and would give each child a Christian name, and severely punished a child for any infraction of the rules. In the classroom, students learned how to read and then learned subjects such as history, science, and arithmetic.[51] Officials believed that Indians could not master these topics, David Adams noted, but they hoped that even an "elementary acquaintance held out the promise of liberating the child from the mind-dulling weight of tribal tradition."[52]

Along with academic subjects, reservations provided instruction in the "rehabilitation" of natives' spirits. Although some American Indians had converted to Christianity prior to arriving at their reservations due to missionary efforts, most carried with them their own tribal beliefs about the nature of God. The BIA agents disallowed any manner of traditional native religion, and school officials inundated students with strict religious training. Students went to church services several times a day, with multiple prayer meetings at night, and teachers made students recite Bible verses repeatedly in English and with no explanation, even though many students did not understand what they meant.[53]

Reservations also turned their attention to adult natives. The goal here was to transform natives from nomadic hunters into farmers. If Indians farmed, the thinking went, they demonstrated the rejection of their old life. To facilitate that metamorphosis, the Dawes Severalty Act of 1887 divided reservation land into allotments and awarded those small plots to individual natives for farming. The government hoped that Indians would no longer see themselves as a tribe that hunted, but rather as individuals who farmed. Experts of the day also believed that this transformation would demonstrate to Indians that they no longer needed extensive amounts of land for subsistence and that they would thus be willing to relinquish control of the extra land.[54] Agricultural practices were not new to Indians; many tribes had farmed prior to their fur trapping partnerships with Great Britain and France. The problem now, according to Calloway, stemmed from the impractical expectations of the Dawes Act: "One hundred and sixty acres per head of household was rarely sufficient for Indians to make a living. . . . The United States tried to transform Indians into farmers overnight on poor lands at the very time when white American farmers on good lands were struggling to make ends meet. Most Indians could not get loans to develop their allotments because they lacked collateral; they could not use their 160-acre plots as collateral because the government held the deed for twenty-five years." With virtually no way to sustain themselves by farming, forced to lease part of their allotment, which was then grabbed by white settlers, and denied any legal recourse to the Dawes Act, Indians suffered from increased poverty and psychological malaise.[55]

Native Americans' reactions varied to this treatment. However, the response that most troubled officials involved the emergence of a new religious movement on reservations in 1889. Initial proponents of the "Ghost Dance" religion prophesied that God wanted Indians to live peacefully with one another and whites, and for natives to continue embracing tribal culture. If they followed these dictates, they would be reunited with their dead loved ones and live as free people in another life. As part of a ceremony, participants performed a "ghost dance" they believed would lead to their salvation.[56]

The BIA officials were concerned about the interpretation of the Ghost Dance religion by certain tribes. According to Richard Morris and Philip Wander, the Sioux "believed that God's promise was an explicit indictment of the dominant society," which led them to the "equally militant belief" that all white influence needed to be purged from Indian life.[57] The Ghost Dance, thus, was the complete reversal and remediation of the imposed rehabilitation of the natives by the government. In 1890, officials outlawed the Ghost Dance and sent troops to arrest Sitting Bull, who they believed advocated the religion; this Sioux leader was already infamous for his participation in Custer's defeat at the Little Big Horn River several years earlier.[58] During the arrest, army troops killed Sitting Bull; fearing their religious beliefs would lead to more violence after his death, hundreds fled the Sioux reservation. Soon captured near Wounded Knee Creek in South Dakota, army soldiers demanded that the Sioux disarm. Although they complied, a gun accidentally discharged and the soldiers opened fire, killing hundreds.[59] Not by coincidence, the soldiers involved in the massacre were part of a reconstituted army unit that had been with Custer.[60] Regardless of the soldiers' guilt, whites illustrated their disgust of Ghost Dance participants by displaying Wounded Knee survivors as exhibits at the Atlanta Exposition in 1895.[61]

Some whites believed the events surrounding Wounded Knee proved that assimilation had failed,[62] but others viewed this event, as well as life generally for natives, sympathetically. They recognized that the government's attempts to acquire land and to "rehabilitate" Indians had crushed them physically, spiritually, and emotionally. This recognition reflected another dominant mythic image of Indians. Aside from natives portrayed as merciless barbarians, popular culture also identified them as "noble savages."

From as early as Columbus's era, Europeans romanticized the indigenous people of North America. For Europeans, and their American cousins, these denizens of the wilderness appeared child-like, innocent and naive, and unaware of the niceties of civilization such as clothing, Christian religion, and personal belongings. Perhaps the most popular "noble savage" was Pocahontas. The sixteenth-century adventures of a "civilized" Indian princess who saved the European John Smith from execution represented an indelible part of Indian-white relations through the early twentieth century. Pocahontas, descended of royalty—beautiful, innocent, and mysterious—created a romantic protagonist for the national myth. "Not a season went by," Raymond Stedman reported of the popular media of the eighteenth and nineteenth centuries, "that some author, or artist, or playwright . . . did not call upon her image."[63]

What made the "noble savage" popular? The idea of "civilized" natives provided some comfort to whites who were fearful of darker-skinned neighbors; the "noble savage" image proved that Indians could be "tamed" through assimilation. Whites saw this mythic figure as possessing traits and abilities they themselves desired, such as honor, bravery, and the facility to commune freely in nature. Early whites imitated Indians' "nature" abilities: on the frontier, settlers adopted the "primitive" ways of the natives to survive.[64] In later decades, whites added parts of Indian culture to their amusements and hobbies, "playing Indian" as a means to adopt and to preserve the "noble savage" idea.[65] In a way, this imitation resolved the contradiction in the nation's treatment of natives. It allowed whites to preserve the romantic idea of Indians while simultaneously killing them in reality.[66]

Regardless of whether the nation believed Indians to be bloodthirsty marauders or "noble savages," one myth positioned them as inferior and unredeemable, and the other depicted them as a people rejecting their culture and thus destined to vanish from the face of the earth. Naive intentions to "help," and the superficial co-optation of parts of their culture aside, the nation had cast Native Americans into a political and cultural limbo, identifying them as virtually useless to American destiny. Myths about Native Americans left no room for them to thrive in the modern era.

One would believe that Roosevelt would offer similar insights. He appeared the consummate cowboy, that is, dismissive of natives and their ways.[67] He noted with pride that as a rancher in the Dakota badlands in the mid-1880s, he single-handedly faced down a group of young native warriors who accosted him.[68] However, despite his much-heralded image as a mythic enemy of frontier "savages," his public rhetoric provided a moderating force in white notions about Indians' identity.

In fact, his public discourse endorsed a grand, mythic vision that positioned natives as viable and necessary candidates for American identity in much the same way he exemplified immigrants. By placing Indians within his version of Americanism, Roosevelt relabeled their "savagery" as a mythic manifestation of the "rugged individualism" that immigrant heroes had demonstrated on the frontier. In doing so, he moved Native Americans one step closer to attaining a more secure place in the national identity.

Re-Imagining Native American Legend

By the end of the nineteenth century, countless novels and essays featured Indians as inhuman fiends, engaged in a violent life-or-death struggle with resolute settlers on the unknown vastness of the North American continent.[69] The stories detailing the frontier "myth of 'savage war'" blamed the natives for instigating a "war of extermination."[70] Particularly, the media made scapegoats of Indians, depicting them as the malicious perpetrators of frontier injustices who were themselves solely responsible for their fate, thus absolving white society of any wrongdoing. This "myth of the savage native" rendered it virtually impossible for most white Americans to identify the mass of "red" Indians as anything other than "inferior human beings."[71]

The media also focused on the romantic image of Native Americans. It praised the "noble savage" when he or she exhibited the genteel civility of white culture.[72] This image, however, also cemented their inferior status. By appearing to reject their old culture, they affirmed that it was indeed unworthy. Moreover, the media emphasized the paternalistic nature of the "White man's burden" to help with Indians' transformation from savagery to civility. According to John Coward, "even the well-meaning concern for Indians ... positioned them as 'poor Indians' and promoted the idea that they were unable to take care of themselves and needed the support and protection of whites."[73] As a result, white society determined Indians' fates similar to that of an insensitive parent dealing with a hapless, and largely unwanted, child.

Ironically, either identification of Indians served the same goal: the elimination of their physical and cultural presence from American society. So-called uncivilized natives deserved displacement and extermination. The existence of "noble savages" affirmed the notion of a people whose original culture was worthless. Therefore, Indians appeared as either frightful or fanciful, with both images allowing the nation to continue its practice of taking Indian land and destroying natives in the process.

Roosevelt's mythic allusions did resemble other popular media in providing graphic descriptions of stereotypical Native American savagery. According to *The Winning of the West,* Indians demonstrated an "inhuman love of cruelty for cruelty's sake" in raids on settlements. "They were cruel beyond all belief," he wrote in 1889, in which "helpless women and children suffered the same hideous fate that so often befell their husbands and fathers."[74] Reminiscent of the "deeds of the Holy Inquisition," Indians engaged in "hideous, unnamable, unthinkable tortures" with their captured foes. In a typical scenario Roosevelt offered, Native Americans stealthily approached a settlement and shot people as they worked in the field. Once they had secured the area, they butchered any wounded men, children, and old women. As the Indians marched the remaining prisoners back to their camp, they tomahawked anyone who could not maintain the pace. Most prisoners, he chronicled, were stripped naked, burned on different parts of the body, scalped, stoned, and, if they survived, were bartered to others.[75]

Native Americans' fiendishness seemed to have no bounds. According to Roosevelt's narrative history, such cruelty represented a typical pastime of the frontier immigrants' foes. Mentioning acts almost "too horrible to mention," he described in gruesome detail what hapless settlers faced: "Not one man in a hundred, and not a single woman, escapes torments which a civilized man cannot look another in the face and so much as speak of. Impalement on charred sticks, finger-nails split off backward, finger-joints chewed off, eyes burnt out— these tortures can be mentioned, but there are others equally normal and customary which cannot even be hinted at, especially when women are the victims." Roosevelt echoed the "captivity narratives" of his time, describing how Native American antagonists raped white women and then sold them as concubines to other Indians. When Indians released a woman, they sometimes forced her to carry "around her neck as a horrible necklace the bloody scalps of her husband and children."[76]

Despite these horrors, though, Roosevelt's novelized tales challenged the outright condemnation of Indians. Unlike other authors, he also featured Indians not just as "savages," but also as welcomed antagonists—beings with physical skills to be lauded. Furthermore, according to Roosevelt, Indians were not solely to blame for their actions. He deflected audience condemnation away from his accounts of extreme Indian behavior by offering a scapegoat of his own: morally weak whites who had pushed natives into responding so violently. In a way, he contextualized Indians' acts as righteous in their ferocity—a fitting response for those who embraced a martial ethic.

By the "time the English had consolidated the Atlantic colonies," Roosevelt wrote, natives epitomized the "most formidable" foes "ever encountered by colonists of European stock."[77] They demonstrated what he believed to be the prime trait for American advancement: martial prowess. He clearly admired what many Indians had accomplished on the frontier battlefield. He declared that the Iroquois tribes "held their own against all comers for two centuries." Other tribes "stayed for a time the oncoming white flood, or even drove it back; in Maine, the settlers were for a hundred years confined to a narrow strip of seacoast. Against the Spaniards, there were even here and there Indian nations who definitely recovered the ground they had lost."[78] If true American identity sprang from physical hardihood during the frontier experience, he argued that natives too demonstrated that critical trait.

Roosevelt celebrated Native Americans as the consummate opponent in the nation's mythic origin. To applaud their physical prowess, without endorsing what many considered their "savagery," he depicted frontier natives, at times, metaphorically. Such depictions removed human deliberateness from their actions, casting them more as mysterious entities whose abilities were beyond human ken. In *The Winning of the West,* for example, he portrayed them as a supernatural force. "Wrapped in the mantle of the unknown . . . they seemed to the white settlers devils and not men," able to disappear "into a wilderness that closed over their trail as the waves of the ocean close in the wake of a ship." Soldiers were helpless in the "dense woodland . . . as they would be if at night they had to fight foes who could see in the dark." Roosevelt's metaphoric depictions rendered Indians preternatural, almost a part of the environment itself. "A white might outrun [Indians] for eight or ten miles," he observed, "but on a long journey they could tire out any man, and any beast except a wolf." He concluded, "Their silence, their cunning and stealth, their terrible prowess . . . make it no figure of speech to call them the tigers of the human race."[79] Roosevelt accomplished two ends with his metaphoric descriptions. He tapped into the allure of the unknown wilderness and its inhabitants, promoting "savage" strength as a fundamental element of frontier life and, as he argued on many occasions, American life. Furthermore, his accounts merged Indians with the environment itself, rendering any conscious maliciousness on their part moot. They became a force of nature for Roosevelt. At times, they appeared no different from any of the environmental challenges that early settlers faced, such as wild animals or harsh weather. It would be ludicrous to blame natives for deliberate acts, as it would be to blame any (super) natural "act of God." This allowed readers to admire martial strength while tamping their anxiety about the problematic consequences such strength wrought.

Obviously, Roosevelt did not completely absolve Native Americans for their so-called outrageous practices. He observed that some, such as the Cheyennes, "have more often been sinning than sinned against."[80] However, he also undercut his audiences' knee-jerk conclusions about native "savagery" by indicting whites. He dismissed some Indian acts of violence, for example, by portraying them as dupes of Great Britain's intrigues.[81] Furthermore, he clearly denounced those Anglo-Saxon whites who acted immorally when dealing with Native Americans. Commenting on the Nez Percé, Roosevelt declared that the "most cruel wrongs have been perpetrated by whites upon perfectly peaceable and unoffending tribes."[82] In the 1888 *Ranch Life and the Hunting Trail*, Roosevelt admitted that in dealing with tribes, "we have erred quite as often through sentimentality as through wilful [*sic*] wrongdoing." Although he revealed that there have been many "atrocities" committed by Indians, he noted he "could recite a dozen instances of white outrages which, if told alone, would seem to justify all the outcry raised on behalf of the Indian." Particularly, those dishonorable whites who engaged in outrages against Indians seemed even more severe, Roosevelt noted, given natives of the caliber of some of the Cherokee, who is "nowadays as good as a white," and some of the Pueblo, who he called "thrifty, industrious, and peaceful as any European peasant."[83] In a moment of enlightened insight, he saw that the trouble between both parties stemmed from the "tendency on each side to hold the race, and not the individual, responsible for the deeds of the latter."[84]

Roosevelt argued that Indians were not simply a "red mass" of cruelty and inferiority. If looked at individually, some demonstrated exemplary traits. In fact, his insight spoke to what he considered critical to American development: individual responsibility. As he had argued about immigrant frontier folk, "blood" lineage only went so far to explain success or failure in America. Individual responsibility, as evidenced by the heroic exhibition of strength and will to do right, provided the true means to win an equal place in the nation. Now, he asked readers to look beyond the stereotypes they attributed to Indians as a "tribe" and instead to look at some of them as individuals who possessed the same sterling traits as did frontier heroes.

To do that, Roosevelt co-opted the meaning of the "noble savage." Traditionally, that term reflected white audiences' understanding that most Indians were "barbaric," but that a few individuals were "civilized," such as Pocahontas. The depiction concentrated on an Indian's adoption of white culture, and his or her resulting martial passivity within it. This mythic notion spelled doom for natives as it affirmed the weakness and dissolution of their own culture.[85] When Roosevelt described Pueblo natives as "thrifty, industrious, and peaceful," he undoubtedly invoked this traditional interpretation of the idea. However, his conception of the individual "noble savage" differed substantially. He re-imagined the term by linking individual Indians' "savagery"—their strength and will as warriors—to the idea of nobility. This version of the "noble savage" echoed his "strenuous life" philosophy as a foundation for American life. Moreover, it provided a counterpoint to the belief that the dissolution of martial strength was a necessary component for national identity. Roosevelt worried enough about the nation's seeming embrace of materialism and its rejection of physical vigor without challenging whites who promoted martial weakness in Indians as a sign of cultural advancement.

Roosevelt linked nobility to a responsible individual who stood steadfast against powerful forces. In that way, some Indians appeared similar to their counterparts in the Frontier Myth, the heroic settlers. Indians, in fact, demonstrated strength of sinew and of character—the hallmarks of Americanism. Just as he heralded an individual immigrant as an exemplar of American spirit, he likewise proffered individual natives in that role. For example, in *The Winning of the West,* Roosevelt admired a Shawnee chief named Cornstalk, who was a "mighty warrior" and a "man who knew the value of his work and prized his honor."[86] This individual not only embodied Roosevelt's martial philosophy, but he also demonstrated high character. Given the lament of Roosevelt about the moral decay of the modern era, he offered Cornstalk as a necessary icon for white culture.

Roosevelt saved his most effusive praise for an Iroquois named Logan, who epitomized the potential that some Indians brought into the American community. Logan represented the mythic American ideal—martially adept, morally strong, and cognizant of treating others with respect:

> He was a man of splendid appearance: over six feet high, straight as a spear-shaft, with a countenance as open as it was brave and manly, until the wrongs he endured stamped on it an expression of gloomy ferocity. He had always been the friend of the white man, and had been noted particularly for his kindness and gentleness to children. Up to this time he had lived at peace with the borderers, for though some of his kin had been massacred by them years before, he had forgiven the deed—perhaps not unmindful of the fact that others of his kin had been concerned in still more bloody massacres of the whites. A skilled marksman and mighty hunter, of commanding dignity, who treated all men with a grave courtesy that exacted the same treatment in return, he was greatly liked and respected by all the white hunters and frontiersmen whose friendship and respect were worth having.[87]

The fact that both Cornstalk and Logan had long since died could allow audiences to see them within the traditional, passive, romanticized past of the "noble savage." Nevertheless, what Roosevelt highlighted were the quintessential traits of Americanism that such "red" men had exhibited, similar to what frontier immigrants had demonstrated in becoming Americans.

The popular media's description of Indians as "savages," and "nobly civilized" was problematic. Both depictions threatened to cement natives' place on the lowest rungs of national society. Roosevelt did his fair share of articulating both descriptions. However, he addressed this social tension by also offering a middle ground. Audiences could move away from the extremes of either hating all Indians because of their supposed barbarity or romantically celebrating them for their passivity. Instead, he asked audiences to consider his interpretation of their "savagery" as noble and a trademark feature of Americanism. Indians' physical vigor distinguished them as martially capable, and their willful character placed them in the mold of frontier immigrant heroes.

Roosevelt's intolerance, at times, appeared as deep as any other nineteenth-century, upper-middle-class white man. For example, he and the nation embraced the same logic of the Frontier Myth to explain Indian displacement. Specifically, that logic blessed the westward crushing of Indians since they failed to "use" the land (i.e., make an economic profit from it).[88] Native Americans' seeming unwillingness to put the land to use, as well as those "sentimentalists" who objected to taking that land, galled Roosevelt. The "man who puts the soil to use," he fumed in *The Winning of the West*, "must of right dispossess the man who does not, or the world will come to a standstill." He cautioned against false sentimentality in this regard, and he chastised those who questioned the morality of warring against the indigenous people of the frontier. "It is, indeed, a warped, perverse, and silly morality," he offered, "which would forbid a course of conquest that has turned whole continents into the seats of mighty and flourishing civilized nations."[89] The Frontier Myth, for him and others, reconciled American values with Anglo-Saxon racism and greed regarding the conquest of western lands.

Despite Roosevelt's intense passion on this point, however, he recognized the negative implications of this reasoning in the modern era. In justifying whites' behavior, it also created unpleasant and destructive identities for both whites and Indians. The consequences of a fractured and fractious national community concerned Roosevelt, and the greed and ill character that suffused the supposed solutions to the "Indian problem" highlighted a self-serving materialism that he would consider poisonous to national life. He had addressed, this, in part, with his retelling of immigrants' struggles on the frontier, casting their story as more about heroism than plunder. Now, he would recast the mythic interpretation of Indians, which had positioned them as savage and inferior participants in the national experiment. Roosevelt's public rhetoric highlighted these two popular depictions of Indians and revealed a middle ground, a mythic interpretation that merged them within his notion of Americanism. Just as immigrant settlers had demonstrated their strength and will and had earned the opportunity to become Americans, he argued that the natives of his mythic anecdotes likewise exhibited such traits. By extension, then, they would deserve some opportunity for consideration as American citizens.

Even if audiences accepted Roosevelt's synthesis of those competing frontier images, there were problems. As the country entered the twentieth century, Indians did not appear as hardy protagonists worthy of a more revered place in the national hierarchy. Robbed of their lands, livelihoods, and societies for centuries, many of them suffered from physical and cultural malaise. Their emasculated condition confirmed the paternalistic need for whites to shoulder the burden of care for people whom assimilation had failed. Roosevelt's subsequent response may have been a different form of paternalism, but he continued to engage the frontier to explain how Native Americans, in fact, were Americans.

Constructing Native American Destiny

Roosevelt reinterpreted the meaning of natives' "savagery" to resemble the martial vigor of Americanism. For example, writing of his tours to reservations, he celebrated such events as the Hopi Snake-Dance, which pitted men against venomous snakes in an hours-long ritual. In describing the rituals, he concluded that they were not just "relics of an almost inconceivably remote and savage past," but more important, were a representation of a mystical "symbolism which has in it elements that are ennobling and not debasing."[90] For Roosevelt, these rituals preserved the sense of the wild, frontier universe, something that Indians offered as a meaningful contribution to the modern nation. The physical danger of such Indian rites—their tests of man against nature—constituted a "real" way to "play Indian" in the modern world. As co-participants in the Frontier Myth, natives had a place, although contested, in the nation's history. According to Roosevelt, they possessed both the strength of body and of character that he believed necessary for any race or ethnicity to win some level of equal respect in the community. Yet, many racists at the turn of the twentieth century still considered Indians collectively, as a group that shared an "uncivilized" character.

This stemmed, in part, from the public's understanding about life on reservations. Despite the abuses Indians faced, and the human response to resist such treatment, many Americans believed that it was Indians' low character that prevented their rehabilitation. High incidents of alcoholism on reservations marked all Indians as worthless drunks, an "uncivilized" state also attributed to "inferior" classes of people, such as immigrants.[91] Others believed that Indians' laziness allowed them to grow too dependent on the largesse of the federal government.[92] Still others looked at Indians susceptibility to disease as a manifestation of their inherent racial weakness.[93] Whatever the belief, the nation considered the character of Indians unfit, making them ill-suited for attaining American identity. Roosevelt responded to these ideas by arguing that Indians' character was not the problem—whites were to blame for lack of progress on the reservation.

As was his penchant, Roosevelt celebrated decent character by castigating those who failed to display it. He condemned officials that he believed hindered the advance of Indians. During a dinner address in 1893, the young civil service commissioner commented on conditions at an Indian reservation he had toured. He raised his displeasure with political appointees who served as agents on the reservation. "I came away impressed," Roosevelt remarked sarcastically, "with the outrageous iniquities of the spoils system as applied to the management of our Indian affairs." Unlike in white society, he continued, natives could not "demand" the retirement of "incompetent" or morally "bad" agents. He sympathized with Indians who saw the "working of the spoils system . . . [as] a curse and an outrage," and which made the "road leading upward from savagery . . . more difficult and infinitely more stony for the poor feet trying to tread it."[94] Although Roosevelt had engaged similar castigations against materialistic corporate business owners, he did not cast the public as impotent necessarily. His strategy this time depicted Indians in that way. While he identified white greed and stupidity as morally reprehensible, he implied that Indians were of weak will as well. According to him, they seemed unable to make better progress on the "road leading upward from savagery" due to the machinations of others. Basically, his circular argument affirmed the idea that reservation Indians were not truly of rugged stock since they relied on too much help and could not stand up for themselves when treated unjustly.

This was not the first time that Roosevelt echoed the paternalistic attitude that many Americans felt toward Native Americans.[95] Sometimes he publicly categorized Indians as similar to children, a "group of beings who are not able to protect themselves." According to him, natives could only excel with a "helping hand."[96] Even when Roosevelt used the "bully pulpit" to chastise weak character in whites, he perpetuated the stereotype of Indians suffering from such flaws as well. As president, he continued the tradition of previous chief executives in blaming whites for "Indian problems" on reservations.[97] Of course, claiming that whites prevented the social and cultural progress of natives once again affirmed the Indians' lack of strong character. In his "Fourth Annual Message," he blamed the "slow advance" of reservation Indians to the "unsatisfactory character of the men appointed to take immediate charge of them," men who engaged in "flagrant dishonesty."[98] Speaking at a private club later in his presidency, Roosevelt called to task local governments who could not afford "to do less than justice to the Indian." He called on them to "make it your work to see that your own State courts, your State officials, carefully preserve the rights of the Indian, and that you try to give him the chance to which he is entitled."[99] While whites may be responsible for many "Indian problems," Roosevelt confirmed the idea that Native Americans were weak-willed since they only made slow progress, albeit, in a corrupt system. Clearly, his statements about Indians needing "helping hands" and only making "slow advances" reflected a then-common prejudice about Native American character.

Roosevelt exacerbated the tension surrounding the debate about Indians' place in the nation. By repeatedly visualizing the opposing positions and their consequences in the starkest terms, he made them unpalatable as realistic possibilities—whites forever stuck taking care of Indians who could not seemingly help themselves. As he usually did, though, Roosevelt had simply set the extreme contours of the public debate, allowing him room to offer a position that, in contrast, would appear moderate.

By the turn of the twentieth century, Indians, collectively, were "red others," seemingly helpless children who constituted the "White Man's Burden." That image rooted whites in the uncomfortable and expensive position of caretaker and consigned all natives to the unwanted and marginalized role of weak-willed wards of the state. For Roosevelt, this could not stand; the social cohesiveness of the nation was at stake. He addressed white racism and "red" despondence by offering his audiences what they might believe to be a middle ground. Although he stated, "We must protect and guard [Native Americans] up to a certain point," he also declared that "when all, humanly speaking, is done that can be done, we must turn them loose."[100] In other words, America's paternalistic role, while necessary, could eventually end because Indians were proving ready to take their place in the larger society.

During his presidency, Roosevelt took two positions in response to popular conceptions of Indians appearing weak and needy. First, he argued that some natives were proving their character and were thus ready to receive respect as Americans. They were re-embracing the "rugged individualism" of American identity. Second, Roosevelt alleged that Indians who no longer needed a "helping hand" were ready to enjoy an equal status with whites. Specifically, he promoted a controversial form of Native American equality—intermarriage with whites. Through that act, Indians would attain a respected place in the national hierarchy.

First, Roosevelt attacked the public's belief that natives were helpless children. The "time has arrived," he declared in his "First Annual Message," to "recognize the Indian as an individual."[101] According to him, some of them exhibited the requisite hardiness of character. He argued that like the frontiersmen of old, some natives had shown "in a degree greater than ever before, an appreciation of the necessity of work." In fact, he revealed in his "Fourth Annual Message" that the government had been "reducing the amount of subsistence to the Indians." In turn, this forced them, "through sheer necessity, to work for a livelihood." Though seemingly harsh, Roosevelt considered it useful since many Indians learned the "habits of regular industry."[102] More important, though, this theme argued that not all natives were alike. Just as some immigrants proved ready for American identity by a show of "rugged individualism," Roosevelt argued that some Indians had likewise proven themselves in hard conditions.

Now, what Roosevelt called "reduced subsistence," many Indians probably considered starvation.[103] Trapped on reservations, they received little enough assistance given the number of crooked, incompetent, and uncaring BIA agents. Still, he considered the "ration system" on reservations to promote "beggary" and "pauperism," thus reaffirming his idea that individuals needed to be willing to work hard; for him, this character trait constituted a national virtue.[104] So he assured whites that many individual Indians were worthy of American identity because they had embraced a hardy work ethic, albeit forced. Likewise, natives could hope that their demonstration of "regular industry" readied them for their eventual release from the reservation system.[105]

The one "helping hand" that Roosevelt did not begrudge Indians was education. As president, he linked it to their character development. Not just any education, Roosevelt believed, but an appropriate one: vocational training. Similar to the myth he would spin regarding African Americans and education, he argued that vocational training had made a difference in fostering character. "In the schools the education should be elementary and largely industrial," President Roosevelt offered in 1901, with the "need of higher education" being "very, very limited." To that end, teachers needed to deliver this industrial training with the individual, and his location, in mind: "Every effort should be made to develop the Indian along the lines of natural aptitude, and to encourage the existing native industries peculiar to certain tribes, such as . . . canoe-building, smith work, and blanket work."[106] Offering only vocational education may have indicated Roosevelt's class bias—various racial and ethnic groups laboring in their place based on their "natural aptitude"—but it was also consistent with his belief that too much higher education robbed the individual of the rough-and-tumble grit necessary for citizenship. In that regard, he affirmed the importance of fostering a will for hardy effort rather than the effeminate work of the intellect.

Far from being "children," Roosevelt surmised, individual natives epitomized people of high character. They demonstrated the frontier-inspired, homespun virtues central to his conception of American identity. In his published letter accepting the vice presidential nomination in 1900, Roosevelt alleged that there existed "Indians which have so far advanced that it has been possible to embody them as a whole in our political system." There existed "men of Indian blood" who served with distinction in high-ranking business, political, and military positions. He appeased racists by acknowledging that some Indians might "still be too wild" to be accorded the rights and privileges of citizenship. However, he repeatedly declared that there "are individuals among the Apaches, Pawnees, Iroquois, Sioux, and other tribes," whose accomplishments reflected that they were ready to stand "on an absolute equality with all our citizens of pure white blood."[107]

Roosevelt's invocation of "blood" equality represented his second response to popular conceptions about Indians' unfit character. For him, Indian blood mixed with white blood possessed transformative power. This element reflects one of the most powerful symbols in a culture's myths. Blood routinely embodies the means for people to revitalize themselves physically and spiritually.[108] Roosevelt said as much about immigrants and the infusion of their blood. Now, the blood of First Americans could likewise rejuvenate a new generation. The traditional belief that Roosevelt was contented with Indians' expulsion from American society, or their outright extermination, seems unlikely.[109] Roosevelt actually invoked the mythic potential of Indian blood as a way to offer them a place in the nation and, more important, to inject a biological hardiness in Americans he believed suffering from the malaise of the modern era. Some Indians, like some immigrants, had demonstrated their physical hardihood and good character and had thus deserved what Roosevelt considered "equality." He offered a simple solution to giving Indians an exalted place in the national identity: allow them to intermarry with whites without the outcry from racists. Biological assimilation, in a way, constituted the ultimate manifestation of equality.

For many people at the time, the idea of Indian and white intermarriage seemed blasphemous. Roosevelt, however, appeared amused by these racist notions and repeatedly challenged them. As a civil service commissioner assessing conditions on reservations, he noted, "half-breeds are very much further advanced than the Indians proper, and that in a great number of cases they are on a complete level with the whites."[110] Again using the frontier as his mythic touchstone, he explained that the nation's storied past revealed the validity of such unions. "In the old times," he noted about early American frontiersmen, "all had Indian wives; but nowadays those who live among and intermarry with the Indians are looked down upon."[111] Roosevelt believed it to be an advantage for both races, in that such marriages resulted in the type of citizens he heralded in his myth of Americanism. He noted for his readers of *Ranch Life and the Hunting Trail* that: "Here and there on the border there is a certain amount of mixture with the Indian blood; much more than is commonly supposed. One of the most hard-working and prosperous men in our neighborhood is a Chippewa half-breed; he is married to a white wife, and ranks in every respect as a white. Two of our richest cattlemen are married to Indian women. . . . In several of the most thriving Northwestern cities men could be pointed out, standing high in the community, men who have a strong dash of Indian blood in their veins."[112] Obviously, Roosevelt's attention to "half-breeds" and the ability to identify a "strong dash of Indian blood" acknowledged skin color as a salient factor in American identity. The frontier "proof," however, trumped the idea that "red" stained "white." Thus, he asked audiences to look beyond skin color and accept Indians' presence (and blood) as a necessary ingredient for the advancement of both groups.

Roosevelt identified mixed blood as a sign of other advantages as well. "In portions of the Indian Territory," he wrote in his "Second Annual Message" to Congress, "the mixture of blood has gone on at the same time with progress in wealth and education." In fact, "there are plenty of men with varying degrees of purity of Indian blood who are indistinguishable in point of social, political, and economic ability from their white associates."[113] His mythic allusions to the transformative power of mixed blood argued that America benefited from the legendary essence of natives, while natives themselves gained the civilizing influence of white culture. Some Native Americans found the issue of assimilation into white culture problematic. They resented and resisted the destruction of their tribal identities for a questionable place in American identity.[114] Yet, others realized that they needed to learn to live with a new, national identity and not a tribal one.[115] For whites, accepting Indians' essence in the national bloodstream constituted a moderate position given the specter of blacks in white America. Social and legal acceptance of miscegenation between whites and blacks was impossible; the mythic belief that a single drop of African American blood made a person "all black" rendered any biological union damning to whites.[116] Since many Anglo Americans considered themselves racially opposite to African Americans, and considered Indians racially opposite to blacks, they inadvertently positioned natives closer to their end of the racial spectrum.[117] Roosevelt strategically moved that closeness of Indians and whites to its logical and frontier-inspired conclusion—racial fusion. This constituted his version of equality for Native Americans.

The moral of Roosevelt's mythic treatment of Native Americans appeared straightforward. Indians were not simple "savages," not noble to the point of unmanliness, and they were not needy, inept children. He overturned those extreme positions, transforming Indians instead into protagonists deserving recognition for their martial hardiness and moral character. According to him, they represented an important link to the nation's frontier past and embodied the mythic essence he considered essential to its future. By contextualizing Indians within the myth of Americanism, he celebrated the idea of their "blood" transfusion to the nation. Both whites and natives could rest assured, then, that all would be Americans, pure and simple.

Conclusion

Little did Native Americans realize that when explorers arrived on the North American shores in the 1500s, their centuries-old customs would soon be under assault. Little did they know that their relationships with settlers would expose them to biological and cultural influences that would decimate their lives. Little did they contemplate that their "red" skin would mark them as mythological "others," uncivilized hindrances to be exterminated or exiled.

Whatever his feelings about Indians, Roosevelt saw them as a potential resource that could invigorate the American nation, if whites accepted them. To that end, he offered his own mythic treatment of Native Americans. He placed them within his frontier-inspired myth of Americanism, positioning them between two extremes in the public's mind. On the one hand, he downplayed the "merciless" nature of Indians' "ferocity" on the frontier by having them also appear as admired archetypes of physically vigorous, strong-willed warriors. Moreover, when Roosevelt condemned immoral immigrants for their part in the hostilities, and depicted Indians as metaphoric and "natural" parts of the frontier universe, he partially absolved the natives of wrongdoing. On the other hand, his rhetoric countered the notion that Indians languished on reservations as helpless and inferior "children." According to him, these individuals had "grown" into Americans by determinedly working with what they had on reservations. Because Native Americans had proven their worth, he deemed it ludicrous to prevent them from biologically mixing with whites. In this way, Indians found the evidence of their "equal" status. Their essence in the nation's body, Roosevelt alleged, would help the nation to move more quickly toward its destiny.

Roosevelt used his public rhetoric to shape a diverse collection of people— white and nonwhite alike—into one mythical, cohesive identity. To do that, his discourse highlighted the social contradictions of Native Americans' place in the nation. Rather than dismiss Indians as troublemakers or worthless, his celebration of their character demonstrated their viability as Americans, balancing both white hate and white guilt, and native "savagery" and native despair. As a result, he resolved the question of the nation's identity within the confines of Americanism.

Clearly, Roosevelt's rhetorical treatment of Indians perhaps hurt them as much as any other racist dialogue of the day. His portrayal of their supposed savagery echoed other popular works of the time, perhaps affirming rather than submerging that notion in the public's consciousness. His public rhetoric promoted white superiority by forcing a "helping hand" toward "child-like" natives who he believed needed to "prove" their maturity. Although he literally threw Indians into the "melting pot" to add their biological essence to whites, he, like others, traded their cultural uniqueness for a proscribed and problematic place in American identity. As myths can do, though, Roosevelt's Americanism simultaneously offered desired change for one group and reestablished the status quo for another. Specifically, his Americanism promoted the values important to the nation, offered Indians the opportunities for success, reconciled the loss of their cultures as a natural manifestation of newfound "equality," and affirmed the notion of white superiority.

4

Shaping the African American Image

~

Americanism and the "Negro Problem"

The turn of the twentieth century represented a low point in American race relations, given the rampant discrimination toward, lynching of, and outright contempt for African Americans.[1] Across any number of media, whites communicated to blacks that they constituted an unnecessary and unwanted burden on national development. As one of the most outspoken, controversial, and powerful leaders of the day, Theodore Roosevelt bucked the trend that cast blacks as virtually worthless. His performance on the national stage, however, earned him a precarious legacy in regard to African Americans, race, and national identity.[2]

On a number of occasions, Roosevelt appeared to be a staunch supporter of African American progress. As governor of New York State, he signed legislation that made it illegal to segregate public schools. As president, he closed a Mississippi post office when whites prevented the black postmistress from doing her job. He also successfully fought for three years to appoint an African American as the collector of customs in South Carolina. Furthermore, he became the first chief executive to invite an African American, Booker T. Washington, to dine with him at the White House.[3]

For each mark of distinction Roosevelt achieved, he compiled more than a few moments of disgrace. As president, he named fewer blacks to federal appointments than his predecessor did. In the infamous Brownsville case, he dishonorably dismissed scores of African American soldiers from the army for allegedly attacking that small Texas town and assaulting its citizens, despite the fact that the evidence against the soldiers was inconclusive. Furthermore, his presidency also coincided with one of the most violent periods in white mob attacks against black citizens, with Roosevelt remaining silent about it much of the time.[4]

Several scholars explain Roosevelt's behavior as resulting from his supposed ambivalence to blacks. According to Thomas Dyer, Roosevelt considered the "'Negro problem' as a very special dilemma." However, despite representing a "moderating force in an age of high racism," Roosevelt, like others of his era, "harbored strong feelings about the inferiority of blacks."[5] As H. W. Brands noted, Roosevelt "really *was* torn as to where wisdom resided on the race question." In regards to lynching in particular, Roosevelt had "mixed feelings." He saw it simultaneously as a "horrendous punishment" that whites visited on blacks, and an "inevitable corrective to the failing of the formal criminal justice system."[6] Roosevelt worried about finding the proper place and role for blacks in America. For instance, he believed in blacks' innate inferiority, yet still thought that African Americans could hold political office.[7] In other words, Roosevelt seemingly expressed his vexation with a confusing set of actions and statements.

The conclusions that offer Roosevelt's statements as contradictory to his policies, or that label him simply as a racist, or as a political opportunist, dismiss too quickly his rhetorical attempt to mediate the problematic racial issues of the day.[8] African Americans represented too large a group to let languish as "inferior" citizens. While "objectionable" immigrant populations could be restricted, and Indian populations had fallen to approximately 300,000 by the turn of the twentieth century,[9] blacks numbered a whopping 8.8 million.[10] Despite all the "back to Africa" talk, blacks were not going anywhere.[11] Thus, although Roosevelt believed in the inherent virtues of Euro-Americans, he understood that the "Negro problem" would have to be resolved before the nation could advance toward what he considered its destiny.[12] Furthermore, any resolution regarding blacks would need whites' blessing, or at the very least, their grudging acceptance.

Perhaps more important, Roosevelt wanted a martially strong and virtuously resolute nation that respected the principle of equality. In other words, he wanted a nation that epitomized his version of Americanism, one that, whether or not he or anyone else liked it, would have to include blacks in some fashion. As a result, he employed a rhetoric that could appease both white and black audiences and that respected the racist beliefs of whites while defending the equal treatment of blacks. Despite Roosevelt's seeming vacillation on the issue, both races considered him their champion.[13] He promoted his version of Americanism within an atmosphere of hostility and fear expressed by blacks and whites about each other. The question is: How did he navigate the tensions surrounding race and national identity so that both groups could see themselves as Americans, pure and simple?

Roosevelt strategically kept those contradictory tensions active in an attempt to keep the public debate from polarizing any further. Using myth, he balanced an overtly racist ideology with what he may have considered "pie in the sky" reform regarding blacks, focusing instead on a middle ground—Americanism. Despite the problematic outcomes, he provided African Americans an identity that moved beyond their antebellum depiction. He not only created an opportunity for them to achieve a more valid place in society, but he also appeased whites that blacks were not moving too far beyond their station.

Contrary to the claim that Roosevelt excluded African Americans from national mythology,[14] Roosevelt placed them in the mythic frontier settings that had previously been the sole domain of whites. He portrayed African Americans as representatives of the "strenuous life" who distinguished themselves on the frontier battlefield. Rather than focus solely on their physical prowess, though, Roosevelt also highlighted the virtuous nature of black individuals within the frontier mythos, celebrating their strength of character. Perhaps recognizing that whites considered blacks an inferior mass, he anointed select blacks as exemplars who demonstrated the type of character that immigrant settlers exhibited when they served their frontier community; specifically, he welcomed qualified blacks to participate in political life. For remaining African Americans, he tailored his mythic treatment of black identity with elements borrowed from the competing ideologies articulated by W. E. B. Du Bois and by Booker T. Washington. Roosevelt offered vocational education—an education the frontiersmen respected—as the means to popularize the idea of successful, hard-working blacks. Such imagery could inspire African Americans to elevate themselves in society, as well as to mollify whites that blacks were not advancing too quickly. Finally, Roosevelt's depiction of lynching as an odious example of lawlessness rightfully cast blacks as victims. However, he also depicted lynching as a sometimes-necessary form of "frontier justice." This perpetuated certain racist stereotypes yet demonstrated how equality would have to be earned by African Americans. Engaging frontier-inspired elements in his public discourse, Roosevelt opened a mythic place in national identity for blacks, one that positioned them between the competing tensions of fear and hatred that nonwhite people faced in modern society.

Race and Opportunity in the Post–Civil War Era

Having endured the oppression of American slavery for over two hundred years, African Americans hoped that the North's victory during the Civil War marked the beginning of their freedom and all the opportunities it might bring.[15] Whites, particularly southerners, quickly dispelled such hopes. Through popular, political, and criminal means, whites continued to denigrate African Americans in an attempt to excise their presence from national life. Particularly, ex-slaves still found themselves the subject of a national mythology that questioned, if not outright denied, their humanity and their right to equality.

Before the American Revolution, most whites regarded blacks as inhuman and thus inherently inferior.[16] Despite gaining their freedom after the Civil War, racist myths about African Americans continued to flourish. James Robertson noted that the "function of the myths of race and color in America" following the end of slavery maintained a "vision of black Americans as outsiders in American society, as people beyond the frontier."[17] Since the frontier represented the mythical universe in which immigrant settlers and, to a certain extent Native Americans, found national identity, placing blacks "beyond" it affirmed their alien nature. According to Thomas Gossett, the popular literature about blacks after the Civil War revealed an "undisguised hatred of the Negro which [portrayed] him as little if any better than a beast."[18] Such literature emphasized the idea that ex-slaves were less than human. "The idea that black people were physically and mentally very close to animals," Mia Bay noted, "was widely disseminated among whites" following the Civil War. According to Bay, "during these years blacks were routinely depicted as ape-like figures in political cartoons, popular art, and advertising.... Images of animal-like black children being menaced by crocodiles and black men and women grinning like monkeys graced postcards, souvenirs, and advertisements."[19] Blacks' status as brutes made them unworthy candidates for respectful consideration in the nation's identity.

One of the most potent media for fueling these depictions was the new movie industry. People seemed in awe of this new technology and were particularly receptive to long-held beliefs of white superiority and racial inequality presented to them in the form of moving pictures.[20] Like the printed media, movies portrayed African Americans as woefully inferior. According to John Kisch and Edward Mapp, a "troupe of crude, insulting, racist images stumbled across the screen: dimwitted, comic, contorted coons, [and] loyal, submissive, doltish toms." Perhaps the more effective means to ostracize blacks from American culture rested in white actors wearing a black face, "making the characters all the more grotesque and alien." These stereotypes existed long before the films of the early twentieth century, but the movies allowed them to reach broader audiences and reaffirmed such images in the public's mind.[21]

These mythic depictions of black inferiority continued in the so-called scientific literature. Many pseudo-scientific tracts appeared throughout the late nineteenth and early twentieth centuries that explained black inferiority in biological terms. For example, one medical textbook argued that educating ex-slaves would be impossible since that would damage their brains, leading to an overdeveloped area of their heads, which would in turn throw off their equilibrium.[22] These "facts" supported claims of inferiority made by advocates of Darwinian theory. Bay noted that Social Darwinists took the "survival of the fittest" idea to "arrange the races in a racial hierarchy that placed black people on the bottom as perennial losers in the evolutionary struggle."[23] Eugenicists, those believers in improving racial types through controlled breeding,[24] perpetuated the myth that blacks had proven their inferiority since they had not reached the intellectual and social heights as had whites. Marouf Hasian concluded that the work of eugenicists frequently argued that African Americans had "failed miserably in the race of life," continually squandering their chance "to prove their worth."[25] Strategically, whites argued that blacks were incapable of contributing to national life and, if true, meant that there was no need to assist them in trying to reach a goal that nature had determined was unreachable.

Despite these depictions, many African Americans believed that they would enjoy the benefits offered by the myths of freedom and equality, specifically participation in political life.[26] However, they found little relief in this area since whites attempted to bar them from that civic arena.[27] Bristling at the northern-enforced Reconstruction plans, many southern states adopted harsh laws that returned African Americans to an enslaved status. These "Black Codes" prevented ex-slaves from holding political office, required them to get permission to move from place to place, created conditions that made it easier for them to be arrested for vagrancy and, being unable to pay the fine for that offense, would be forcibly hired out as labor for an indefinite period of time.[28] The landmark Supreme Court case in 1896, *Plessy v. Ferguson,* established legalized segregation between the races. The resulting "Jim Crow" laws called for "separate but equal" accommodations, separating blacks from whites on trains, in hospitals, factories, restrooms, and other public facilities. According to Joel Williamson, segregation acted as a political "device for putting down feelings of self-esteem among black people, first by exclusion and then by relegation to inferior accommodations."[29] While not "officially" codified at the national level, the federal government implicitly approved of Jim Crow statutes by allowing segregation in the nation's capital. By the end of the nineteenth century, blacks had essentially been "abandoned by all three branches of the federal government and largely left to the tender mercies of oligarchic white southern state governments."[30]

One of the most potent means to perpetuate black inferiority was through physical violence, particularly lynching. African Americans seemed powerless victims of this gruesome, criminal act. Real or imagined crimes, most notably violations of white womanhood by black men, frequently spurred lynchers. "The cry of rape, appealing to the most extreme fears and hatreds," Herbert Shapiro wrote, drew upon "racist myths concerning black male sexuality," acted as a "summons to the mob," and justified the brutal act of lynching.[31] White law enforcement personnel and citizens alike lynched over one thousand blacks near the turn of the twentieth century, with an average of 187 lynched each year between 1889 and 1898; before 1917, the number of lynchings did not drop below 50.[32] In many ways, targeted blacks became unwilling stars in a macabre show: "The lynchers, characteristically, were not content merely to kill the victim; the act of lynching was often transformed into a public spectacle, and sometimes hundreds or thousands of whites from the surrounding countryside would come to town to observe the event. . . . Before death came the victim was tortured, tormented by having limbs or sexual organs amputated, by being slowly roasted over a fire. . . . After death pieces of the charred remains would often be souvenirs to the mob whose members desired a keepsake as a remembrance of the notable happening."[33] Lynching once again made the African American man appear to be devoid of human identity, with no real difference between himself and some rabid animal. "In the myth of the black beast rapist," Williamson observed, the message about race and sex was "exceedingly clear—that black men were to be kept away from white women, precisely because black men were . . . sexual creatures."[34]

As whites struggled to shape the ex-slave's character in the public mind, blacks did too. They had a more difficult job if only due to the numbers of credible writers and their access to media outlets. While there was a recognized singular white voice in the negative depictions of African Americans, the black community hardly spoke with one voice. African American rhetors clashed with one another just as they attempted to gain ground against white racist propaganda used against them. Two recognized leaders of the African American community at the time, Booker T. Washington and W. E. B. Du Bois, voiced their own competing conceptions of black identity in modern America.

Tapping into the myth of American progress—the idea that rewards come to those who struggle for them[35]—Washington, the "Wizard of Tuskegee,"[36] affirmed the belief that blacks could attain material prosperity similar to whites if given the opportunity. To that end, he established the Tuskegee Institute in

1881 to provide African Americans industrial and agricultural education training. He recognized that such skills would not only give blacks the means to attain some form of economic viability through the country's burgeoning manu-
facturing industry, but it also placated whites who did not want their ex-slaves
educated beyond the level of manual laborers.[37]

W. E. B. Du Bois, a contemporary of Washington, chafed at Washington's
ideas. Du Bois promoted another identity that was more controversial. Specifically, he called on blacks to embrace their distinctiveness as a group, essentially
resisting assimilation. Blacks needed to advance economically, obviously, but
their talents rested not just in using farm implements. For him, ex-slaves needed
to develop their own innate gifts, and when they did, they could contribute to
the aesthetic culture of America and the world. Engaging the myth of equality,[38]
Du Bois promoted a form of cultural pluralism where the essence of blackness
would maintain its spiritual and intellectual integrity alongside that of whites,
equal to it in every way.[39] He emphasized his idea of advanced education as the
means to success for black Americans. This type of training would take gifted
blacks and educate them as leaders of their community.[40] As John Weaver concluded, however, Du Bois's call for "gifted black children" to be "educated to become leaders [and] not servants" sent a "chill down white spines."[41] Allowing
blacks to engage in intellectual pursuits similar to that of whites privileged the
African Americans in a way that was abhorrent to whites. Whites, grudgingly,
might allow blacks to work as blue-collar laborers, but such behavior affirmed
blacks' "beast of burden" nature, and continued to keep them subservient to the
supposed intellectual superiority of whites. African Americans as physical and
sexual "brutes" appeared to be the extent of their national identity.

As competing arguments about black identity in American culture continued, Theodore Roosevelt matured. Born in 1858, he observed first-hand the
place of African Americans, as well as the various remedies offered for their
situation. Like many whites of his time, he accepted the stereotypical portrait
of the ex-slave. As a child, he perceived similarities between his family's black
servants and those servants presented in the popular press as being childlike in
their devotion to their white employers. His Harvard education reinforced cultural beliefs about the superiority of the white race.[42]

Race played a key role in Roosevelt's thinking about American identity.
Roosevelt deemed the white race central to the nation's advance to greatness;[43]
so, African Americans, with their dark skin and supposed inferiority, did not
qualify to become an equal ingredient in the "melting pot." Dyer echoed this
point, arguing that Roosevelt believed African Americans could never enter the
national bloodstream in the same way that certain immigrant groups and Native
Americans could.[44] Roosevelt may have promoted the notion of "equality for all"

as a distinguishing characteristic of national identity, but Roosevelt also wanted a nation comprised of a "complex blend of racial hybridity and purity." As a result, scholars have concluded that Roosevelt worked little to include blacks in the social fabric of the nation.[45]

Although Roosevelt accepted the notion of black "equipotentiality" in matters other than social intercourse, "he always made it clear," Dyer wrote, "that the distance from the black racial position to the status of the superior races remained great and that blacks had only begun to traverse it."[46] Yet, Roosevelt also embraced other ideas. Despite the "kindly condescension" he had for African Americans, Joseph Gardner observed that Roosevelt considered Abraham Lincoln the "greatest hero in American history" for the stand the "Great Emancipator" took regarding the slaves. Like Lincoln, Roosevelt "believed passionately in emancipation and the gradual improvement of the black man's lot."[47] Roosevelt also possessed a legendary sense of fairness.[48] His sense of fair play may have rested uneasily next to his awareness that blacks, inferior or not, suffered injustices and were denied legitimate opportunities.

How African Americans could prove themselves and traverse the road to equality became the subject of much of Roosevelt's discourse. The racist mindset at the time marginalized blacks as subhuman outsiders, preventing them from attaining any form of success; this, in turn, Roosevelt argued, inhibited the progress of the nation itself. However, Du Boisian notions of equality scared many whites. Roosevelt kept these tensions in play to reconcile what he considered an appropriate identity for African Americans. Neither side could win out, nor could the public debate continue as it had. Thus, he addressed the "special dilemma" of the "Negro problem" mythically, redefining black potential through the lens of the frontier.

Redefining the "Seething Mass"

Roosevelt defined American identity by offering frontier protagonists as archetypal representatives of the nation's citizenry. Immigrant pioneers, as well as Native Americans, exhibited the requisite traits that he believed gave America its power and prominence as an ideal community.[49] For him, these legendary men and women embodied Americanism. According to Roosevelt, they not only demonstrated the "rugged individualism" and hardy character necessary in any great society, but they also recognized the need to work together equally and to create an existence greater than the sum of their individual lives. The appealing nature of such protagonists in Roosevelt's public discourse, as well as the community they created, provided audiences with the means to identify with such characters.[50] His emphasis on immigrants' roles in founding the nation's mythic history, as well as envisioning Native Americans as necessary elements in that history, positioned both groups as viable candidates for American identity.

African Americans, on the other hand, proved more difficult to consider as ingredients in the "melting pot." One of the key elements of national identity revolved around race. The tendency to use physical differences, primarily skin color, to distinguish "races" has been a human tendency for thousands of years.[51] In America's case, Congress legally established the relationship between whiteness and citizenship in 1790.[52] By the end of the nineteenth century, the nation had become obsessed with explaining how traits, both superior and inferior, were inherent and tied to skin color. Whites resisted the idea that a person's environment and social education mattered.[53] As a result, lighter skin not only became a prerequisite for entrance into the national community, but it also acted as an indication of innate superiority.

The dark skin of African Americans appeared to be an insurmountable obstacle for their acceptance in the American community. "In the Alice-in-Wonderland mythic logic" employed by racists, Robertson observed, the "colors are moral polarities: 'pure white' is the most superior, and 'pure black' . . . the most inferior."[54] That attitude, in varying degrees, extended to all ex-slaves. For a number of whites, the skin color of African Americans made them, as a group, unworthy of any type of equal consideration after the Civil War. According to Williamson, whites saw African Americans as a "seething mass of black atoms," indistinguishable in their inferiority.[55] Considered by whites as a mythic and inferior mass, blacks inhabited the lowest rungs in the national hierarchy. Roosevelt, though, attacked the notion of African Americans' "mythic inferiority" by extending his version of Americanism to them. He placed them in frontier settings to establish their martial hardiness, just as he did with immigrants and American Indians. Furthermore, he responded to the notion of blacks as a worthless mass with his own identifications of individual "Negroes" who demonstrated high character.

Although the Frontier Myth defined American identity, Roosevelt avoided connecting blacks directly to that story. He did not place African Americans in the Frontier Myth. During the timeline of the traditional frontier story, blacks were slaves and were thus unfit for any consideration. Consequently, the Frontier Myth became the sacrosanct domain of native-born whites, as well as those immigrants and Indians who "became white." Roosevelt, though, did the next best thing. If he could not include blacks in the frontier universe, he could place them in *a* frontier setting. Given that the legacy of the frontier emphasized the clash between civilization and savagery, he celebrated those blacks who fought in such clashes after America's domination of the North American continent.

In 1899, Roosevelt published *The Rough Riders*, an account of his experiences in the Spanish-American War. On more than one occasion in that book, he played into racist notions. For instance, he noted that the "colored soldiers" seemed "peculiarly dependent upon their white officers," and in another case erroneously identified black soldiers as retreating under fire when they were actually taking the wounded for treatment.[56] On other occasions, though, he lauded select individuals. He noted that some blacks became "non-commissioned officers who can take the initiative and accept responsibility precisely like the best class of whites." In fact, some blacks distinguished themselves to the point that Roosevelt's Rough Riders, who had a "strong color prejudice, grew to accept them with hearty good will as comrades." This anecdote highlighted the tension in race relations and provided a moderating lesson to Americans: some blacks could "measure up" to whites, and both could live comfortably together when they all embraced the hardy lifestyle of the frontier or its battlefield substitute. According to Roosevelt, his white soldiers were so impressed with the "colored soldiers" that they were "entirely willing, in their own phrase, 'to drink out of the same canteen.'"[57] The Rough Rider never called for this wartime interaction between the races to become the basis for social relations in modern society. Rather, the exhibition of the frontier spirit simply demonstrated that some blacks could endure the mythic "strenuous life," and rightly earned respect for that ability from whites.

Roosevelt depicted a frontier setting that provided a unique transformative experience. In fact, he saw humanity's struggle in the wilderness as the key to American identity.[58] It comes as no surprise, then, that he lauded individual African Americans for proving their worth in the rugged wilderness. Roosevelt, making the connection between blacks and *a* frontier, celebrated them in the same way that he praised immigrants when he included them in America's frontier history. In *Outdoor Pastimes of an American Hunter*, published in 1905, Roosevelt related the story of Holt Collier, a "negro hunter" whom he admired: "He was a man of sixty and could neither read nor write, but he had all the dignity of an African chief, and for half a century he had been a bear-hunter, having killed or assisted in killing over three thousand bears. . . . When ten years old Holt had . . . killed his first bear. In the Civil War he had not only followed his master to battle as his body-servant but had acted under him as sharpshooter against the Union soldiers."[59] The anecdote about Collier served two purposes. Depicted as exhibiting the requisite martial character of American identity, the same trait that the mythical supermen of *The Winning of the West* demonstrated, Collier acted as an exemplar that provided blacks a way to see themselves as part of the nation's story. Furthermore, the Collier anecdote assured whites that they had nothing to fear from black ruggedness: that trait seemed only to appear in defense of whites, an image hearkening back to the subservient relationship with blacks that whites had enjoyed decades earlier.

Roosevelt had long admired individual fortitude, and so he celebrated the fact that African Americans had demonstrated the physical vigor necessary in war and wilderness. His "strenuous life" philosophy—invoking the mythic frontier of a life filled with danger and strife that needed strength of arms to meet it—permeated much of his discourse. "In this life we get nothing save by effort," Roosevelt declared in the "The Strenuous Life" speech, and it was the effort of the man "who has those virile qualities necessary to win in the stern strife of actual life," that benefited the nation.[60] Yet, Roosevelt did not spend a great deal of time on this aspect of Americanism in relation to African Americans. In a sense, African Americans had already proven their ruggedness by enduring the burden of slavery. Perhaps more important, reminding audiences that the "seething mass" of blacks was a near mythic, physical force would exacerbate white anxiety. Thus, Roosevelt's rhetoric turned, for a time, to establishing blacks as individuals rather than as an indistinguishable group. Given the perception that they, as a group, were morally inferior, he highlighted how individual blacks demonstrated virtuous character in service to the community, another hallmark feature of Americanism.

In Roosevelt's mythic conception of the nation, participation in civic life reflected a fundamental service for all upright Americans to undertake. Settlers on the frontier, he wrote in *The Winning of the West*, demonstrated a keen appreciation for civic duty. A person needed to work "in combination" with others, devoting a "reasonable share of his time to doing his duty in the political life of the community." The frontier universe shaped their "characteristic capacity for combination," noting that immigrants in the Tennessee region worked vigorously to develop the first "written constitution . . . ever adopted . . . by a community composed of American-born free-men."[61] He lauded "pure and simple" citizens of moral conscience who served their community by entering politics. And he wished that "more of our good citizens would go into politics" with the "same spirit with which their fathers went into the Federal armies." He positioned the people who upheld their political duty as similar to the frontier settlers, virtuously demonstrating a "fearlessness, honesty, and common sense to do [their] best for the nation."[62]

Therefore, beyond martial capability, Roosevelt argued that the individual needed to demonstrate strength of character as well. The successful person not only had the "ability to fight well," but also possessed the "capacity to subordinate [his or her] interests . . . to the interests of the community."[63] For him, political involvement not only epitomized a person's service to the nation, but it also acted as a marker for good character. "No man has a right to shirk his political duties," he charged an audience in 1893. By embracing that duty, a person deserved the "high praise of being called a good American citizen."[64] A citizen with hardy virtues actively participated in politics, and he illustrated that individual African Americans could play in that arena as well.

The prevailing notion, particularly among southern whites, was that not all blacks were capable, or wanted, in politics.[65] Yet, Roosevelt still believed that a "few blacks had acquired . . . the necessary characteristics for participation in politics."[66] These exemplars would establish a limited black presence in politics, providing a middle ground between what Williamson called a "striking persistence of black activism" and whites' knee-jerk rejection of that notion.[67] This middle position allowed whites to tolerate just a few individual blacks as worthy for political life, even though they could continue to believe that the mass of African Americans may not be. It also showed African Americans the proscribed levels to which they could aspire as political leaders.

Roosevelt distinguished individual blacks among that "seething mass," using select members of that race as exemplars—as a form of "proof." Rather than argue directly that whites should consider all African Americans as worthy, he rhetorically aimed to situate only some blacks in his myth of Americanism. His strategy of "inclusion via exemplars" allowed his myth of individual black success to act as a moderating position between the extreme tensions of white racism and black despair. The advancement of a few African Americans would not threaten white audiences since they could still maintain their racist views about the larger mass of blacks. On the other hand, blacks could see the measured advance of some of their race as an indication of their own inclusions in national life. Thus, the strategy of "inclusion via exemplars" allowed Roosevelt to balance African Americans' need to feel included in the nation's life, while simultaneously attending to whites' desire for the "seething mass" to be largely excluded from American culture.

One of Roosevelt's earliest speeches gave voice to his concern that African Americans were denied the opportunity to enter the political process. As a delegate to the 1884 Republican National Convention, Roosevelt decided to support the appointment of John Lynch, a black congressman from Mississippi, as temporary chairman of the Republican National Committee.[68] Invoking his hero Abraham Lincoln, Roosevelt reminded the audience that the convention was in the same city in which the Republican Party had nominated the man "who broke the fetters of the slave and rent them asunder forever." Roosevelt called for the conventioneers to do the "fitting thing" and choose "one of that race whose right to sit within these walls is due to the blood and the treasure so lavishly spent by the founders of the Republican party."[69]

Roosevelt's declaration for Lynch promoted several ideas. First, it showed that blacks such as Lynch met his mythic requirement for good character by politically serving the community. Second, it supported a black man for a symbolically important—albeit not truly powerful—position in a national political party. Finally, as the legacy of Lincoln, Roosevelt emphasized that blacks were truly free to take their place in the larger culture. Roosevelt's support for Lynch's nomination made it appear that whites could grant blacks a greater level of freedom than they currently enjoyed.

Roosevelt highlighted the place of black leaders in government throughout his early career. As a civil service commissioner from 1889 to 1895, he fought for reform in the system, emphasizing the need to provide appointments to the most qualified candidates, and not to those with the political connections that routinely benefited whites.[70] Writing for the *Atlantic Monthly* in 1891, he praised the reforms in the appointment process that created a system with an "utter disregard of color."[71] To that end, he appointed several African Americans to federal posts, and he recognized their leadership in the popular press. This resulted in qualified blacks comprising a fourth of the new appointees from the South. "Under the civil service law," he declared at an 1893 banquet, "we have thrown open the door" to blacks and provided them an "avenue of employment in public service." Commissioner Roosevelt boldly claimed that African Americans stood on equal ground with whites, shown "no favoritism . . . if they prove themselves worthy." As commissioner, he had "absolutely refused to consider the question of color. I have put no man ahead because he was a colored man . . . if he was the most competent to fill the position. . . . I have treated him simply and solely as I would treat any other American citizen."[72] Roosevelt's hyperbole about disregarding color in favor of ability contrasted starkly with the racist assumption of black inferiority. By establishing the extreme positions in this debate, Roosevelt's promotion of the individual blacks who could qualify for civil service positions appeared to be an appeasing middle ground for both blacks and whites. Blacks could see the select few who acquired political office as the realization of Du Bois's notion of cultivating black leadership, while whites still maintained a dominant presence in civil service work.

Although Roosevelt engaged the Du Boisian idea of establishing limited African American leadership, he admired the man who was ideologically opposed to Du Bois. Roosevelt began a working relationship with Booker T. Washington in 1898 and frequently consulted Washington about racial issues.[73] When Roosevelt became president, he brought Washington's counsel along with him and used the rhetorical nature of the executive office to promote his version of the black leader's message.

Roosevelt ascended to the presidency in 1901 after an assassin struck down President McKinley. The youngest president to date, Roosevelt brought an awareness to the executive office that it could be used to inspire, as well as administer, a nation. In the pivotal work "The Rise of the Rhetorical Presidency," James Ceaser, Glen Thurow, Jeffrey Tulis, and Joseph Bessette noted that presidential leadership in the modern era reflected a form of executive speech "that soars above the realm of calm and deliberate discussion." Recitations of dry, policy-making processes by chief executives gave way to a presidential leader who "constantly exhorts in the name of a common purpose and a spirit of idealism."[74] Roosevelt, the first of the modern rhetorical presidents, keenly appreciated this concept, and deftly combined it with a manipulation of the era's mass media. Using all the rhetorical power of his position, he ensured dissemination of his message about the place of blacks in the nation's destiny.[75] Education would be the road on which African Americans, as Roosevelt had argued for immigrants and natives, could progress from "seething mass" to truly American.

Prior to his presidency, Roosevelt had established the idea that education was "essential" to the "healthy growth" of the nation. Early frontiersmen, he wrote in *The Winning of the West,* were "anxious to give their children a decent education." Even poor people, he wrote, "who were still engaged in the hardest and roughest struggle for a livelihood, showed appreciation of the need of schooling for their children."[76] Although advanced education was important, he believed that it also tended to sap martial vitality. Instead, a "really good" education, one that challenged the mind while not neglecting the "fighting virtues," appeared to be crucial to Roosevelt.[77] Thus, people served their country by acquiring a "really good" vocational education. Roosevelt carried the idea of education as service to the nation into his presidency, especially as it pertained to carving out a place for blacks in the American identity.

African American leadership of the day offered Roosevelt two very different views of black education. Given his goal of melding disparate groups into a unified American whole, Roosevelt could hardly adopt the more radical view of W. E. B. Du Bois. Du Bois demanded advanced education for his "talented tenth," a handful of gifted blacks who would gain an excellent education and in turn would lead their race to its rightful place in society.[78] But Du Bois's "talented tenth" would create a black mirror image of the extant white social and political hierarchy. This would not encourage blacks to assimilate into Roosevelt's Americanism, nor would it assure nervous whites that blacks would not overreach their bounds. Roosevelt instead articulated Booker T. Washington's message that African Americans could find their place in the nation through in-dustrial education and vocational work, opportunities that, in turn, were open to any black who took up that challenge. While Roosevelt argued that individual African Americans could aspire to some limited form of political leadership, the "seething mass" would win American identity through education.

As the young president was apt to do, he drew the media's attention to that message by visiting Washington's Tuskegee Institute in 1905. "It is of the utmost importance," Roosevelt declared before the Institute's audience, "that the ne-gro be encouraged to make himself a citizen of the highest type of usefulness." That "usefulness" came from both races recognizing the opportunities in the South. Given a "scarcity not only of common labor, but of skilled labor, it be-comes doubly important to train every available man to be of the utmost use, by developing his intelligence, his skill, and his capacity for conscientious ef-fort." Not only would blacks help themselves, but they also demonstrated their good character by selflessly serving the community. According to the president, Washington's Institute developed the right kind of American: "Every black man who leaves this institute better able to do mechanical or industrial work adds by so much to the wealth of the whole community and benefits all people in the community." He asked both whites and blacks to transcend their stereotypes of each other and to achieve their destinies "not as races" but as "American citi-zens."[79] As president, he gave Washington's message a salience that even the black leader could not have achieved.

As Roosevelt argued about Indians' opportunity in the modern nation, vo-cational training became the means and limit for the mass of African Ameri-cans to gain a respected place in the nation. He promoted the same argument that Washington offered in his Cotton States Exposition address in 1895: give the majority of blacks the opportunity to work as they did before gaining their freedom—as laborers, farmers, and other common workers.[80] Roosevelt's appeal allowed whites to continue seeing the "seething mass" of blacks as traditional "beasts of burden," which could lessen whites' anxiety given that he also identi-fied a limited number of blacks who deserved political office. In turn, he offered the "seething mass" the opportunity to engage in hard work and to achieve ma-terial success—the modern manifestation of the frontier experience.

Roosevelt continued the theme of education advancing the nation in rela-tion to African Americans in his 1906 "Annual Message" to Congress. He argued for whites to support the chance for blacks "to get a good elementary education," since it acted as the foundation of the "whole political situation." To get white support, he invoked the myth of the black as criminal, a salient fear in whites at the time. Through education, he argued, blacks would commit less crimes since it was the "lowest and most brutal criminals . . . who have had either no education or very little." It was thus in society's best interest for blacks to be vocationally educated. Roosevelt again turned to Booker T. Washington for inspiration: "Of course the best type of education for the colored man, taken as a whole, is such education as is conferred in schools like . . . Tuskegee; where the . . . young men and young women, are trained industrially as well as in the ordinary public-school branches."[81] Strategically, Roosevelt framed the education of African Americans as part of the "white man's burden." Such a depiction placed whites again in the comfortable role of "overseer," yet provided blacks with an appealing notion that their aspirations for a better life seemed possible.

Although some whites may have been willing to grant blacks a better life, it did not involve any consideration of real equality. Whites looked at African Americans' skin as an impassable boundary between them.[82] Scientific, popular, and political discourse unanimously decried the notion of equality between the races.[83] Roosevelt, though, spoke repeatedly about equality for blacks, even though he did not want truly equal relations with them any more than most other whites did.[84] Yet, equality was part of Roosevelt's trinity in Americanism. Given its importance to him as a fundamental virtue for the identity of the nation, he may have felt compelled to talk about it in relation to blacks, who were, like it or not, citizens. His goal, though, was to reconcile the virtue of equality with the fact that African Americans could never enter the "melting pot" and exist equally with whites. Thus, he needed a way to discuss equality so that blacks could believe its promise without exacerbating fears in whites that it might actually occur.

Roosevelt's well-known articulation about the need for an individual to have fair opportunities to achieve success came in his "Square Deal" speech in 1905. While it referred to the corporate practices that enhanced the rich at the expense of the poor, his address reflected his belief in a code of justice that should extend to anyone he deemed worthy. The president stated, "It is not in the power of any human being to devise legislation or administration by which each man shall achieve success or have happiness." However, he declared, every man should be given "as nearly as may be a fair chance to do what his powers permit him to do; always provided he does not wrong his neighbor."[85] He extended the benefit and the burden of this idea to African Americans.

Roosevelt contextualized equality and a "square deal" within the frontier exhibition of individual fortitude. Because of his admiration of martial ability, he lauded the "colored soldiers" with whom he served at Santiago. "A man who is good enough to shed blood for the country," he observed at the Lincoln Monument in 1903, "is good enough to be given a square deal afterward."[86] He also recognized those African Americans of high character whose determination allowed them to work and to prosper as their talents allowed. Speaking before the National Negro Business League in 1910, Roosevelt praised the organization for teaching blacks "not to whine or cry about privileges" that they did not have, and congratulated those who concentrated on "making the best of the opportunities" that came their way. With equal opportunities, both blacks and whites would prove the adage, "all men up and not some men down."[87] Unfortunately, Roosevelt's affirmation of the "square deal" for African Americans who demonstrated individual fortitude trapped blacks in an untenable position. Offering the almost Darwinian "square deal" to people recently freed from centuries of slavery placed the burden of securing equality on the very people who had no power to demand it. Opportunities in the South, for example, were hardly equal given that blacks' constitutional and civil liberties were violated with every attempt to exercise those opportunities.[88] Furthermore, blacks could not challenge their "equal" treatment, or lack thereof, without appearing to "whine or cry," which Roosevelt identified as a lack of frontier character, and would thus render them unworthy of American identity.

Another tactic of President Roosevelt to promote a "square deal" involved offering unconditional declarations of "equal treatment for all" when talking about what blacks could expect in modern America. "There is but one safe rule in dealing with black men as with white men," he wrote in his "Sixth Message" to Congress, "that is, to treat each man, whatever his color, his creed, or his social position, with even-handed justice on his real worth as a man." This national ideal ensured that a good man, of whatever color, has "the right to his life, his liberty, and the pursuit of his happiness as his own qualities of heart, head, and hand enable him to achieve it." Without that as a goal, he cautioned, "evil will surely come in the end to both races."[89] His unequivocal declarations of blacks and whites finding equality together undoubtedly heartened blacks who had given him their support in the 1904 election and had maintained their allegiance to him during his second term.[90] Simultaneously, given the widespread white sentiment against equality, Roosevelt's unflinching pronouncements seemed absurd. As a result, whites understood his calls for unfettered equality as patently false and uttered only to appease blacks.[91]

Roosevelt had to keep blacks mollified and moving toward the promise of some level of consideration, while not overly threatening whites' sensibilities in that regard. The challenge of those conflicting positions was evident in his engagement of the lynching issue. As with education, he contextualized that lawless act within the frontier setting, giving it legitimacy in which to mediate the tensions surrounding blacks' viability to become equal partners in white America.

"Frontier Justice" in Modern America

Roosevelt faced a complex and interrelated set of challenges. He needed to create a place for blacks in America's identity that they would accept and work toward; otherwise, they might constitute what Booker T. Washington described as a "veritable body of death, stagnating, depressing, retarding every effort to advance the body politic."[92] In that regard, blacks saw the specter of lynching as barbaric and threatened to bolt from the South, leaving it in economic chaos.[93]

Yet, whites considered black men as savages who lusted after white women, and lynching became the default punishment for any black man who "touched" a white woman. According to Williamson, in the antebellum culture of the late nineteenth century, southern white men had "pedestalized white women in their minds," essentially removing them as sexual partners. As a result, Victorian mores caused white men to feel guilt if they attempted intimacy with white women. For white men, the black male was the "only man on earth who had sex with Southern white women without inhibition, to the exhaustion of desire . . . without guilt. Black men had achieved what white men . . . had lost—'no-fault' sex." Black men became scapegoats for the guilt that white men felt in regard to their intimate relations with white women; lynching the black scapegoat was the only solution to purge that guilt.[94]

Moreover, lynching epitomized lawlessness and "mob" rule, and that frightened Roosevelt.[95] He wanted a stable society of strong-armed and strong-willed citizens who respected one another, with each race in its proper place. If he seemed to take a side in the debate on race, equality, and identity, he would alienate the other. To resolve this dilemma, Roosevelt returned to myth. He blasted the indiscriminate use of lynching as evil, while simultaneously redefining it as a frontier symbol that explained why African Americans had not progressed further toward earning their equality. This represented a traditional function of myth in society. He used that symbol to reconcile values and actions that seemed contrary to one another. Consequently, that mythic frame created the illusion of a stable community, moving toward its destiny with a singular mind despite the diversity and supposed inferiority of races.

Using the power of the "bully pulpit," President Roosevelt condemned lynching. He frequently wrote letters about the issue that he suspected newspapers would publish. One letter he wrote in 1903 to Winfield Durbin, governor of Indiana, did become public. Durbin had been one of the few governors to use the state militia to quell a race riot.[96] Not only did the president thank the governor for his stand against lynching, but Roosevelt also used the opportunity to highlight the illegitimate use of lynching. The president lauded Durbin for the "admirable way" that he "vindicated the majesty of law." From here, Roosevelt quickly turned to the "peculiarly hideous forms so often taken by mob violence when colored men are the victims." He called on the audience to recognize the "inhuman vengeance" taken by a mob and to acknowledge how that represented a form of anarchy in American culture. Such acts, accompanied by "dreadful torture" of the victim, started the nation down a road of tyranny and degeneracy. "The spirit of lawlessness grows with what it feeds on," Roosevelt warned, "and when mobs with impunity lynch criminals for one cause, they are certain to begin to lynch real or alleged criminals for other causes.... Surely no patriot can fail to see the fearful brutalization and debasement which the indulgence of such a spirit and such practices inevitably portends."[97]

After a bloody race riot in 1906, Roosevelt devoted a substantial portion of his sixth "Annual Message" to condemning mob violence and warning Congress of the dangers such actions presented to civilized society.[98] As he typically did with those people he thought immoral, the president vilified them. "The spirit of lynching," he wrote, "throws into prominence in the community all foul and evil creatures who dwell therein. No man can take part in the torture of a human being without having his own moral nature permanently lowered." Roosevelt particularly disdained the demagogues with "evil temper" that indulged in the "inflammatory and incendiary speeches and writings which tend to arouse mobs and to bring about lynching." He declared that they were an insidious force that spurred rampant lawlessness by giving "prominence . . . to the hideous deed" and exciting "other brutal and depraved thoughts."[99]

Roosevelt's hyperbolic statements on lynching served several strategic ends. First, his blistering condemnations positioned lynchers at the outer extreme of inhumanity, far from others in the white race. The majority who did not engage in lynching would not feel indicted or even concerned since such seemingly extreme matters did not relate directly to them. Second, like his unequivocal statements on equality, Roosevelt demonstrated patent unambiguous support for African Americans, even as whites would likely view the president's statements as overblown and thus insincere. Perhaps more important, he separated lynching from any manifestation of hatred between the races. Lynching was simply the act of evil men, not necessarily racist ones. This last move would allow him to contextualize the act in new ways.

His strident indictments notwithstanding, Roosevelt struggled with the issues of equality and lynching. He articulated the promise of "all men up," but he also believed that blacks would never receive the same social consideration as whites by virtue of their skin color.[100] In addition, he, like many other whites at the time, accepted the "conventional wisdom" that some blacks deserved lynching for their supposed sexual aggression against white women.[101] Although one biographer noted that the president "admitted that long-term justice for the Negro concerned him more than any other issue," it was not necessarily for altruistic reasons.[102] For Roosevelt, the lawlessness and deviancy perpetrated by both sides, real or imagined, exacerbated an already volatile and unproductive situation regarding race relations. Thus, he redefined the meaning of lynching, legitimizing its use in certain circumstances. In that way, both he and other whites could feel some comfort that lynching did not represent the nation's descent into social chaos. Blacks also would learn that lynching was not simply a punishment for supposed sexual deviancy, but a symbol for how well they worked to serve the nation as respected citizens within it, such as by identifying suspected criminals within their community.

To do that, Roosevelt turned again to the familiarity of the frontier. For him, early immigrants' experiences on the mythical and untamed North American continent became benchmarks for the establishment of social order in America. As a frontiersman in his own right, he looked at justice and punishment as something needing swift delivery. Communities on the frontier, he wrote in *The Winning of the West,* usually enforced a "rough-and-ready justice of its own," as there was, in most cases, no legal authority that could administer quick justice. This justice called for "severe" punishment, taking the form of "death or whipping. . . . Occasionally, torture was resorted to" and, in the case of some lynching, he admitted, "the effect [had] been healthy for the community." In the frontier universe, "lynch-law" was the preferred means to uphold righteousness. According to him, it was about "good men" who "banded themselves together as regulators [to] put down the wicked with ruthless severity."[103] Roosevelt had re-envisioned lynching, not as a sign of white depravity, but as a mythic symbol that brought stability to the community.

While Roosevelt affirmed that justice should be "under the law, and not the wild and crooked savagery of a mob,"[104] it was not necessarily a "mob" if whites dispensed the "swift justice" of the frontier. The moral of this frontier allusion appeared simple: blacks needed to identify criminals among the "seething mass" who perpetrated sexual outrages. If they were unwilling to serve the larger community in that way, lynching became a legitimate means to force them into compliance. Lynching thus joined the other means of assimilation and Americanization that Roosevelt and others used to coerce nonwhites' allegiance to the national culture and to demark their place within it.

During a 1905 tour of the South, President Roosevelt offered his conception of "frontier justice" to both black and white audiences. While at Tuskegee, Roosevelt played down the brutality of lynching, focusing instead on the causes of it as a "misunderstanding between the races." He stressed that the best way to deal with these crimes was to "have a prompt . . . consultation between representatives of the wise, decent, cool-headed men among the whites and the wise, decent, cool-headed colored men."[105] These statements reflected what Williamson noted as Roosevelt's tendency to "pull one way and then the other so as to maintain a general equilibrium between contending forces."[106] Although he mollified blacks by depicting them as generally law-abiding and able to meet equally with whites, Roosevelt also fed white stereotypes that assumed blacks, as a matter of course, were raping white women, and that other blacks knew the guilty parties but had refused to speak. The next day at a city park in Little Rock, Arkansas, the president emphasized black criminality, as he blessed the "frontier justice" of whites. He identified the black rapist as the "worst enemy of the negro race" for committing "an unspeakably dreadful and infamous crime against the victim" and "against the people of his own color." Roosevelt charged "every reputable colored man" to "hunt down that criminal with all his soul and strength." If not, whites would balance the scales.[107]

Roosevelt's attempt to negotiate a middle ground between "contending forces" worked against African Americans. Any articulation on his part of their supposed criminality, or their conspiracy of silence, fed racist fears. Despite the condemnation of lynching in his 1906 "Annual Message," he undoubtedly reinforced the myth of the black rapist in the same address. He stated that the "greatest existing cause of lynching is the perpetuation, especially by black men, of the hideous crime of rape," a crime he considered "even worse than murder." He absolved whites for their participation in "frontier justice," and placed the burden of change on African Americans. If "respectable colored people" were unwilling to serve the community by hunting down the criminal, they deserved what they got. Roosevelt wrote: "Every colored man should realize that the worst enemy of his race is the negro criminal, and above all the negro criminal who commits the dreadful crime of rape; and it should be felt as in the highest degree an offense against the whole country, and against the colored race in particular, for a colored man to fail to help the officers of the law in hunting down with all possible earnestness and zeal every such infamous offender." Unless blacks learned "not to harbor their criminals," the "atrocious offenses" of lynchings would keep occurring.[108] Thus, black solidarity, perceived as any reluctance on the part of blacks to identify one of their own as a "black beast rapist," justified "frontier justice."

Black criminality, the solidarity and silence of African Americans, and the potential of "frontier justice" converged in the events at Brownsville, Texas, in August 1906. Some Brownsville townspeople alleged that African American soldiers from the Twenty-fifth Infantry stationed at the nearby Fort Brown assaulted them, shot and killed one citizen, wounded a police officer, and destroyed property. This event culminated the volatile interactions that had occurred between some soldiers and the townspeople over the previous two weeks, including discrimination, beatings, and the local newspaper account of an unknown black solider attempting to force himself upon a white woman. Roosevelt called for an investigation of the shooting incident. For several months the army attempted to determine which soldiers had done the shooting, assuming from the beginning that the soldiers had done the shooting rather than investigate what may have actually happened that night. The army collected enough contradictory evidence to establish reasonable doubt on the soldiers' involvement in the incident. Yet, the report submitted to the president concluded that the African American soldiers were guilty of the crime and of the conspiracy to keep the actual perpetrators from being revealed. Roosevelt responded in November by discharging all 167 men of the unit.[109]

Stunned by the president's order, both races declared their disapproval. One of the most active voices came from Congress. Senator Joseph Foraker, known as "Fire Alarm Joe," took up the soldiers' cause.[110] Early in the December 1906 Congress, he attacked Roosevelt, questioning the president's ability to use an Executive Order to convict and to punish men who had "served for thirty years faithfully and honorably."[111] Incensed, Roosevelt shot back two weeks later with a fiery message to Congress defending his actions in dismissing the soldiers. In that message, he perpetuated the myth of black criminality. Furthermore, he condemned those soldiers who stood by silently. For him, any reluctance to serve the communal good represented as great an evil as any that actively attempted to violate it.

The president wrote that he was happy to present the "facts as to the murderous conduct" of the soldiers. He admitted that blame undoubtedly rested equally on the soldiers and the townspeople. It was the troops, however, that had engaged in "atrocious conduct" and in a "lawless and murderous spirit." Their act, the president declared, was "unparalleled for infamy in the annals of the United States Army." Roosevelt's pronouncements undoubtedly engaged whites' greatest fear—rampaging blacks set to violate white society: "In short, the evidence proves conclusively that a number of the soldiers engaged in a deliberate and concerted attack, as cold blooded as it was cowardly; the purpose being to terrorize the community, and to kill or injure men, women, and children in their homes and beds or on the street, and this at an hour of the night when concerted or effective resistance or defense was out of the question."[112] For Roosevelt, perhaps even the greater crime involved the soldiers' "conspiracy of silence for the purpose of shielding those who took part in the original conspiracy of murder." As a result, he declared, it was these "comrades of the murderers" who have "rendered it necessary" to dismiss them all from service. In Roosevelt's belief, this seemed more than fair. As in his 1906 "Annual Message," when he warned blacks to cooperate with authorities, he had likewise cautioned the soldiers that unless they assisted in hunting down criminals from their race, they would suffer the consequences. In fact, the president admitted that he did not bring the full weight of "frontier justice" to the soldiers, since punishment for their crimes should have been death.[113] Essentially, Roosevelt's mythic form of justice spurred him to "lynch" the soldiers in the only way that he could—through swift and uncompromising dismissal.

Following a year of Senate investigation led by Foraker into the events of Brownsville, a congressional committee concluded that the president had acted justifiably in dismissing the soldiers; some on the committee provided dissenting views.[114] Despite this affirmation, Roosevelt sent a "Special Message" to Congress in 1908 that reflected a slight change of heart. He explained that the soldiers' "conspiracy of silence" resulted from them being "cowed by threats" from the actual wrongdoers.[115] Of course, such an argument still highlighted black criminality and solidarity as a reason for "frontier justice" being served. The president called for the reinstatement of those African Americans who would now tell the truth about that night in Brownsville. A few soldiers were reinstated in 1910, but it was not until the Nixon administration that all the soldiers were given honorable discharges.[116]

Years after he left office, Roosevelt continued to argue that his myth of "frontier justice" signified not hatred, but attempts to stabilize relations between the races. He briefly mentioned the Brownsville incident in a published letter to the Illinois State Federation of Labor. In that 1917 letter, he condemned the July riots in East St. Louis where white mobs attacked hundreds of blacks, murdering many of them.[117] In directing the government to address similar problems between labor organizations and workers, Roosevelt called for authorities to act more quickly to "put down violence with ruthless resolution, whether it be of white against black or black against white." He offered Brownsville as a representative example of justice coming swiftly and roughly, regardless of skin color. He reiterated the charge that black soldiers had "shot up" that Texas town and that other black soldiers conspired with the shooters to remain silent about it. Their quick dismissal, he alleged, was not a sign of racism. Rather, the soldiers' dismissal reflected the fact that "justice would be invoked against wrong-doers without regard to the color of their skins."[118]

Roosevelt stayed on message regarding race relations and the need for "frontier justice." Shortly before his death, he spoke before W. E. B. Du Bois and a mixed audience at Carnegie Hall. He admitted the unfairness of life in America for blacks. "Too often the white man is guilty," he concluded, "of the dreadful injustice of putting on the whole Negro race the responsibility for the Negro criminal." Regardless, blacks had a responsibility to serve the community and "hunt down, hunt out, the colored criminal of every type."[119] Only then could blacks progress toward some level of equality in the nation and become Americans, pure and simple.

Conclusion

Theodore Roosevelt's discourse about race, African Americans, and national identity, at first glance, seem inconsistent. In discussing lynching, for example, he sometimes appeared more concerned with that act leading to whites' descent into barbarism rather than with the degradation and torture that blacks experienced. Similarly, he probably fueled whites' fears about the "Black criminal" and the inferiority of the "seething mass" by perpetuating those images, particularly in the way that he acted during the Brownsville affair. On the other hand, his defenses of African American appointees to federal positions, calling for an unequivocal "square deal" for blacks, as well as his open admiration of Booker T. Washington, heartened blacks in ways they had heretofore not known. His discourse, as a result, seemed confounding.

Roosevelt's goal through much of his public career was to bring into existence what he considered a nation of virtuous warriors who would stand side by side with one another. He needed to solve the "Negro problem," to find a place for blacks where they could prove themselves and make an "equal" contribution to the nation. To do that, he used a mythic rhetoric that could appeal to both blacks and whites. Situating blacks in his frontier-inspired version of Americanism, a mythic story usually reserved for whites, Roosevelt exaggerated the already polarized positions of race and identity. By widening that space, he was better able to create and to negotiate what seemed to be a middle ground that could appease both audiences. He accorded to blacks the status of second-wave frontier heroes, an aspect he considered fundamental to American citizenship, but that allowed whites the opportunity to keep their hallowed spot in the traditional Frontier Myth. He illustrated that individual African Americans were of good character, giving blacks *limited* authority in the political arena, reminiscent of early settlers who also believed participation in civic life was important. Furthermore, he, like Booker T. Washington, depicted blacks as a "seething mass," but one that seemed worthy of at least vocational education opportunities. By contextualizing this type of education as the kind promoted on the frontier, he strategically muted W. E. B. Du Bois's call for blacks to have advanced education. Finally, Roosevelt condemned lynching, but still blessed it when whites used it to mete out "frontier justice." His mythic treatment of African Americans and their place in the nation's identity attempted simultaneously to provide them an appealing role while not necessarily alarming whites.

5

From Hero to Traitor to Good Citizen

Americanism and the Campaign against the Hyphen

By the advent of the First World War, Theodore Roosevelt had spent decades invigorating the debate about immigrants, race, ethnicity, and American identity. In his myth of Americanism, he highlighted the fundamental elements of national identity that immigrants and nonwhites needed to exhibit—physical strength, moral character, and acceptance of the idea that a person had to earn equality.

No group had been more lauded by Roosevelt for embracing Americanism than had German immigrants. Even as Germany raced to war in 1914, Roosevelt wrote in a private letter that "on the whole, I think that of all the elements that have come here during the past century the Germans have on the average represented the highest type."[1] For him, with their martial prowess and cultural achievements, German immigrants distinguished themselves as the embodiment of true American citizens. During times of war, however, even the "right" kind of immigrants can be again viewed as foreigners, and native-born Americans now looked suspiciously at their neighbors of German origin.

To Roosevelt's chagrin, many German-Americans seemingly rejected their mythic American identity. They instead chose to hold too vigorously to their Old World heritage, pointedly using the hyphen to symbolize the parity between their ethnic origins and their adopted American culture. Roosevelt saw their hyphenated self-reference not just as an insult, but also as a warning that the country could devolve into a "tangle of squabbling nationalities, an intricate knot of German-Americans, Irish-Americans . . . Italian-Americans, each preserving its separate nationality." As a result, he concluded, "there is no such thing as a hyphenated American who is a good American. The only man who is a good American is the man who is an American and nothing else."[2] Hyphenated Americans flagrantly displayed the treachery of divided loyalties at a time when such divisions were literally matters of life and death. Thus, he could not let the use of the hyphen go unchallenged, especially from the group he had most respected.

There could be no equivocation on the issue of hyphenated Americans, in Roosevelt's view. To show his determination and commitment to a unified America, Roosevelt linked his rhetorical campaign to force German immigrants to discontinue the use of the hyphen with his campaign to push for America's participation in World War One. He reminded Americans that their frontier ancestors had fought a war with savage Indians and that they now needed to continue that fight with the equally barbaric Germans. By invoking the myth of "savage war" and casting Germany as a savage and demonic power, Roosevelt asserted that German immigrants who used the hyphen signaled their allegiance to that corrupt power. Those hyphenated Americans were "professional" traitors, people loyal to Germany who never intended to assimilate in America. They engaged in overt sabotage of the American war effort or emasculation of the martial vigor of America by calling for neutrality in the conflict. Because of the direct association Roosevelt drew between Germany as an "enemy of God" and German immigrants who dismissed the notion of a God-blessed "melting pot," he could spur the nation to war and compel German-Americans to discard the hyphen. Roosevelt's fervent casting of German immigrants as great heroes of the frontier in American history did not preclude a rhetorical reversal that would take aim at them as enemies of a unified American identity. Citizens who spoke of unmanly peace or failed to drop the hyphen risked the violence and indignity that would come to any who refused to become Americans, pure and simple.

Germans in American History and Rooseveltian Mythology

Virulent racism haunted virtually all immigrants' attempts to establish themselves in America. The prejudice against Native Americans and blacks could be easily traced to a belief that darker skin color meant inferiority. Other immigrants who began arriving on the shores of this nation were met with a kind of racism that labeled their physically white groups as "white niggers," and they were treated accordingly.[3] They were assumed to be capable of only the most unskilled labor and were segregated from white Americans politically, economically, and educationally. The Irish, Jews, Italians, and other immigrant groups were each placed at the bottom rung of American society, with only the obviously nonwhite groups, such as Mexican or Asian, being held in more disdain.[4] Generally, native-born white Americans feared that their country would act as a dumping ground for the lesser races and ethnicities from other countries.[5]

On the other hand, Americans welcomed German immigrants. Racially speaking, many Anglo-Saxons traced their heritage to the noble Teutonic traditions of Germany.[6] Thus, Germans found a welcoming environment, one that allowed them to establish themselves as the preeminent immigrant group in America.[7] Their many contributions infused the martial, cultural, and political fabric of the nation. La Vern Rippley noted that German-Americans distinguished themselves during their adopted country's Revolutionary War: Forming the "largest single nationality in America next to the British, Germans proved to be among the toughest troops in the line wherever gritty engagements with the British regulars occurred."[8] They likewise fought in great numbers during the Civil War. Siding primarily with the Union, German officers on both sides of the conflict acquitted themselves with distinction.[9] In fact, their martial exploits made them valued citizens across the new nation.[10]

America also felt German influence in numerous cultural avenues during the nineteenth and early twentieth centuries. German-American singers and musicians enriched the aesthetic atmosphere of the nation. German singing societies in the 1800s acted as major participants in the evolution of the United States into a "musical mecca." These societies built concert halls, initiated choral festivals, and were the first to bring professionally lavish musical productions to common workers.[11] German-Americans also heavily influenced national customs regarding food and drink. Many people frequented the popular *delikatessengeschaefte,* or delicatessen, to sample German-made food. The beer gardens, as well as the beer brewing industry, also popularized this social facet of German culture. Furthermore, many of the American culinary customs at Christmas originated with German immigrants.[12]

German intellectuals also introduced their home country's pedagogical practices, profoundly changing the American school system. In the lower grades, German influence led to the introduction of the kindergarten and the emphasis on physical education in public schools. The German language itself was taught in elementary schools until the Great War. American universities patterned themselves after institutions of higher learning in Germany, promoting the elimination of "denominational influences," recruiting the best scholars and teachers for discrete disciplines, and affirming an active research spirit in the academic community.[13]

Of all immigrant groups in America, Germans dominated the foreign-language press in the 1800s and early 1900s. Carl Wittke noted that the "German-language press was not only the most numerous among the foreign language papers" in America, "but the most ably edited and the most widely read."[14] For the most part, the German-American press helped immigrants assimilate into American culture. Newspapers and journals routinely described the politics and history of their new country. According to Albert Faust, German newspapers appeared "strongly patriotic in all matters concerning national or local politics," siding primarily with the Democratic Party through the mid 1800s.[15] Not only dominant by number, Germans played a pivotal role in the development of the American press. German immigrant Johann Peter Zenger helped to establish the concept of a free press; Joseph Pulitzer, of Hungarian and German descent, contributed much to the standard form of daily newspapers; and German immigrant Adolph Ochs founded the *New York Times*.[16]

With strides in education, media, and popular culture, German immigrants actively participated in American politics. According to Faust, the "first protest ever made in the United States against Negro slavery came from the Germans in their original settlement." They spearheaded reform in the civil service to prevent non-merit-based appointments. German societies also attacked the idea of temperance, arguing for the personal freedom to drink alcohol on the Sabbath.[17] At the beginning of the twentieth century, the National German-American Alliance (NGAA) coordinated the political activism of state and local organizations. The NGAA, with membership in the millions, advocated against particularly stringent immigration legislation, promoted woman's suffrage, and worked against the prohibition movement.[18]

Given the prominence of Germans in American culture, they notably appeared in the country's mythology. For Roosevelt, German immigrants represented the prototypes for his mythic heroes: strong, determined, and warlike. As Gary Gerstle observed, Roosevelt saw the German invaders of Great Britain as "warriors above all," and found them reminiscent of the early American settlers who waged "relentless war against the savage Indians who claimed these lands as their own."[19] Roosevelt looked with admiration on those ancient warriors of "Germanic stock."[20]

Roosevelt specifically brought German immigrants into America's idealized story of epic struggle and destiny. Like the mythic heroes of old, German newcomers battled the unknown and provided boons to the larger American community. Commenting on their sacrifices in a 1903 speech, Roosevelt clearly admired German pioneers: "they had to encounter bitter privation, had to struggle against want in many forms; [and] had to meet and overcome hardship."[21] Particularly, German immigrants used their martial prowess in service to the frontier community by successfully fighting the indigenous people. In fact, he lauded the Germans as the "most noted hunters and Indian fighters" of all immigrant groups.[22]

Roosevelt popularized German martial spirit prominently in his myth of Americanism before World War One. Just as the iconic heroes of myths demonstrated their abilities in contests with the unknown, so too did Roosevelt's Teutonic knights. Early in *The Winning of the West*, Roosevelt established Germans' worth in the American saga by retelling their native history. Akin to some supernatural force of nature, the Germans "swarmed out of the dark woodland east of the Rhine" centuries ago, exhibiting the "warlike prowess of the stalwart sons of Odin" and conquering everything in their path. Even Rome, the mighty "imperial city of Italy," he admitted, "acknowledged the sway of kings of Teutonic or Scandinavian blood." Norse men were not the only figures of legendary martial prowess. Writing for *Outlook* magazine in 1911, Roosevelt revealed that the heroines of German myths were themselves "splendid and terrible [and] fit to be the mothers of a mighty race, as stern and relentless as their lovers and husbands." According to him, these Norse heroines were likewise capable of the "demonic" and "fearsome rage" that distinguished immigrant men in America's mythic origin.[23] Roosevelt's celebration of the German warrior spirit positioned Germans, like Anglo-Saxons, as the nation's progenitors and gave them an importance beyond any other immigrant group. They acted as the standard by which to judge all newcomers.

However, America's heroes proved not just to be militarily proficient. They also demonstrated the moral character representative of Roosevelt's Americanism. These heroes for a modern age enriched the community with their customs and homely virtues. In his narrative history of New York, published in 1891, Roosevelt credited Germans with playing a pivotal role in that city's development. He praised those immigrants as: "thrifty, hard-working, and on the whole law-abiding, and they not only rose rapidly in the social scale, but as soon as they learned to speak our language by preference ... they became indistinguishable from the other Americans with whom they mixed. They furnished leading men to all trades and professions, and many founded families of high social and political distinction. They rendered great service to the city by their efforts to cultivate a popular taste for music and for harmless public pleasures."[24] Roosevelt lauded the new German heroes for bringing ethical and social benefits to America. For example, he thanked his audience during a 1910 post-presidential speech in Berlin for the "German strain in our blood." Americans had "taken from you, not only much of the blood that runs through our veins, but much of the thought that shapes our minds." He admitted, "for generations American scholars have flocked to your universities, and, thanks to the wise foresight of ... the present Emperor, the intimate and friendly connection between the two countries is now in every way closer than it has ever been."[25] His narrative accounts of German immigrants answered nativists' concerns that immigrants polluted the body politic. According to him, German blood infused America with a moral essence that distinguished that group as critical to national development.

Roosevelt routinely spoke of America benefiting culturally from transplanted Germans. More important, he regularly pointed to nativist racism as the primary force inhibiting Germans' immigration and assimilation. He openly questioned nativist sentiment that identified American Germans as immoral criminals. During a speech before the New York Assembly in 1884, he announced that the "large class of Germans . . . are in the main decent, reputable, and law-abiding." Even when non-Germans emulated the German habit of "drinking ales and beers," those people contributed little to the "criminal class."[26] Roosevelt himself proudly admitted that he was "partly of German blood" and that he held the utmost "respect and honor" for American citizens of German origin.[27] In fact, Roosevelt went so far as to declare that "there are not, and never have been, in all our land better citizens than the great mass of the men and women of German birth or descent who have been or are being completely merged in our common American nationality."[28] Roosevelt's promotion of the prominence and promise of German immigrants stressed a critical point to all immigrants: newcomers deserved such accolades when they merged with the American culture.

To Roosevelt, Germans exemplified the ideal stock for America because the German race historically enriched an existing nation, but did not replace it. He once again turned to his frontier narrative to establish the point. "The German tribes conquered Europe," Roosevelt wrote in *The Winning of the West,* but they "did not extend the limits of Germany nor the sway of the German race." Instead, their essence simply fortified the people they encountered. Ancient history demonstrated that the "Latin nations . . . strengthened by the infusion of [German] blood, sprang anew into vigorous life, and became for the time being the leaders of the European world."[29] He pointed to evidence of German blood enriching Americans. Germans, he alleged, were notable in the "upbuilding of New York," transforming the character of public schools, playing a vital role in the Civil War, and demonstrating that the "folk of German birth or origin" loyally served their inherited flag.[30] Roosevelt argued that the vigor of Teutonic blood would energize the American spirit, but would eventually acquiesce to it. For him, this was not simply an observation, but a command.

During the late nineteenth and early twentieth centuries, Roosevelt generally lionized German influences in America. His descriptions of German physical vigor, homely character, and undoubted assimilation distinguished them as icons of Americanism. According to him, they constituted fundamental ingredients in the forge of American citizenship. As was Roosevelt's penchant for keeping social tensions in play during public debates, he paralleled his celebratory rhetoric with a discourse of admonition against German newcomers who refused to assimilate.

The Fall of German-Americans

The American nation benefited from and respected the accomplishments of German immigrants throughout much of its history. Yet, there also existed a constant suspicion directed at Germans. For instance, Benjamin Franklin railed against them in the late eighteenth century when they, as a group, voted against some of his political allies. According to him, the new nation appeared in danger of being "Germanized" if it was not careful.[31] As one scholar noted, "it almost seemed to their fellow Americans that the German element had been stirring up trouble ever since their arrival." Many Americans decried German workers' support of American socialism. Events such as the Haymarket Riot of 1886 marked the German-born as anarchists and the "most disruptive [element] in American society."[32] Furthermore, with the influx of German Jews in the mid-nineteenth century, coupled with strong anti-Semitism in America, Germans found themselves as ostracized victims in much the same way that whites disenfranchised African Americans.[33]

Perhaps the most volatile element involved German immigrants' adamant refusal to discard certain elements of their Old World culture. The second wave of German immigrants that arrived in the nineteenth and early twentieth centuries constituted one of the largest foreign groups in American history. Two consequences resulted. First, with so many Germans arriving at one time, they found comfort together by remaining isolated from the cultural mainstream. Second, because of the isolation, this group wanted to retain its cultural heritage. Rather than assimilate as completely as their predecessors did, second-wave German immigrants sought to promote the "dream of a unified German civilization" by injecting their culture into American life.[34] They believed that they could infuse the existing American culture with their Old World ideology to create a multicultural identity. German-Americans rejected the idea of the "melting pot," arguing that citizenship, as an American, was distinct from their ethnic background; they symbolized this idea with the hyphen.[35] German immigrants believed that American culture benefited from an *intact* German heritage and used the hyphen to designate their promotion of cultural pluralism.

Even more than its political activism, the NGAA gave prominence to the idea of a cohesive German culture in America. Despite their willingness to be assimilated, members of the NGAA wanted to ensure that their *Deutschtum*—

their sense of community around their Old World heritage—was sustained. To that end, the organization recommended teaching German in public schools, and advocated the creation of "educational societies"—such as The German-American Historical Society—to reaffirm German culture to new immigrants and to teach all citizens of German-American accomplishments. Although the organization stated in its constitution that it worked for the preservation of the German spirit in America, it also firmly acknowledged the "need to remain American first" and "German second" while it accomplished that goal.[36]

Regardless of its stated goal, the NGAA made a number of rhetorical missteps that undermined its message of "America first and German second." Many Americans were already disgusted with German-Americans who sought to keep their Old World culture intact. The NGAA exacerbated that anxiety with a rhetoric that seemed to support Germany instead of the United States as the Great War loomed in Europe. When Germany declared war against Russia following the assassination of Archduke Ferdinand of Austria in 1914, the NGAA publicly supported the German position. As its members saw the American press turn decidedly pro-British, they stridently objected.[37] Charles Hexamer, president of the NGAA, reviled American sentiment for the British at a meeting in late 1914: "As a native American I must confess that I have not been proud of my country lately. A country that prays for peace on Sunday and supplies England and her allies with arms . . . on every other day of the week, is, to say the least, hypocritical. . . . I must confess that I as a native American, who fervently loves this land of liberty, am nauseated by the lick-spittle policy of our country, which allows England to pull our nose, to slap our face, and then licks the hand that smites us."[38] In addition to such fiery rhetoric, other activities also called into question the ultimate loyalty of some German-Americans. Between 1914 and 1917, the NGAA actively provided relief for German and Austrian soldiers by raising money for them.[39] The organization also used the German-American press to channel propaganda from the German government.[40] According to Charles Johnson, such newspapers attempted to "tell Germany's side of the story" with an almost "unbounded carelessness . . . in the face of growing pro-Allied opinion." Such an "unbounded carelessness" may explain why the NGAA provided no definitive statement of its feeling about German submarine warfare, particularly after the sinking of the *Lusitania*. "Its indecision," Johnson concluded, "led Americans supporting the Allied cause . . . to become convinced that the NGAA considered sinking passenger liners in war zones justifiable."[41] The NGAA's rhetoric challenged America's political and ideological position in the coming war, adding further evidence that German-Americans privileged only the first half of the hyphenated label.

The NGAA made continuous declarations of loyalty to the United States and ceased various pro-German activities once America declared war against Germany.[42] Nevertheless, it and all things German became the target of local and federal governmental investigations, and the object of the public's wrath. Similar to the Americanization process on reservations for Indian children, public school teachers engaged in a series of overtly hostile acts designed to intimidate German children into renouncing their heritage.[43] Senate hearings led to the dissolution of the NGAA, and state legislatures revoked the charter of many German-American organizational entities. The passage of the Espionage Act in 1917 targeted the German-language press, giving postal inspectors the authority to label any mailed German newspaper as treasonous. Thousands of German-Americans found themselves detained indefinitely while government-sponsored groups, such as the American Protective League (APL), conducted investigations into the loyalty of citizens of German descent. Although the APL "failed to catch a single bona fide German spy," Frederick Luebke revealed, "it succeeded in creating a climate in which persons with German names or accent or of German birth were objects of suspicion and alarm."[44] More violent in its approach, public groups—i.e., "mobs disguised as volunteer patriotic organizations"—routinely terrorized German-Americans with threats, beatings, public humiliations involving tar and feathers, church and book burnings, and lynching.[45] Anything remotely connected with Germany came under attack in America, including the German language outlawed in schools to the infamous name change of sauerkraut to liberty cabbage.[46] These shifts in the rhetorical tenor of many Americans toward Germans were evinced in Roosevelt's public discourse as well.

Despite his numerous public statements about German ethnicity enriching but not dominating existing cultures, Roosevelt still worried about second-wave Germans and their tendency to hold on to their heritage. As H. W. Brands revealed, Roosevelt "had no patience . . . for what a later generation would call multiculturalism."[47] Since the goal of Americanism ran counter to the German belief in maintaining its own heritage, Roosevelt warned those of German origin to adhere to the tenets of his philosophy. Specifically, he reminded Germans that they should follow the example of their ancestors and simply infuse American culture with their strength and will, while discarding their Old World allegiance in the process.

Roosevelt acknowledged in 1891 that by the turn of the nineteenth century, the "descendants of the Old German immigrants had become completely Americanized." At the turn of the new century, however, the blame rested on the "new swarms of Germans" who "revived the use of the German tongue . . . often forming the entire population of certain districts" and clinging "pertinaciously to their own customs." As a result, the new group failed to earn equal status because they resisted assimilation. This group constituted a "sodden, useless lump" that "remained mere foreigners, speaking an alien tongue" that marked them for a "lower grade in the body politic."[48] Redemption was available, Roosevelt argued, when they let go of their old ways, which then allowed them to move "up to the same level with the native-born."[49] German cultural independence proved inconsistent with Roosevelt's vision of the American national identity. Rhetorically, he highlighted German assimilation at one end of the cultural continuum and the problematic nature of German-American independence at the other; then he offered a resolution to the tension.

Well before the war began in Europe, Roosevelt outlined the means for redemption. As their frontier ancestors had done, modern Germans needed to put aside their allegiance to their European birthplace. To that end, he took issue with the German tendency to use the "hyphen." "The one essential for success," Roosevelt penned in 1890, "is that our citizens should act as Americans; not as Americans with a prefix and qualification—not as Irish-Americans, German-Americans, Native Americans—but as Americans pure and simple."[50] According to him, America did not "wish German-Americans . . . who figure as such in our social and political life. . . . We have no room in any healthy American community for a German-American."[51] In a speech on American citizenship in 1893, Roosevelt identified a good friend of his who was German by birth. However, this man proved to be a "good" American because he no longer used the hyphen. According to Roosevelt, the man appeared "just straight United States as if his ancestors had come over here in the *Mayflower* or in Henry Hudson's yacht." Despite being from a foreign country, men like this did not try to "perpetuate their language and customs."[52] In Roosevelt's view, the hyphen acted as a wedge that threatened to tear apart the integrity of American identity.

Roosevelt offered German-Americans the opportunity to become Americans again and to infuse the nation with their vigor and character, granting them the benefits of equality that such assimilation brought. But as the conflict abroad spread, and German-Americans continued to promote their cultural independence, he decided to force their compliance. Prior to the Great War, Roosevelt addressed the tension caused by nativists' fear of immigration and immigrants' fear of assimilation by offering Germans as the favored middle ground—as foreigners who chose to embrace Americanism. Now, because they seemed to remain in isolated pockets together, speaking their old language, heralding their culture at the expense of American culture, and supporting Germany's actions abroad, Roosevelt would make them pay a high price. With the events in the summer of 1914, Roosevelt's rhetoric positioned Germany and German-Americans together as villains in the Frontier Myth, a mythic story the immigrants once owned as the quintessential heroic immigrant group on the frontier. With their new status as the nation's enemies, German-Americans were pressured to purge themselves of the hyphen, which would symbolize their true assimilation into the American community.

Savage War, God, and German-Americans

Roosevelt waged two major rhetorical campaigns during the last years of his life. One involved pushing the United States to enter the Great War. William Harbaugh noted that within three months of Germany's invasion of Belgium, Roosevelt had "thrown himself into the mightiest struggle of his career—the campaign to persuade the American people to enter World War I." In fact, Harbaugh credited the ex-president as doing "more than any other citizen including [President Wilson] to condition the American people to the coming of war."[53] The other crusade Roosevelt undertook involved pushing German immigrants to assimilate. To that end, he called on them to renounce what he believed to be their allegiance to their birth country. "As a national campaign for Americanization commenced," Thomas Dyer remarked about the era of World War One, "Roosevelt led the chorus demanding that ethnics shed old ways." At this time, ethnicity seemed to be less about race and more about nationalism.[54] For Roosevelt, it was simple: new arrivals to America's shores would find equality when they assimilated and embraced the nation's founding principles. German-Americans seemed to resist this idea by using the "hyphen" to designate their national identity. According to Brands, Roosevelt "saw the campaign against the hyphen as being even more important than the campaign for preparedness."[55] Strategically, though, Roosevelt combined the two campaigns. By vilifying the German nation, he rhetorically pressured German immigrants to distance themselves from their Old World culture. Immigrants signified that distance, as well as their allegiance to the United States, when they discarded the hyphen.

Roosevelt had spoken for years against the hyphen and German immigrants' seeming refusal to assimilate fully into the American body. For him, "we must have in this country but one flag, the American flag, and for the speech of the people but one language, the English language."[56] Likewise, he led the charge for the United States to declare war on Germany. Each campaign empowered the other: the war against Germany "hysterically speeded up" the Americanization of German-Americans.[57] In linking German combatants in Europe with German immigrants in America, Roosevelt made the immigrants' ability to hold on to their birth culture more problematic than ever. Conversely, the presence of deceitful Germans in America buoyed the idea that Germany itself was a threat to decent nations everywhere.

To demonize the German nation and to spur America's participation in the struggle abroad, Roosevelt invoked the myth of "savage war." Specifically, he depicted the Germans as merciless barbarians threatening the borders of civilization, placing them in the same role that Indians had played a century before in the myth of the frontier. According to Richard Slotkin, the Frontier Myth's description of "savage war" depended on the idea that particular races are "inherently disposed to cruel and atrocious violence."[58] Similarly, "images of savagery" frequently infuse America's rhetoric of war. "It is difficult to imagine," Robert Ivie observed, "a more powerful call to arms than one based on the image of savagery."[59] "Civilized" forces, then, convinced themselves that they were morally justified to exterminate their diabolical, irrational, and "uncivilized" counterparts. The violence between American "civilization" and the "barbarity" of other cultures empowers the myth of "savage war." "What is exceptional in American culture is the mythology of violence," Slotkin wrote, "the special meaning given to violence of a certain kind." By invoking the "savage" nature of Germans, Roosevelt reiterated the frontier ideology of American culture and made his position regarding national identity that much more compelling; true Americans understood that they were extraordinarily disposed for battle in order to dominate inferior ("savage") groups.[60] Indians may have been the first enemy to crush, but America's myth of "savage war" foretold that they would not be the last.

There would be no environmental wilderness for the site of this struggle. But Roosevelt's depiction of the warring forces invoked the mythical "border" between savagery and civilization. This constituted the place where frontier heroes traditionally struggled to defeat the "dark side" of human nature.[61] This national myth reflected a powerful frame in which to cast existence and to initiate action: when faced with "savage" forces, civilized people must fight them and, according to Roosevelt, only the martially vigorous and morally determined cultures would survive. The nation would achieve its destiny if it exhibited what he considered the tenets of Americanism in this modern struggle.

In Roosevelt's public rhetoric, wars became more than just contests between humans. Modern wars still reenacted the age-old battle between good and evil. Joseph Campbell found that combatants hold a "belief that God, the creator and sole governor of the universe, was absolutely and always on the side of a certain chosen community." As a result, earthly contests were "Holy Wars, waged in the name and interest of God's will."[62] America's relationship with God had existed since the Puritans' mythic errand into the frontier. According to Sacvan Bercovitch, the "myth of America" allowed early settlers to re-envision "God's country" from a "*New* England . . . into the United States of America."[63] The Creator's will thus helped the community to attain a host of benefits, including progress, national unity, prestige, and security. America's mythic history, such as that illustrated on the frontier, naturalized the idea that violent action against godless "savages" brings these needed benefits to "civilized" people.[64]

Roosevelt exacerbated the tensions regarding national identity, emphasizing that the struggle was no longer about assimilation versus immigration, but now rose to the mythic level of righteous good versus monstrous evil. Despite creating these extreme positions, Roosevelt also pointed to the means to resolve this conflict. As he did countless times before when negotiating the tension between ethnicity, racism, civic duty, and national identity, he would offer Americanism as the middle position that would ease the nation's anxiety about its responsibilities in the world and about immigrants, and he would communicate to immigrants their need to assimilate.

To execute his campaign for America's involvement against Germany's malevolence and to break German-Americans' intractability regarding their assimilation, Roosevelt invoked two mythic themes: "savage war" and the blessing of a higher authority. The German nation had proved its savagery by using bombs and torpedoes to terrorize innocent civilians. Just as savage, in Roosevelt's view, were the immigrants he came to identify as "professionals"—German immigrants who supported Germany's aggression from within America itself. These traitors used the hyphen as a weapon by which they would attempt to confound and cripple patriotic sentiment. If the hyphenated Germans discarded their allegiance to the Old World and stood with "real" Americans against their "savage" enemy abroad, they would become an equal part of a nation guided by the hand of God—a nation that epitomized the ultimate expression of mythic existence.

Roosevelt characterized Germany's actions as "savage" by labeling them as cataclysmic affronts against God. This represented the ultimate proof that the culture was not "civilized," given its purposeful violation of God's will. Soon after the German invasion of Belgium in August 1914, he described the event in biblical proportions. "Hell yawned under the feet of these hard-working . . . men and women," he wrote, "and woe smote them as it smote the peoples we read of in the Old Testament. . . . Through the rents in our smiling surface of civilization the volcanic fires beneath gleamed red in the gloom."[65] In fact, he judged that "Germany had sinned against civilization by her conduct toward Belgium and her method of carrying on the war."[66] Roosevelt's statements, hyperbolic as they were, muted the geopolitical issues and focused on the notion that the German nation was morally wrong for its actions. Just as the Puritans linked their mythic mission in the wilderness to biblical scripture, invoking the moral authority to act against the "uncivilized" Native Americans in the process,[67] Roosevelt likewise depicted the Germans as "savages." As a result, America needed to reaffirm its mythical and moral origin by entering the war and civilizing this enemy as it did with the Indians centuries before.

Germany's barbaric conduct, according to Roosevelt, was nearly unparalleled in the annals of history. He informed the press in 1915 that Germans were like the buccaneers of old who mercilessly attacked defenseless ships. In this case, Germany had engaged in an inhuman act against the *Lusitania:* "When the *Lusitania* sank some twelve hundred non-combatants, men, women and children, were drowned. . . . Centuries have passed since any war vessel of a civilized power has shown such ruthless brutality toward non-combatants, and especially toward women and children. The Moslem pirates of the Barbary Coast behaved at times in similar fashion. . . . But none of these old-time pirates committed murder on so vast a scale as in the case of the *Lusitania.*"[68] Roosevelt again highlighted the inhumanity of Germans but, perhaps more important, he articulated a critical reason for America to enter the struggle abroad. America's mythic history of "savage war" was not simply between immigrants and Indians; it reflected the larger cultural anxieties that any group of settlers faced in creating and pitting their civil religious culture against the indigenous peoples' supposed barbarism.[69] Implicitly, he argued that America manifested the civilizing power of Christianity and it needed to fight against the Germans, who were worse than the unchristian and uncivilized Moslem pirates.

Roosevelt catalogued an array of offenses by Germans, featuring them as bloodthirsty warriors and vicious criminals. "The devastation of Poland and Serbia," he wrote in 1915, "has been awful beyond description and has been associated with infamies surpassing those of the dreadful religious and racial wars" of the 1600s. According to him, the Armenians had "suffered atrocities so hideous that it is difficult to name them, atrocities such as those inflicted upon conquered nations by the followers of Attila and of Genghis Khan."[70] When not displaying the ferocity of ancient warlords, Germany appeared as a common criminal who preyed on the helpless. For instance, the attack against Belgium resembled the "highwayman who holds up a passer-by or a blackhander who kidnaps a child."[71] Seeming to exhibit the worst of human behavior, Germans were responsible for "Belgian women and children . . . suffering the last extremities of infamy and outrage; English women and children . . . being killed by the bombs of German war vessels and aircraft; and our own women in Mexico [who] had been subjected to nameless infamies."[72]

These descriptions of German "savagery" resembled the anecdotes that Roosevelt told about life on the frontier with Indians. His rhetoric reminded Americans of the similarity between the atrocities committed by Native Americans and the heinous behavior he revealed about Germans. In fact, he noted in one article that the German practice of "murder and torture and rape" would have "appealed to an old-time Apache Indian."[73] Particularly, Germany's presence in Belgium and the "infamies" it supposedly practiced against women and children hearkened audiences back to Indian captivity narratives that frightened readers in the nineteenth century and which cemented the image of the "savage" as an enemy to exterminate.[74] Given America's mythic history with defending the border between savagery and civilization, Germany's actions demanded U.S. participation in the war.

Strategically, Roosevelt affixed the blame on the German government and not the citizens. In fact, he believed that German citizens suffered their institutional regime as well. "Germany's social system," Roosevelt wrote for the *Kansas City Star* in late 1917, "was based upon the duty of the average man to cringe before the insolence of his superiors and his right himself to behave with insolence to his inferiors."[75] Thus, the despicable actions by Germany were no simple whims, but an institutionally derived evil. Roosevelt noted in another article months later, the "hideous inequities committed by Germany during the present war have been deliberately ordered by the German Government as part of its deliberate campaign of '*Schrecklichkeit*,' or 'horror'." This marked the German government as "utterly debased."[76]

On this issue, President Wilson and Roosevelt were in agreement. Though Wilson and Roosevelt both denigrated the German government's role in the war, and excluded that country's citizens in their condemnations, they had different motives. According to Richard Barnet, Wilson believed that "public opinion precluded any course other than neutrality."[77] At that time, American involvement in the war in Europe would have been quite unsettling to the nearly one-quarter of America's population who had been born abroad; to see their birth nations attacked by their adopted nation would have felt traitorous. Roosevelt, on the other hand, wanted the United States to go to war and used the German government as a foil. By offering it as a monolithic evil, he placed America in the role of protecting innocent people from a "savage" institution. He positioned the nation to revisit again its mythic role as a stalwart sentinel at the boundary between civilization and barbarism.

Roosevelt's common rhetorical practice appeared to be the creation of extremes. Once the outer edges of the debate had been set, he would offer a middle position between them. So, with the savage German government at one end, he placed "traitorous" German immigrants at the other. Specifically, he indicted those immigrants who dared to use the "hyphen" as a means to designate their nationality. Like Germany, they too found themselves in a mythical context that called into question their loyalty to their adopted country, to God, and to Roosevelt's Americanism.

During 1915–1918, Roosevelt took aim at what he called the institutional or "professional" German-American who refused to be assimilated. "Any effort to keep alive different nationalities and different tongues in this country," he admonished in one speech, "merely means an effort to turn us from a nation into a polyglot boarding house, where dollar hunters of many different races devote themselves to squealing fury to getting all they can out of the trough." According to him, this meant that "whatever soul allegiance [hyphenates] have is paid to some nation on the other side of the water."[78] Thus, the use of the hyphen came to represent not a German awareness of the multicultural potential of the nation, but a link to an institutionally evil government and a symbol of corruption used by German-Americans to destroy the integrity of the United States.

Roosevelt connected "professional" German-Americans to the enemy nation abroad, depicting each as offenders against God and violators of God's will. "Professional" German-Americans worked for the devilish and immoral country that currently waged war against the "civilized" countries of the world. "Professors of every form of hyphenated Americanism," Roosevelt announced in 1915, "made active war" from inside the country by preaching peace. These men and women served not God, but "Baal." Their refusal to denounce Germany for its actions in Belgium and Armenia made them "active agents of the devil."[79] Specifically, any person who "in the name of peace" advocated the "refusal on the part of the United States to furnish arms . . . to those nations who have had the manliness to fight," Roosevelt declared, "is serving the devil and not the Lord."[80] He also likened "professional" Germans to a well-known, biblical unbeliever. Retelling the story of Lot's wife, Roosevelt replaced her with German-Americans "who, instead of adopting an attitude of hearty and exclusive loyalty to their land" tried to "look backward to their old countries." As a result, they became "pillars-of-salt citizens, who are not merely useless, but mischievous members of our commonwealth."[81] Anyone calling for peace, German immigrants in particular, became the antithesis to the Rooseveltian idea that martial fitness was essential to the nation's destiny. Specifically, by casting them as a biblical affront to that mythic element of Americanism, he potentially elevated his philosophy to the level of a civil religion.

Roosevelt blamed "professional" entities for serving Germany's interests from within America: "I do not approve of American citizens of German descent," he wrote in 1916, who formed "organizations to force the United States into practical alliance with Germany because their ancestors came from Germany." Roosevelt declared that "the German-Americans who call themselves such . . . have shown that they are not Americans at all, but Germans in America. Their action has been hostile to the honor and interest of this country."[82] In his published letter to the Progressive National Committee declining its nomination for the 1916 presidential election, Roosevelt attacked "professional" German-

American entities who he believed prevented his nomination in the Republican Party. According to him, the "professional German-Americans . . . are acting purely in the sinister interest of Germany" by refusing him the Republican nomination. Instead, they sought to "make the American President in effect a viceroy of the German Emperor." To that end, they have "shown their eager readiness to sacrifice the interest of the United States" by adhering to the "politico-racial hyphen which is the badge and sign of moral treason to the Republic." Roosevelt even went so far as to support Charles Hughes—the Republican nominee—because he believed that Hughes' character made him "incapable" of being "influenced by the evil intrigues of these hyphenated Americans."[83] Use of the hyphen simply meant disloyalty. "These professional German-Americans and Pro-Germans," he declared, "are Anti-Americans to the core. They play the part of traitors, pure and simple."[84] German immigrants who used the hyphen automatically aligned themselves with a country that Roosevelt and others condemned. But Roosevelt's rhetoric helped turn the hyphen from a simple display of cultural recognition and multicultural intent to a sign of insidious allegiance and virulent anti-American sentiment.

Roosevelt also attacked the "professionals" of the German-American press. Once heralded in America, he now emphasized their allegiance to a diabolical nation. "These hyphenated American newspapers," he revealed in 1916, "have shown that their entire loyalty is to that portion of the compound term which precedes the hyphen."[85] As proof, Roosevelt offered an investigation conducted by a "patriotic" paper, the *Philadelphia North American*. To establish the objectivity of that paper, as well as to affirm that he welcomed the "right" type of immigrant, Roosevelt revealed that the investigation was conducted by an "American of Scandinavian birth." According to that newspaper, hyphenated newspapers proved unscrupulous, "behaving as enemies of the United States, sneering at and misrepresenting our country, and violently attacking our allies . . . and praising and upholding Germany and the Kaiser in extravagant terms." Whether German-American newspapers acted from ignorance or ignominy, Roosevelt wanted them to cease publication; no newspaper, he believed, should be "published in the tongue of any of our enemies."[86] As German language newspapers faltered through self-censorship or revenue loss, German-Americans lost much of their voice in the public forum, and they were deprived of an important symbol of their culture.[87] Roosevelt's attack helped to take away one more obstacle to German assimilation in the nation.

Such disloyal Americans of German descent struck at the mythic core underpinning Americanism, the need for martial vigor. According to Roosevelt, the despicable actions of "professional" German-Americans represented an attempt at "national emasculation" that had to be stopped. He assured readers of *Fear God and Take Your Own Part*, his collection of pro-war essays, that such statements were "not a figure of speech, or a hyperbolic statement." Such statements, he claimed, came from the "leaders of the hyphenated-American movement in this country [who] are also leaders in the movement against preparedness." As proof, he offered the following: "I have before me a little pamphlet, circulated by a 'German-American' organization. . . . This pamphlet is a bitter attack upon the policy of preparedness for the United States, and a slanderous assault on those advocating this American policy. It is, therefore, an effort *in the interest of Germany* to turn the United States into a larger Belgium— an easy prey for Germany."[88] American emasculation appeared evident given German-American organizations freely debasing their adopted country. Roosevelt pointed to a "so called 'German-American' mass meeting" in Milwaukee where the president of the meeting stated that their organization's "purpose was 'to spread German ideals' throughout the country," convincing people to see the "hyphen an honor."[89] According to Roosevelt, "The German-American Alliance and all similar organizations should immediately be broken up by Congress. . . . Our people would do well to remember that even when such organizations keep quiet . . . they are certain to revive and to work against America with the utmost malignity." Thus, "the time to crush them" he warned in 1918, "is now."[90] For him, German-Americans who used the hyphen were clearly traitors to the nation. Casting them as agents of a demonic power abroad sent to weaken the United States played on the age-old fear many nativists held about immigrants generally.[91]

Roosevelt's most damning indictment of German-Americans, however, may have come with his interpretation of the term "professional." "Professional" immigrants were traitors who worked as direct agents for Germany. Beyond the issue of loyalty, however, this label resonated subtly within the larger cultural issue of manhood as an American ideal. Roosevelt despised the "over-civilized effeminacy" developing in the nation due to its focus on materialism and commercial gain.[92] During Roosevelt's era, Jackson Lears wrote, educated businessmen suffered "nervous prostration," a medical disorder caused by the "monotony of routinized, subdivided labor . . . [and] from the unprecedented speed with which railway and telegraph allowed people to transact business."[93] With so much time spent in the office, middle- and upper-class "professionals" neglected their connection to nature and the rough-and-tumble experiences it provided. Roosevelt and others would call for these men to join church camps and gyms to experience "muscular Christianity," making a "Christian commitment to health and manliness" as the means to revitalize their flagging physical vigor.[94] The term "professional" acted as an indictment, and when Roosevelt used it to describe German proponents of the hyphen, he argued that they were not just traitors, but unmanly, and hence not true Americans. Roosevelt's simplistic identification of traitors by their use of the hyphen encouraged many of his true Americans to enact "frontier justice" against their fellow citizens. Rage against the "savage" foreign power flooded American streets with racist mob violence against any American of German heritage, regardless of hyphenation.[95]

Roosevelt called the violence perpetrated against "good" German immigrants an outrageous disgrace; he made no call for a cessation of aggression against immigrants who chose to use the hyphen. He declared that "such a discrimination is itself profoundly anti-American" since it "cruelly wounds brave and upright and loyal Americans."[96] When German immigrants refused to use the hyphen, they proved themselves worthy of the accolades bestowed to any "good" citizen. In fact, Roosevelt claimed, "all good Americans should feel a peculiar pride in the fine and gallant loyalty with which the great majority of the Americans of German descent have come forward to do their part to win this war against the brutal and merciless tyranny of the Prussianized Germany."[97] The great German soldiers of the Frontier Myth had carved a place of honor for early German immigrants. Though Roosevelt did not solely convince large numbers of German-Americans to enlist, many of those citizens seemed eager to prove their loyalty by enlisting to fight in the Great War. By setting the extremes of the debate between a demonic German government and disloyal "professional" traitors subject to the whims of mob violence, he created a situation in which immigrants had virtually no choice but to prove their allegiance through enlistment.

Roosevelt made the choice of Americanism and physical vigor even more compelling by assuring audiences that the Creator watched over their martial exploits in the war. Moreover, his rhetoric provided Germans in America the chance to align themselves with a country blessed by God. "We are the citizens of a mighty Republic," Roosevelt wrote in a 1916 essay, "consecrated to the service of God above, through the service of man on this earth." This became pivotal in Roosevelt's writings: the nation received its godly blessing when it upheld the principles of Americanism and exhibited the requisite strength to do its mythic duty. The country needed to resist the pacifists who preached "sloth and cowardice under the high-sounding name of 'peace.'" Their peace, Roosevelt warned, meant rebuking the tenets of the Bible; the duty of a nation to be prepared "has never been put in stronger form than by St. Luke in the direction that 'He that hath no sword, let him sell his garment and buy one.'" Just as the Savior "armed himself with a scourge of cords and drove the money-changers from the Temple," Roosevelt told Americans to stand against the misdeeds of

Germany and the German hyphen users.[98] Martial righteousness placed Americans next to God.

Roosevelt tied character, the second tenet of Americanism, to God as well. Americans failed to show their character if they did not demonstrate a "fear" of the Almighty by fighting against the savage aggressors of Germany. "In the true sense of the word," Roosevelt explained, "fear" meant to "love God, respect God, [and] honor God" by doing His will. Before America's entrance into the war, Roosevelt chided the nation that it did not fear God given that it sat "idly by while Belgium" was overrun.[99] Americans needed to show "fear"—that strength of will—and join the conflict overseas. German-Americans could prove their character and their loyalty by engaging in the war as well. "The storm that is raging in Europe," Roosevelt penned in 1916, "is terrible and evil; but it is also grand and noble. Untried men who live at ease will do well to remember that there is a certain sublimity even in Milton's defeated archangel, but not whatever in the spirits who kept neutral, who remained at peace, and dared side neither with hell nor with heaven."[100] Roosevelt argued that the commitment to martial action was important, perhaps even more important than the side a person chose. Even Lucifer, according to Roosevelt, was to be commended for having the courage to fight. As a result, German-American peace advocates who called for American neutrality proved more loathsome than the Devil himself. Roosevelt's hyperbole made a fundamental point: a nation blessed by God had to fight, and there was no room in such a nation for citizens with divided loyalties.

Roosevelt found a compelling moral for the nation's story in the modern era. Nativists and immigrants both needed to find the martial character and moral strength to stand against the foes of God. By embracing those aspects of Americanism, forged in America's mythic history, they would realize their destiny together. "We must not prove false to the memories of the nation's past. We must not prove false to the fathers from whose loins we sprang, and to their fathers, the stern men who dared greatly and risked all things that freedom should hold aloft an undimmed torch in this wide land. . . . Let us show ourselves worthy to be their sons. Let us care, as is right, for the things of the body; but let us show that we care even more for the things of the soul. Stout of heart, and pledged to the valor of righteousness, let us stand four-square to the winds of destiny."[101] Just as the Frontier Myth offered a new life to those strong enough to seize it, Roosevelt recognized that when all citizens embraced Americanism, it would "mark the rebirth of our nation," a nation "dedicated to orderly freedom and to the cause of justice for all men."[102] And with the simple act of eliminating the hyphen, German immigrants could share in that rebirth and become once again Americans, pure and simple.

Conclusion

The Germans represented the most star-crossed of immigrant groups to arrive on American shores. When the first German settlers arrived in Virginia in 1608 little did they realize that they would be heralded as the "right" kind of immigrant, only to become one of the most feared and hated groups in the nation.[103] Theodore Roosevelt lent his voice to the public debate on Germans in America, juggling several rhetorical themes that emphasized their significance, abetted their fall, and offered them the means for their redemption in American culture.

During his early years as a public advocate, Roosevelt invoked the "good" German in his myth of Americanism. Early German settlers courageously met the unknown evils on the North American frontier. In all of America's major military encounters, Roosevelt reminded his audiences that German immigrants had proven themselves as accomplished warriors. He also argued that they provided an enriching cultural element to America. In fact, their intellectual and aesthetic character helped to transform the political, educational, and social landscape of the United States. German blood had been infused in the American body for the better, making them equal participants in the nation's destiny.

Roosevelt had heralded German newcomers as "good" immigrants, essentially countering the racist calls for strict immigration controls. They "proved" that immigrants, of the right type, were necessary for American development. Yet, as one of their greatest champions, Roosevelt also proved to be one of their harshest detractors. Second-wave German newcomers seemingly refused to assimilate, rejecting, in a sense, their honored status as the premier immigrant group in the United States. For Roosevelt, this could not stand. Thus, he sought to force German-Americans to assimilate, which would be symbolized by their dropping the hyphen. This would constitute their rejection of cultural independence.

Roosevelt's strategy involved linking German-Americans to their home country during the Great War. When that conflict began, Roosevelt wanted the United States to participate. To that end, he placed Germany as the antagonist in the myth of "savage war," similar to the Native American foes that early settlers fought on the North American frontier. Casting Germany as a "barbaric" and godless enemy, he hoped to reawaken the country's memory about their mythic role in defending the borders of civilization against such savagery. Moreover, Roosevelt connected that demonic government to German-American immigrants. He labeled the latter as "professionals" who used the hyphen to identify their allegiance to a corrupt German nation, as well as to signify the unmanliness of their actions in America. For him, the hyphen was synonymous with betrayal, a betrayal similar to the one the German nation had perpetrated on the civilized world. If German-Americans turned their backs on their birth country by ridding themselves of the hyphen, Roosevelt offered them an equal place in the God-blessed nation.

For some, Roosevelt's strident Americanism put him in the "bad" company of rabid nativist groups who raved about the negative influence of immigrants.[104] However, that considers only one aspect of Roosevelt's public rhetoric.

Roosevelt created rhetorical extremes in public debates, to keep the opposing poles in tension with one another so that he could offer a solution that would seem balanced or moderate by comparison. Much of his mythic rhetoric about national identity created near impossible criteria for nonwhites and foreigners to meet. His discourse exaggerated their merits as a way to construct their place in the nation's identity or overstated their flaws to limit the benefits of citizenship to them. In this case, he hailed their vitality in the American body while condemning their "hyphenated" venom in the nation's spirit. To reconcile the tension, he offered what seemed a reasonable compromise: German immigrants had to discard the hyphen. Mythically, it reaffirmed the notion of Americanism. However, it also meant that German-Americans turned their backs on their heritage, gave up on their ideas of an intact German culture, and denied their dreams of a multicultural community in their adopted country.

There is no question that Roosevelt's rhetoric was harsh. He demanded much from immigrants, whether they had the will to give themselves up to Americanism or not. When they did, though, he "guaranteed" them that they too could take their place, as equals with other native-born whites—as Americans, pure and simple.

Conclusion

Identity and Myth in the Twenty-first Century

From the beginning of the American Republic, the nation has suffered from a sort of dual identity involving race and citizenship. Gary Gerstle commented in *American Crucible* that this duality constituted the "true American dilemma—a national identity divided against itself."[1] Representative of that division, Gerstle pointed to Theodore Roosevelt. According to Gerstle, Roosevelt promoted a form of "racial nationalism" that discriminated among groups based on their perceived racial and ethnic "inferiorities." On the other hand, Roosevelt's celebration of "civic nationalism" welcomed the "right" group into the national community, a community that gained its identity from a set of patriotic ideals.[2] The scholarly body of work on Roosevelt would agree that Roosevelt never closed the gap between race and civic virtue.

Whether he gained some political benefit for engaging a narrative that enfranchised aliens and "others," and despite the flaws and at times harshness of his discourse, Roosevelt did negotiate civic and racial/ethnic traits into one American identity. He promoted what he termed "Americanism": the understanding that American citizens needed to exhibit strength and character in order to earn equality. To popularize that concept, Roosevelt embedded it in a rhetorical form fundamental to the formation and longevity of a community— myth. Given his penchant for all things frontier, he grounded Americanism in the lore of the Frontier Myth, a centuries-old narrative that features heroes who embody the essences of martial strength and high character. These heroes contend with malevolent forces, and in the process illustrate values—such as equality—that would help guide them all to their grand destiny. Roosevelt's invocation of mythic elements provided nativists the framework for "otherness" and whiteness to coexist in one identity, however uneasily. Moreover, he educated immigrants, Native Americans, and African Americans as to their responsibility in earning the opportunity for American identity.

Roosevelt told the story of immigrants newly arriving to the North American continent in his multivolume history, *The Winning of the West*. He strategically placed immigrants in roles predominately held by nativist whites: that of mythic heroes who helped to forge the American nation. These new, legendary individuals who dedicated their strength and morality in service to a community of equals promoted both immigration and assimilation as necessary to the nation's sense of self.

Roosevelt also turned his attention to the tragedy of Native Americans. He took a dim view of how the nation had hounded them almost to extinction and harassed them in the popular culture. Challenging the notion of Indians as worthless or lazy "savages," his mythic version of Americanism portrayed many as individuals who contributed much to the nation. Not only did Roosevelt admire Native Americans' martial vigor, but he also argued that they demonstrated character consistent with Americanism by renouncing their "savage" culture. Because of this, he claimed, they also proved worthy to merge biologically with whites, something he abhorred in any other nonwhite race.

Roosevelt addressed the plight of African Americans as well. Co-opting the rhetorical positions of both Booker T. Washington and W. E. B. Du Bois, he provided African Americans with a mythic, individual identity akin to that of whites. Blacks fulfilled the requirements of Americanism by demonstrating their physical prowess and by engaging in the morally worthwhile world of politics; consequently, he argued, they had earned *some* level of equality. Yet, the cost for not demonstrating the "right" behavior resulted in blacks becoming victims of lynching, a mythically legitimized act of "frontier justice."

Of all the racial and ethnic groups, Roosevelt directed most of his admiration and ire toward German-Americans. Although he heralded German immigrants initially as the "right" type of immigrant who embraced Americanism, he also punished those who sought to hold on to the "hyphen" to designate their dual identity. He demonized German-American immigrants by including them as belligerents in the frontier-inspired myth of "savage war," a myth he also used to spur the United States into battle against Germany in World War I. Roosevelt rhetorically set the United States, and all the "good" immigrants, against the German government, and the "professional" and unmanly German-

American traitors who dared to maintain some semblance of allegiance to their birth country.

Roosevelt's rhetorical juggling of ethnicity, race, and identity depicted not only a unified community, but it also kept those discrete elements prominent in the public debate, further demarking who could and who could not be an American. To that end, he took the debate about such matters to their extremes. He routinely employed hyperbole to demonstrate the ludicrousness of keeping all immigrants and nonwhites from national identity, as well as to quash pleas for overly sympathetic treatment of "inferiors" before they attained a level of equality that he did not believe they deserved. Roosevelt found the middle ground between the rhetorical positions he polarized by identifying individuals within each disenfranchised group to herald as "good" examples. Certain "good" Indians, blacks, and immigrants epitomized the nation's inclusiveness for those who "proved" themselves worthy. They also reaffirmed the idea that those select individuals had risen above the majority in their disenfranchised groups, conceding the racist notion that the majority of the group was in fact inferior.

Along with his rhetorical strategies of using hyperbole and "good examples," Roosevelt's juggling act became manifest most in his public discourse about the mythic foundations of America. His mythic treatment of various groups provided a place in the national identity for people usually dismissed from it, while still comforting the gatekeepers of that identity that all was still well. Claude Levi-Strauss noted that myths are necessary to maintain a community's stability: as a community becomes more "homogenized, the more internal lines of separation become apparent; and what is gained on one level is immediately lost on another."[3] Faced with increases in immigration and the grudging assimilation of native nonwhites, Roosevelt created myths that he hoped would provide stability through the focus on Americanism writ large. He had to placate the ruling elite by assuring them that they would not lose by their inferiors' gains; he had to offer enough gain to the disenfranchised to command their agreement while not truly threatening the power of the elite. Roosevelt's rhetorical situation was not replete with apparent solutions. By forcing a superficial homogeneity on a population whose members were not afforded true equality, Roosevelt may appear at best naive and at worst duplicitous. Indeed, from a twenty-first-century perspective, the shameful nature of that mythically constructed homogenization through the odious act of forced complete assimilation could be viewed merely as the expression of Roosevelt's latent and patent racism. The complexity of such issues as ethnicity, race, and national identity as well as Roosevelt's rhetorical responses to them should not be reduced to so simple a characterization.

Roosevelt's mythic discourse about ethnicity, race, and identity illuminated his role as a significant participant in the debate defining "American" at a critical moment in the nation's history. Of course, his use of myth evinced that while myths do uplift, they can also obfuscate. Roland Barthes observed that myths abolish the "complexity of human acts" and create a "world which is without contradiction because it is without depth." They give people a blissful clarity "which is not that of an explanation but that of a statement of fact."[4] With strength, character, and earned equality as its bases, Roosevelt's mythic "melting pot" synthesized an uncomplicated, consistent, and cohesive place for all the individual ingredients: blacks, Indians, and immigrants found a better status in the national hierarchy; whites still maintained the power of "frontier justice" and exclusivity.

Given the enormity and destabilizing nature of the racism and hopelessness during his era, Roosevelt created a wondrous mythic reality for both whites and nonwhites. His retelling of the Frontier Myth provided nativist and disenfranchised listeners alike with access to the national identity, an access that appeared natural, inevitable, and available to all. Simply put, Roosevelt's mythic rhetoric helped people feel good about who they were by reminding them of the opportunities they had to become Americans, pure and simple.

In the right hands, myths provide a common language for disparate individuals and groups to share common experiences and to create a community. In the wrong hands, they maintain a cultural hierarchy that is never quite what it seems.

From Frontier Myth to American Dream

Since Theodore Roosevelt's death in 1919, the United States has passed a host of legislation that has affected the identities of immigrants, Native Americans, and African Americans. For instance, several national quota acts, immigration acts, and refugee-related policies have implicitly argued that some foreign peoples are better equipped to be American than are others.[5] Laws such as the Indian Citizenship Act of 1924 and the 1988 Indian Gaming Regulatory Act finally granted Native Americans full citizenship and gave them some economic control of their destiny.[6] With the 1954 *Brown v. Board of Education of Topeka* Supreme Court decision, the 1964 Civil Rights Act, and the comprehensive Voting Rights Act of 1965, African Americans found greater opportunities in the nation's sociopolitical hierarchy.[7] Despite these judicial and political decisions, the place of "others" in American identity remains contentious as ever.

Roosevelt's rhetoric did not act as a cure for the disease of nativism and racism then or now. However, in some ways, his version of the Frontier Myth remains in the collective unconscious of American culture, particularly in attitudes toward immigration. Mexican president Vicente Fox faced the displeasure of the American public and the lethargy of the George W. Bush administration in 2001 when Fox proposed that the United States give amnesty to millions of illegal Mexican immigrants already residing in America, thus circumventing the traditional citizenship process.[8] A similar immigration reform bill in early 2006 stalled when critics charged that this bill amounted to granting amnesty to illegal immigrants, eliminating the notion of earning American identity.[9] In the post-9/11 United States, assimilating strangers into the fabric of national identity may no longer be the order of the day. When urban legends heighten fears that the next attack will come from resident immigrants who never intended to assimilate, many "others" will undoubtedly face hostility.[10]

Legislative policies currently reflect the nation's fears and identify foreigners as being "on the wrong side of the frontier."[11] In December 2005, the House of Representatives passed a bill that made illegal immigrants subject to criminal prosecution; many considered this move as demonizing foreigners for being foreign.[12] In May 2006, the Senate reaffirmed its support for building a 370-mile fence along the Mexican border. Although some believed the fence might not make a difference in stopping immigrant traffic, they recognized that the fence symbolized the line between American civilization and a wild environment.[13] Within three weeks of the release of "Neustro Himno," a Spanish-language version of the "Star-Spangled Banner," the Senate passed two provisions which declared English the national language, and which deemed English the country's "common and unifying language." Clearly, the Senate privileged the familiar over the foreign, although Senator Jim Inhofe (R-OK) noted that these provisions were only symbolic, were not racist, and were not directed at Spanish citizens.[14]

Utilizing the "bully pulpit" to appeal directly to the national audience, President George W. Bush addressed immigration concerns in a nationally televised speech in May 2006. He identified the elements of a comprehensive immigration reform bill that he hoped Congress would pass. Several frontier-inspired themes were evident. Bush argued that, before all else, America "must secure its borders." To that end, he re-imagined the frontier evil endangering America. He linked illegal immigrants with other morally inferior and "savage" groups such as "criminals, drug dealers, and terrorists" who threatened national security. Bush also pledged to coordinate with the states' governors to deploy six thousand National Guard troops to assist the Border Patrol. Although he assured his audience that America had no plans to "militarize the southern border," the National Guard's tasks of installing fences, building roads, and stopping drug traffic appeared similar to the exploits of the early American frontiersmen who tamed the environment and policed its inhabitants. Finally, Bush faced the issue of the current

11-12 million undocumented immigrants in the country by engaging the Rooseveltian strategy of identifying extremes before offering a middle position: "We
must face the reality that millions of illegal immigrants are already here. They
should not be given an automatic path to citizenship. This is amnesty, and I oppose it. . . . Some in this country argue that the solution is to deport every illegal immigrant. . . . I disagree. It is neither wise nor realistic to round up millions of people. . . . There is a rational middle ground. . . . I believe that illegal
immigrants who have roots in our country and want to stay should have to pay
a meaningful penalty for breaking the law, to pay their taxes, to learn English,
and to work in a job for a number of years."[15] Just as Roosevelt demanded that
people prove their frontier readiness for national identity, Bush called for illegal
immigrants to bear a "meaningful penalty" and demonstrate their strength and
character before expecting to receive citizenship.

While African Americans have their citizenship, they too face the judgment of the frontier. "Frontier justice," one of Roosevelt's most odious mythic
concepts, has remained a shallowly buried corpse whose ghost haunts African
Americans to the present day. In 1991, Judge Clarence Thomas declared that the
sexual harassment charges made against him during his Supreme Court confir-
mation hearings resembled a "high tech lynching for uppity blacks."[16] Not all
lynching, though, has been as metaphorical as Thomas's claim. For example, just
as blacks sometimes found themselves in the wrong place at the wrong time during Roosevelt's era, so too did West African immigrant Amadou Diallo find a
similar fate in 1999. Four white New York City police officers, suspecting Diallo
of being a rapist and believing he was armed, fired forty-one times at him outside his apartment, killing him. Diallo was not the rapist, or a criminal of any
kind, and he carried only a wallet and a pager at the time of the shooting. Because of these facts, the NAACP called for the officers to pay for their "modern-
day lynching." A jury comprised of both whites and blacks who alleged that
their deliberations never "touched on issues of race" acquitted all four officers
of murder.[17] Former president Clinton voiced a common sentiment about the
jury's verdict. Although he accepted that the jury may be correct under given
criminal law, he also stated that "most people in America of all races believe that
if it had been a young white man in a young all-white neighborhood, it probably
wouldn't have happened."[18] And with the incident involving African American
James Byrd, who, in 1999, was dragged to death by three white men in the small
Texas town of Jasper, "frontier justice" continues to resonate in America.[19]

Roosevelt's "inclusion by exemplar" of heroic individuals certainly seems
to have outlasted him. *Newsweek's* 2006 story that America has reached a "real
racial tipping point" cited the prevalence of prominent African Americans in
society. Specifically, the author noted, "With blacks running major corpora-

tions, with two having served in succession as secretary of state and with three having won election to the Senate in the modern age, it is becoming harder to argue that blacks can't succeed at the top."[20] Those handful of exemplars allow the millions of African Americans some hope, while reaffirming the idea that the "seething mass" have far to go.

Although the frontier ideology remains in the public consciousness, appearing in everything from presidential rhetoric to popular movies, its expression has changed, particularly from Roosevelt's version of a stark, uncomfortably provocative and sustained public articulation of race, ethnicity, and identity.[21] Few Americans in a nation that is over 75 percent urban have the opportunity to fight for their piece of the continent and defend it against the forces of evil.[22] Nevertheless, myths represent enduring forms that allow the community to remake itself continually. In contemporary America, the camera lens most often frames the frontier. The *Crocodile Hunter,* a television program starring an Australian adventurer, presents his forced confrontations with various wildlife creatures as mythic battles between man and the environment. The popularity of the television series *Survivor* attests to a continuing desire to combat nature as well as other "tribes" as the means to rise in power and riches above the rest. As pairs of human beings travel the world hoping to win *The Amazing Race,* the entire planct becomes their frontier as they vie to be the first to lay claim to the target land. As the "urban jungle" seems to have replaced the wilderness as the crucible in which Americans are formed, Roosevelt's myth has quite apparently evolved.[23]

Roosevelt's interpretation of the Frontier Myth, along with his version of Americanism, finds contemporary expression as the myth of the American Dream. This mythic "truth"—that a person who achieves financial success in the free market is a real American—has existed as long as Roosevelt's Frontier Myth. The term "American Dream" was given sustained attention in the 1930s and beyond by such prominent rhetors as Franklin Roosevelt, Martin Luther King Jr., Ronald Reagan, and others who claimed it the Founding Fathers' intent.[24] Advocates popularizing the American Dream had mined much of the same territory as did Roosevelt. With the resonance in such cosmological stories as the Puritans establishing a New Israel in North America, and documents such as the Declaration of Independence that affirmed "self evident" rights, America saw its origin as part of a mythic destiny.[25] This new world represented a "dream of a land in which life should be better and richer and fuller for every man," historian James Adams wrote, "with opportunity for each according to his ability or achievement." However, the tenets of the American Dream did not stop there. Adams, who some believe may have coined the term, also noted that each person "shall be able to attain to the fullest stature of which they are innately capable, and be recognized by others for what they are, regardless of the fortuitous circumstances of birth or position."[26] Success, measured in material gain, and equality would come to those "true" Americans who earned it.

In addition, like all myths, the American Dream protects its own validity. If an immigrant or native-born fails to achieve financial security, the Dream is not the problem. Despite the pragmatic inequities in opportunities for far too many people, this myth simply asserts that the person who failed did not try as hard as those of us who succeeded.[27] Furthermore, the mythic nature of this concept makes it quite elastic. It allows Michael Kinsley of the *Washington Post* to write that our "national myth" is dying given the economic turmoil at all class levels, within a month of Alan Reynolds of the *Wall Street Journal* noting that the "American Dream is alive and well" because hard work still determines success.[28] Roosevelt's frontier version of American identity empowers the currently prominent American Dream. Richard Slotkin noted that the "dark side of the Frontier Myth" has always had an economic undercurrent. The nation develops its resources, he argued, and essentially destroys those who oppose the "dominant forms of economic and national organization."[29] Identity, then, becomes established through fiscal heroism, and not through an Americanism defined by the trials offered in a primordial, savage universe. Thus, the Rooseveltian requirement of physical strength, once needed to defeat sworn enemies on the frontier, evolves into the simple mantra of "work hard" in the urban arena. The definition of work may have changed, but race and ethnicity are still as important in the myth of the American Dream as they were to Roosevelt's Frontier Myth. Notions of certain groups' penchants for being lazy not only explain their failure to seize the Dream, but also justify their unworthiness of respectful treatment. Likewise, some nonwhites who are willing to work hard at "the jobs Americans do not want to do" still may not qualify for national identity if they are considered racially or ethnically "too different" from mainstream society.

Roosevelt's articulation of character as a necessary component of Americanism has a current manifestation as an individual's persistence in repeated efforts to realize the Dream; "starting over" is an American theme in which perseverance is evidence of the moral fiber required to achieve national identity. Some racial and ethnic groups may have to start over more frequently, such as the southern victims of repeated hurricanes. However, the Dream does not allow for complaining about circumstances, which would constitute moral weakness and mark one as an "inferior."[30]

Finally, because of the American Dream, equality, one of the most privileged terms in the nation's vocabulary, now expresses race and ethnicity against an economic backdrop; it places haves in tension with have-nots, rather than directly pitting racial and ethnic "others" against white identity as Roosevelt did. Although he opened the debate in stark fashion for citizens to wrestle with the meanings attached to race and ethnicity in relation to national identity, the overwhelming racism and attending violence apparent in his day prevented an honest exchange of ideas and feelings. The shift in the debate toward monetary matters since then allows the rhetoric of the American Dream to evade any reference to racial and ethnic traits when considering an individual's national identity. Native Americans and Hispanic Americans make a good case in point for the prominence of their place, sans race or ethnicity as a determining factor, in the American Dream myth.

Although "superlobbyist" and public relations consultant Jack Abramoff hearkened us back to the Roosevelt era by referring to the Native American clients he defrauded as "monkeys" and "idiots," popular perceptions of American Indians reflect their preeminent, financially based identity in the national Dream.[31] The media has transformed the frontier-like, dusty reservations peopled by "lazy" Indians of yesteryear into tribal-run, Las Vegas-like gambling empires. Current stories of Native Americans, according to columnist Mark Fitzgerald, revealed a decrease in stereotypes and more "sophisticated coverage" that "treated Native Americans 'as people rather than historical figures.'"[32] Instead of Indians' identity coming from a violent clash with civilization and their uncomfortable capitulation to white ways, tribal-run casinos represent a success story of economic assimilation much more subtle than Roosevelt's biological myth. Books such as Brett Fromson's *Hitting the Jackpot: The Inside Story of the Richest Indian Tribe in History* further reinforce the evolution of the frontier persona in the twenty-first century Dream. Fromson wrote that the "true goal of the Pequots has always been to acquire what so many other Americans want— jobs, homes, wealth, social status. In short, the American dream." Furthermore, when asked what it meant to be a Pequot, Fromson noted that one tribe member "answered the question with another question, asking 'What does it mean to be an American?'"[33]

Illegal Mexican immigrants still fall under the baleful gaze of some native-born Americans. Even legal citizens face identity checks from whites, some who allege, "My neighborhood [has] gone from nice, middle-class Americans to almost all Hispanics."[34] However, as some media and elites allege, the assimilation of Hispanics is well under way. Arian Campo-Flores and Howard Fineman of *Newsweek* reported that the new mayor of Los Angeles in 2005, Antonio Villaraigosa, the "first Latino to win the office" in over one hundred years, "energized Latino voters to turn out for him at historic levels" and created the "sort of *multiracial coalition* that has often eluded less-gifted politicians."[35] President for the Center of Equal Opportunity Linda Chavez noted that "Hispanics . . . are very much like other Americans: They work hard . . . and own their own homes. In short, they are pursuing the American Dream."[36] Mexican President Fox identified the new position of Hispanics and Latinos in America's cultural hierarchy, earning him the wrath of Reverends Al Sharpton and Jesse Jackson in the process. In a May 2005 speech, CNN reported Fox praising the "dedication of Mexicans working in the United States, saying they're willing to take jobs that 'even blacks' won't do."[37] Read in a less cynical way, Fox claimed that Mexican Americans—illegal or not—were assimilating the Dream better than were African Americans. Just as Roosevelt rhetorically distanced Indians from blacks to move the Native Americans racially closer to whites, the American Dream moves certain groups apart based on their perceived desire to work hard and to become materially successful. Even President Bush's May 2006 speech recognized that illegal immigrants were "willing to risk everything for the dream of freedom," and his temporary guest worker program provided them the means to continue their quest for it.[38]

In the heavily scientific and technological twenty-first century, myths may not be as apparently integral to American life as they were in the nation's early years. Contemporary America is no longer a vast frontier waiting for heroes of the people to conquer its power and possess its wealth. And yet, the myths constructed by Theodore Roosevelt resonate through the past century to their current manifestations. He demonstrated how myths could celebrate the promise of equality, spurring nonwhites and immigrants forward, while masking the near insurmountable burdens they faced in their quest for an equal place in the nation. Whether his influence is considered to be for good or ill, the relevance of Roosevelt's rhetorical discourses in contemporary American society is unmistakable. He was, for his time, a rhetorical broker of identity who simultaneously simplified and complicated the issues of assimilation, ethnicity, immigration, and race, to ensure the nation's unity, viability, and progress. The tension between individual and national identity may escalate in times of international conflict and may diminish in times of national crisis. However the tension is perceived, in a country of so many racial and ethnic groups, it remains fertile ground for the development of public argument from rhetors of any political bent.

The political potential aside, this issue affects me at a personal level. I know that one day my son, who is biracial, will come to me wanting to know why some people consider him "different," and why he may have to "prove" himself in a way that others will not. I will tell him about the experiences of "Pop," and discuss the context of my father's advice to me. I will even tell him about Roosevelt. I only hope that when my son and I finish talking about the questions surrounding the "pure and simple" nature of American identity, we can both muster something more than a resigned shrug of our shoulders.

Notes

Introduction

1. The quotation in the book title comes from Theodore Roosevelt, "The Duties of American Citizenship, January 26, 1893," in *American Ideals/The Strenuous Life/Realizable Ideals: The Works of Theodore Roosevelt*, National ed. (New York: Charles Scribner's Sons, 1926), 13: 295.

2. Theodore Roosevelt, *Ranch Life and the Hunting Trail* (1888; Lincoln: University of Nebraska Press, 1983); H. W. Brands, *T. R.: The Last Romantic* (New York: Basic Books, 1997), 180–185.

3. Theodore Roosevelt, *An Autobiography* (New York: Charles Scribner's Sons, 1929), 168–203; Kathleen Dalton, *Theodore Roosevelt: A Strenuous Life* (New York: Alfred A. Knopf, 2002), 149–155.

4. Theodore Roosevelt, *The Rough Riders* (1899; New York: Signet Classics, 1961); William H. Harbaugh, *The Life and Times of Theodore Roosevelt* (New York: Collier Books, 1963), 93–109.

5. Roosevelt, *An Autobiography*, 423–460, 502–531; Edmund Morris, *Theodore Rex* (New York: Random House, 2001), 183–192.

6. Theodore Roosevelt, *Through the Brazilian Wilderness/Papers on Natural History in The Works of Theodore Roosevelt*, vol. 5; and Candace Millard, *The River of Doubt: Theodore Roosevelt's Darkest Journey* (New York: Doubleday, 2005).

7. See http://*movies*.about.com/od/dicaprioleonardo/a/roosevelt091205.htm

and http://www.imdb.com/title/tt0477347/. *Ballot Box Bunny,* 1951, I. Freleng, Director, Warner Brothers.

8. William Marina and David T. Beito, "How Teddy Roosevelt Fathered the 'Bush Doctrine,'" *The Independent Institute,* December 9, 2004, http://www.independent.org/newsroom/article.asp?id=1435; Jonathan Alter, "Between the Lines Online: Loud and Clear," *Newsweek,* Web Exclusive, September 20, 2002, http://web.lexis-nexis.com.

9. John B. Judis, *The Folly of Empire: What George W. Bush Could Learn from Theodore Roosevelt and Woodrow Wilson* (New York: Scribner, 2004), 1–9.

10. Harvey Mansfield, "The Manliness of Theodore Roosevelt," *The New Criterion,* vol. 23.7, March 2005, http://www.newcriterion.com/archive/23/mar05/mansfield.htm.

11. Edmund Morris, *The Rise of Theodore Roosevelt* (New York: The Modern Library, 2001), 480.

12. Thomas G. Dyer, *Theodore Roosevelt and the Idea of Race* (Baton Rouge: Louisiana State University Press, 1980), 71, 109, 133.

13. Sarah Watts, *Rough Rider in the White House: Theodore Roosevelt and the Politics of Desire* (Chicago: University of Chicago Press, 2003), 84, 90.

14. H. W. Brands, *The Last Romantic,* 499–500, 762.

15. Throughout the book, readers will encounter terms that designate identity for various racial and ethnic groups. I will use Indian, Native, American Indian, and Native American interchangeably since there is no scholarly, cultural, or popular consensus as to which term is more appropriate. That reasoning holds for my use of African American and black interchangeably. Furthermore, when I use terms such as Italian American and African American, for example, they will appear without hyphens. Again, there is no consensus regarding hyphen use, and I have chosen to forego their use.

16. Samuel P. Huntington, *Who Are We? The Challenges to America's National Identity* (New York: Simon & Schuster, 2004), 221–256; Patrick J. Buchanan, *The Death of the West: How Dying Populations and Immigrant Invasions Imperil Our Country and Civilization* (New York: St. Martin's Press, 2002); John J. Miller, "Keeping Indians Down on the Reservation," *The Week,* February 10, 2006, 12.

17. Holly Bailey, "A Border War," *Newsweek,* April 3, 2006, 24.

18. *The Week,* "Bennett: The Meaning of a Racial Comment," October 14, 2005, 21.

19. Dyer, *Theodore Roosevelt and the Idea of Race,* 1–15.

20. Dyer's and Watts's books notwithstanding, newer biographies such as Dalton's, and Patricia O'Toole's *When Trumpets Call: Theodore Roosevelt after the White House* (New York: Simon & Schuster, 2005), devote few pages to Roosevelt's relationship with blacks, American Indians, and immigrants.

21. See Dyer, *Theodore Roosevelt and the Idea of Race,* and Brands, *T. R.: The Last Romantic.*

22. Richard Hofstadter, *The American Political Tradition and the Men Who*

Made It (New York: Vintage Books, 1954), 224; Grant McConnell, *The Modern Presidency* (New York: St. Martin's Press, 1967), 70; O'Toole, *When Trumpets Call*, 210–211.

23. Hofstadter, *The American Political Tradition*, 206–237.

24. Theodore Roosevelt, *Fear God and Take Your Own Part* (New York: George H. Doran Company, 1916), 362.

25. Theodore Roosevelt, "New York," in *Hero Tales from American History/Oliver Cromwell/New York: The Works of Theodore Roosevelt*, 10: 361.

26. Dyer, *Theodore Roosevelt and the Idea of Race*, 19.

27. The actual quotation reads, "The rhetorical function is the function of adjusting ideas to people and people to ideas." See Donald C. Bryant, "Rhetoric: Its Functions and Its Scope," in *Contemporary Rhetoric: A Reader's Coursebook*, ed. Douglas Ehninger (Glenview, IL: Scott, Foresman, 1972), 26.

28. Lloyd F. Bitzer, "The Rhetorical Situation," in *Readings in Rhetorical Criticism*, ed. Carl R. Burgchardt, 3rd ed. (State College: Strata Publishing, Inc., 2005), 58–67; Kenneth Burke, *A Rhetoric of Motives* (Berkeley: University of California Press, 1969), 42–43.

29. James B. White, *When Words Lose Their Meaning: Constitutions and Reconstitutions of Language, Character, and Community* (Chicago: University of Chicago Press, 1984), xi.

30. My definition is similar to what Rogers M. Smith labeled a "civic myth." See *Civic Ideals: Conflicting Visions of Citizenship in U.S. History* (New Haven: Yale University Press, 1997), 33–34.

31. Richard T. Hughes, *Myths America Lives By* (Urbana: University of Illinois Press, 2004), 2.

32. Richard Slotkin, *Gunfighter Nation: The Myth of the Frontier in Twentieth-Century America* (New York: Atheneum, 1992), 10.

33. Slotkin, *Gunfighter Nation*, 11–12.

34. Janice H. Rushing, "The Rhetoric of the American Western Myth," *Communication Monographs* 50 (March 1983): 16.

35. Benedict Anderson, *Imagined Communities: Reflections on the Origin and Spread of Nationalism*, 12th ed. (1983; New York: Verso, 2003), 7.

36. M. Lane Bruner, *Strategies of Remembrance: The Rhetorical Dimensions of National Identity Construction* (Columbia: University of South Carolina Press, 2002), 2–3.

37. *CNN*, "Estimated Number of Illegal Immigrants in U.S.," May 11, 2006, http://www.cnn.com; Peter D. Salins, "Assimilation Nation," *New York Times*, May 11, 2006, http://www.nytimes.com/2006/05/11/opinion; Fareed Zakaria, "To Become an American," *Newsweek*, April 10, 2006, 39.

38. *The Week*, "A GOP Split over Immigration," April 7, 2006, 2; Bailey, "A Border War," *Newsweek*, 24; David Streitfeld, "A Job Americans Won't Do, Even at $34 an Hour," *Los Angeles Times*, May 18, 2006, http://www.latimes.com.

39. Streitfeld, "A Job Americans Won't Do"; Teresa Watanabe and Joe Mathews,

"Unions Helped to Organize 'Day Without Immigrants,' " *Los Angeles Times,* May 3, 2006, http://www.latimes.com.

40. Frank Ahrens, "For Mexicans and Americans, A Nudge to 'Think Together,' " *Washington Post,* May 7, 2006, http://www.washingtonpost.com; Bailey, "A Border War."

41. Dan Whitcomb, "LA Immigration Activists Mobilize for Washington," *Washington Post,* May 9, 2006, http://www.washingtonpost.com; Ahrens, "For Mexicans and Americans."

42. Darryl Fears and N. C. Aizenman, "Immigrant Groups Split on Boycott," *Washington Post,* April 14, 2006, http://www.washingtonpost.com; Gary Polakovic, "Marchers Raise Voice in County," *Los Angeles Times,* May 2, 2006, http://www.latimes.com.

43. Dudley Althaus and Cynthia Leonor Garza, "Dreams of Many Ride on Boycott," *Houston Chronicle,* May 1, 2006, http://www.chron.com; Darryl Fears and Krissah Williams, "Boycott Gives Voice to Illegal Workers," *Washington Post,* May 2, 2006, http://www.washingtonpost.com.

44. Erin Texeira, "Some Immigrants Reluctant to Boycott," *Dallas Morning News,* April 30, 2006, http://www.dallasnews.com; Darryl Fears, "After Protests, Backlash Grows," *Washington Post,* May 3, 2006, http://www.washingtonpost.com.

45. Leslie Sanchez, "Boycott? More Like Bullying," *Los Angeles Times,* May 4, 2006, http://www.latimes.com; Ruben Navarrette Jr., "No Such Thing as a Good Immigrant," *San Diego Union-Tribune,* March 29, 2006, http://www.signonsandiego.com.

46. Gregory Rodriguez, "Why We're the New Irish," *Newsweek,* May 30, 2005, 35.

47. Navarrette Jr., "No Such Thing as a Good Immigrant."

48. Laura Wides-Munoz, " 'Star-Spangled Banner' in Spanish Draws Protest," *Houston Chronicle,* April 28, 2006, http://www.chron.com.

49. Ana Veciana-Suarez, "Anthem Debate Hits Sour Notes," *Houston Chronicle,* May 10, 2006, http://www.chron.com; Associated Press, "Bush: Sing 'Star-Spangled Banner' in English," *CNN,* April 28, 2006, http://www.cnn.com.

50. Ralph E. Shaffer and Walter P. Coombs, "Our Discordant Anthem," *Los Angeles Times,* May 2, 2006, http://www.latimes.com; Veciana-Suarez, "Anthem Debate Hits Sour Notes."

51. Erin A. Kaplan, "What Was Lost in the Crowd," *Los Angeles Times,* May 3, 2006, http://www.latimes.com.

52. *National Public Radio,* "Racial Identity in Multi-Ethnic America," Debra Dickerson (8:47–9:31), Part 4, January 6, 2005, http://www.npr.org/templates/story/story.php?storyId=4271005.

53. Richard Feldstein, *Political Correctness: A Response from the Cultural Left* (Minneapolis: University of Minnesota Press, 1997); Marilyn Friedman and Jan Narveson, *Political Correctness: For and Against* (Lanham: Rowman & Littlefield Publishers, 1995); M. E. Banning, "The Limits of PC Discourse: Linking Language Use to Social Practice," *Pedagogy* 4 (2004): 191–214.

54. Bernard Bailyn, *The Ideological Origins of the American Revolution* (1967; Cambridge: The Belknap Press of Harvard University Press, 1992), 232–234.

55. Gordon S. Wood, *The Radicalism of the American Revolution* (New York: Vintage Books, 1993), 186.

56. Daniel J. Boorstin, *The Americans: The National Experience* (New York: Vintage Books, 1965), 182.

57. Bailyn, *The Ideological Origins of the American Revolution*, 241.

58. For what the Declaration of Independence means for the shaping of citizen behavior, see Jim Cullen, *The American Dream: A Short History of an Idea that Shaped a Nation* (Oxford: Oxford University Press, 2003), 37–41. For the text of the Declaration, see http://www.law.indiana.edu/uslawdocs/declaration.html.

59. Daniel J. Tichenor, *Dividing Lines: The Politics of Immigration Control in America* (Princeton: Princeton University Press, 2002), 51; Desmond King, *Making Americans: Immigration, Race, and the Origins of the Diverse Democracy* (Cambridge: Harvard University Press, 2000), 33.

60. William Petersen, Michael Novak, and Philip Gleason, *Concepts of Ethnicity* (Cambridge: Harvard University Press, 1982), 58–59.

61. Gordon S. Wood, *The Creation of the American Republic, 1776–1787* (New York: W. W. Norton & Company, 1969), 72–73.

62. Petersen, Novak, and Gleason, *Concepts of Ethnicity*, 64–65.

63. J. Hector St. John de Crevecoeur, *Letters From an American Farmer*, Letter III, http://xroads.virginia.edu/~HYPER/CREV/letter03.html.

64. Alexis de Tocqueville, *Democracy in America*, vol. 1, "Social Conditions of the Anglo-Americans," chapter 3; and "The Present and Probable Future Condition of the Three Races That Inhabit the Territory of the United States," chapter 18, http://xroads.virginia.edu/~HYPER/DETOC/toc_indx.html.

65. Matthew F. Jacobson, *Whiteness of a Different Color: European Immigrants and the Alchemy of Race* (Cambridge: Harvard University Press, 1998), 30.

66. Reginald Horsman, *Race and Manifest Destiny: The Origins of American Racial Anglo-Saxonism* (Cambridge: Harvard University Press, 1981), 102–103.

67. Smith, *Civic Ideals*, 168; Marouf A. Hasian Jr., *The Rhetoric of Eugenics in Anglo-American Thought* (Athens: University of Georgia Press, 1996), 5, 19, 28.

68. Tichenor, *Dividing Lines*, 12.

69. Thomas F. Gossett, *Race: The History of an Idea in America*, New ed. (New York: Oxford University Press, 1997), 72–73.

70. Philip J. Deloria, *Playing Indian* (New Haven: Yale University Press, 1998), 26, 30–31, 37.

71. A more in-depth discussion of the rhetorical contexts surrounding African Americans, Native Americans, and immigrants will appear in their respective chapters.

72. Ronald Takaki, *Iron Cages: Race and Culture in Nineteenth-Century America* (Seattle: University of Washington Press, 1979), 114.

73. Brian W. Dippie, *The Vanishing American: White Attitudes and U.S. Indian Policy* (Lawrence: University Press of Kansas, 1982), 56–78.

74. King, *Making Americans*, 23.

75. John Higham, *Strangers in the Land: Patterns of American Nativism, 1860–1925* (New Brunswick: Rutgers University Press, 1988), 42–43; Jacobson, *Whiteness of a Different Color*, 55–56.

76. Arthur M. Schlesinger Jr., *The Disuniting of America: Reflections on a Multicultural Society* (New York: Norton & Company, 1998), 142.

77. O'Toole, *When Trumpets Call*, 63.

Chapter 1

1. Philip Gleason, *Speaking of Diversity: Language and Ethnicity in Twentieth-Century America* (Baltimore: Johns Hopkins University Press, 1992), 59, 274.

2. Winthrop Talbot, ed., *Americanization: Principles of Americanism/Essentials of Americanization/Technic of Race-Assimilation* (New York: H. W. Wilson Company, 1917), 8.

3. Gleason, *Speaking of Diversity*, 49–50.

4. The government's attempts to assimilate Native Americans will be examined in more detail in chapter 3.

5. Ronald Takaki, *A Different Mirror: A History of Multicultural America* (New York: Little, Brown and Company, 1993), 47–49.

6. David W. Adams, *Education for Extinction: American Indians and the Boarding School Experience, 1875–1928* (Lawrence: University Press of Kansas, 1995), 17–27.

7. Stephen Cornell, *The Return of the Native: American Indian Political Resurgence* (New York: Oxford University Press, 1988), 42.

8. Samuel P. Huntington, *Who Are We?: The Challenges to America's National Identity* (New York: Simon & Schuster, 2004), 131–132.

9. Kenneth L. Karst, *Belonging to America: Equal Citizenship and the Constitution* (New Haven: Yale University Press, 1989), 84.

10. Neil L. Shumsky, "Zangwill's 'The Melting Pot': Ethnic Tensions on Stage," *American Quarterly* 27 (1975): 29.

11. Gary Gerstle, *American Crucible: Race and Nation in the Twentieth Century* (Princeton: Princeton University Press, 2001), 51.

12. Israel Zangwill, *The Melting Pot: A Drama in Four Acts*, in *The Works of Israel Zangwill: The Melting Pot/Plaster Saints*, Edition De Luxe, vol. 12 (1925; New York: AMS Press, 1969), 184–185.

13. Philip Gleason, "The Melting Pot: Symbol of Fusion or Confusion?," *American Quarterly* 16 (1964): 27.

14. Charles Hirschman, "America's Melting Pot Reconsidered," *Annual Review of Sociology* 9 (1983): 397–398.

15. Gleason, *Speaking of Diversity*, 15–16.

16. Huntington, *Who Are We?*, 132–134.

17. Desmond King, *Making Americans: Immigration, Race, and the Origins of the Diverse Democracy* (Cambridge: Harvard University Press, 2000), 88–90.

18. Gleason, *Speaking of Diversity*, 18.

19. The Americanization Movement and its relation to German-Americans, who were the focus of many outrages, will be explored in more detail in chapter 5.

20. Theodore Roosevelt, *New York*, in *Hero Tales from American History/Oliver Cromwell/New York: The Works of Theodore Roosevelt*, National ed., 20 vols. (New York: Charles Scribner's Sons, 1926), 10: 362.

21. Theodore Roosevelt, "Americans for Americans, May 31, 1916," *The Theodore Roosevelt Collection*, Harvard College Library, TRC-SP-1 (10), Speeches, 1913–1916, 3. Use is by permission of the Houghton Library, Harvard University.

22. Theodore Roosevelt, "The Strenuous Life, April 10, 1899," in *American Ideals/ The Strenuous Life/Realizable Ideals: The Works of Theodore Roosevelt*, 13: 321.

23. Numerous scholars retell Roosevelt's transformation from a frail youth to a strapping young man. See H. W. Brands, *T. R.: The Last Romantic* (New York: Basic Books, 1997), 23–26; Kathleen Dalton, *Theodore Roosevelt: A Strenuous Life* (New York: Alfred A. Knopf, 2002), 48–50; William H. Harbaugh, *The Life and Times of Theodore Roosevelt* (New York: Collier Books, 1963), 15–16.

24. Theodore Roosevelt, *An Autobiography* (New York: Charles Scribner's Sons, 1929), 27–28.

25. Roosevelt, *An Autobiography*, 28–32; Dalton, *Theodore Roosevelt: A Strenuous Life*, 24.

26. See the Theodore Roosevelt Association timeline at http://www. theodoreroosevelt.org/life/timeline.htm.

27. Theodore Roosevelt, "Americanism in Municipal Politics, September 10, 1895," in *Campaigns and Controversies: The Works of Theodore Roosevelt*, 14: 195.

28. Ray A. Billington, *The Genesis of the Frontier Thesis: A Study in Historical Creativity* (San Marino, CA: Huntington Library, 1971), 3, 175.

29. Frederick J. Turner, "The Significance of the Frontier in American History," http://xroads.virginia.edu/~HYPER/TURNER/home.html

30. Turner, "The Significance of the Frontier in American History."

31. Billington, *Genesis*, 78–80.

32. Ray A. Billington, *America's Frontier Heritage* (New York: Holt, Rinehart and Winston, 1966), 13.

33. Theodore Roosevelt to Frederick Jackson Turner, February 10, 1894, in *The Letters of Theodore Roosevelt*, ed. Elting E. Morison, 8 vols. (Cambridge: Harvard University Press, 1951), 1: 363; Theodore Roosevelt to Frederick Jackson Turner, April 26, 1895, in The *Letters of Theodore Roosevelt*, 1: 446; Theodore Roosevelt to Frederick Jackson Turner, April 10, 1895, in *The Letters of Theodore Roosevelt*, 1: 440.

34. Richard Slotkin, *Gunfighter Nation: The Myth of the Frontier in Twentieth-Century America* (New York: Atheneum, 1992), 61.

35. Billington, *Genesis*, 72.

36. Ronald H. Carpenter, "The Rhetorical Genesis of Style in the 'Frontier Hy-

pothesis' of Frederick Jackson Turner," *Southern Speech Communication Journal* 37 (1972): 234; Ronald H. Carpenter, "Frederick Jackson Turner and the Rhetorical Impact of the Frontier Thesis," *Quarterly Journal of Speech* 63 (1977): 123.

37. Mary E. Stuckey and John M. Murphy, "By Any Other Name: Rhetorical Colonialism in North America," *American Indian Culture and Research Journal* 25 (2001): 73–98.

38. Billington, *America's Frontier Heritage,* 14–15.

39. Billington, *Genesis,* 74.

40. See Brooks Adams, The *Law of Civilization and Decay: An Essay on History* (New York: Macmillan & Co., 1895).

41. Quoted in Brands, *T.R: The Last Romantic,* 308.

42. Theodore Roosevelt, "The Law of Civilization and Decay, January, 1897," in *American Ideals/The Strenuous Life/Realizable Ideals: The Works of Theodore Roosevelt,* 13: 242, 259–260.

43. David W. Noble, *The Progressive Mind: 1890–1917* (Minneapolis: Burgess Publishing Co., 1981), 172–173.

44. Gail Bederman, *Manliness and Civilization: A Cultural History of Gender and Race in the United States, 1880–1917* (Chicago: University of Chicago Press, 1995), 11–12, 170.

45. Sarah Watts, *Rough Rider in the White House: Theodore Roosevelt and the Politics of Desire* (Chicago: University of Chicago Press, 2003).

46. Theodore Roosevelt, "The Monroe Doctrine, March, 1896," in *American Ideals/The Strenuous Life/Realizable Ideals: The Works of Theodore Roosevelt,* 13: 177–179.

47. Roosevelt, "The Strenuous Life," in *American Ideals/The Strenuous Life/ Realizable Ideals: The Works of Theodore Roosevelt,* 13: 319, 328, 331.

48. Theodore Roosevelt, "At Chicago, Ill., April 2, 1903," in *Presidential Addresses and State Papers,* Homeward Bound Edition, 7 vols., 1: 266.

49. Recent scholarship argues that presidents have utilized the power of the rhetorical presidency from the beginning of the American Republic. See Leroy G. Dorsey, ed., *The Presidency and Rhetorical Leadership* (College Station: Texas A&M University Press, 2002).

50. James W. Ceaser, Glen E. Thurow, Jeffrey Tulis, and Joseph M. Bessette, "The Rise of the Rhetorical Presidency," *Presidential Studies Quarterly* 11 (1981): 162–163, 168–171.

51. Jeffrey K. Tulis, *The Rhetorical Presidency* (Princeton: Princeton University Press, 1987), 19.

52. Leroy G. Dorsey, "Sailing in the 'Wondrous Now': The Myth of the American Navy's World Cruise," *Quarterly Journal of Speech* 83 (1997): 447–465.

53. J. Michael Hogan, *The Panama Canal in American Politics: Domestic Advocacy and the Evolution of Policy* (Carbondale: Southern Illinois University Press, 1986), 34–54.

54. Harbaugh, *The Life and Times of Theodore Roosevelt,* 439–451, 471–473.

55. Theodore Roosevelt, "Americanism, October 12, 1915," in *America and the World War/Fear God and Take Your Own Part: The Works of Theodore Roosevelt,* 18: 393, 404–405.

56. Theodore Roosevelt, *Fear God and Take Your Own Part* (New York: George H. Doran Company, 1916), 54–55.

57. Dalton, *Theodore Roosevelt: A Strenuous Life,* 18–19.

58. Nathan Miller, *Theodore Roosevelt: A Life* (New York: William Morrow and Co., 1992), 31–32.

59. See Richard Hofstadter, *The American Political Tradition and the Men Who Made It* (New York: Vintage Books, 1954), 225–230; George E. Mowry, *Theodore Roosevelt and the Progressive Movement* (New York: Hill & Wang, 1946), 9–10; Henry F. Pringle, *Theodore Roosevelt: A Biography* (New York: Harcourt, Brace and Co., 1931), 208; Brands, *T. R.: The Last Romantic,* 541–542.

60. Leroy G. Dorsey, "Preaching Morality in Modern America: Theodore Roosevelt's Rhetorical Progressivism," in *Rhetoric and Reform in the Progressive Era, A Rhetorical History of the United States: Significant Moments in American Public Discourse,* ed. J. Michael Hogan, 10 vols. (East Lansing: Michigan State University Press, 2003), 6: 49–83.

61. Noble, *The Progressive Mind,* 172–173.

62. Ronald H. Carpenter, "The Historical Jeremiad as Rhetorical Genre," in *Form and Genre: Shaping Rhetorical Action,* ed. Karlyn K. Campbell and Kathleen H. Jamieson (Falls Church, VA: Speech Communication Association, 1978), 103–117. See also Sacvan Bercovitch, *The American Jeremiad* (Madison: University of Wisconsin Press, 1978), 9.

63. Ernest G. Bormann, "Fetching Good Out of Evil: A Rhetorical Use of Calamity," *Quarterly Journal of Speech* 63 (1977): 130–139.

64. John M. Murphy, "'A Time of Shame and Sorrow': Robert F. Kennedy and the American Jeremiad," *Quarterly Journal of Speech* 76 (1990): 401–414; Kurt W. Ritter, "American Political Rhetoric and the Jeremiad Tradition: Presidential Nomination Acceptance Addresses, 1960–1976," *Central States Speech Journal* 31 (1980): 153–171; Richard L. Johannesen, "Ronald Reagan's Economic Jeremiad," *Central States Speech Journal* 37 (1986), 79–89.

65. Jonathan Edwards, "Sinners in the Hands of an Angry God," in *American Rhetorical Discourse,* 3rd ed., ed. Ronald F. Reid and James F. Klumpp (1988; Long Grove, IL: Waveland Press, Inc., 2005), 66–78.

66. Theodore Roosevelt, "Machine Politics in New York City, November, 1886," in *American Ideals/The Strenuous Life/Realizable Ideals: The Works of Theodore Roosevelt,* 13: 81–82.

67. Sean Cashman, *American in the Age of the Titans: The Progressive Era and World War I* (New York: New York University Press, 1988), 10–12, 38–40.

68. Adams, *The Law of Civilization and Decay,* vii–viii, 32.

69. Alan Trachtenberg, *The Incorporation of America: Culture and Society in the Gilded Age* (New York: Hill & Wang, 1982), 83–84.

70. Gabriel Kolko, *The Triumph of Conservatism: A Reinterpretation of American History, 1900–1916* (New York: Free Press of Glencoe, 1963), 57–58.

71. Gabriel Kolko, *Main Currents in Modern American History* (New York: Pantheon Books, 1976), 16.

72. Theodore Roosevelt, "Highest Level of Prosperity Ever Attained, December 2, 1902," in *The Roosevelt Policy: Speeches, Letters and State Papers, relating to Corporate Wealth and Closely Allied Topics,* ed. William Griffith, 2 vols. (New York: Krause Reprint Co., 1971), 2: 611.

73. Richard L. Watson Jr., *The Development of National Power: The United States, 1900–1919* (Boston: Houghton Mifflin Company, 1976), 108.

74. Leroy G. Dorsey, "Theodore Roosevelt and Corporate America, 1901–1909: A Reexamination," *Presidential Studies Quarterly* 25 (1995): 725–739.

75. Harbaugh, *The Life and Times of Theodore Roosevelt,* 343; Theodore Roosevelt, "The Campaign Against Privilege, January 21, 1908," in *The Roosevelt Policy,* 2: 725.

76. Theodore Roosevelt, "False Standards Resulting from Swollen Fortunes," in *The Roosevelt Policy,* 1: 284–285.

77. Theodore Roosevelt, "Federal Supervision of Railways as an Executive not a Judicial Function, June 22, 1905," in *The Roosevelt Policy,* 1: 276; and Theodore Roosevelt, "Corporate Activity and 'Law Honesty,' October 20, 1905," in *The Roosevelt Policy,* 1: 311.

78. Hofstadter, *The American Political Tradition,* 225, 229.

79. Theodore Roosevelt, "The Administration of William McKinley, September 7, 1900," in *Campaigns and Controversies: The Works of Theodore Roosevelt,* 14: 348.

80. Theodore Roosevelt, "Annual Message, January 3, 1900," *State Papers as Governor and President, 1899–1909: The Works of Theodore Roosevelt,* 15: 44–45.

81. Theodore Roosevelt, "The Man with the Muck-Rake, April 14, 1906," in *American Problems: The Works of Theodore Roosevelt,* 16: 417–418.

82. Theodore Roosevelt, "True Americanism, April, 1894," in *American Ideals/ The Strenuous Life/Realizable Ideals: The Works of Theodore Roosevelt,* 13: 8–11.

83. Roosevelt, "Americanism in Municipal Politics," in *Campaigns and Controversies: The Works of Theodore Roosevelt,* 14: 192, 194, 200.

84. Theodore Roosevelt, "Fourth Annual Message, December 6, 1904," in *State Papers as Governor and President: The Works of Theodore Roosevelt,* 15: 245–246.

85. Theodore Roosevelt, "Sheridan, November 25, 1908," in *The Rough Riders and Men of Action: The Works of Theodore Roosevelt,* 11: 222.

86. Detailed discussions of assimilation and equality issues surrounding foreigners and nonwhites will be discussed in more detail in their respective chapters.

87. Hector St. John de Crèvecoeur, *Letters from an American Farmer* (1792; New York: Fox, Duffield, 1904), Letter 3: 54, http://xroads.virginia.edu/~HYPER/CREV/letter03.html.

88. Roger Daniels, *Coming to America: A History of Immigration and Ethnicity in American Life* (New York: HarperPerennial, 1990), 265.

89. Cashman, *America in the Age of the Titans*, 185–187.

90. Theodore Roosevelt, "A Colonial Survival, December 1892," in *Literary Essays: The Works of Theodore Roosevelt*, 12: 302–303.

91. Roosevelt, "Americanism in Municipal Politics," in *Campaigns and Controversies: The Works of Theodore Roosevelt*, 14: 24.

92. Thomas F. Gossett, *Race: The History of an Idea in America* (New York: Oxford University Press, 1997), 256–270.

93. Edmund Morris, *Theodore Rex* (New York: Random House, 2001), 258–259; Lewis L. Gould, *The Presidency of Theodore Roosevelt* (Lawrence: University Press of Kansas, 1991), 238–244.

94. Leonard Dinnerstein, Roger L. Nichols, and David M. Reimers, *Natives and Strangers: A Multicultural History of Americans* (New York: Oxford University Press, 1996), 99–100.

95. Thomas G. Dyer, *Theodore Roosevelt and the Idea of Race* (Baton Rouge: Louisiana State University Press, 1980), 5-6.

96. Theodore Roosevelt, "Religion and the Public Schools, November 1893," in *American Ideals/The Strenuous Life/Realizable Ideals: The Works of Theodore Roosevelt*, 13: 276.

97. Theodore Roosevelt, "Citizenship in a Republic, April 23, 1910," in *American Ideals/The Strenuous Life/Realizable Ideals: The Works of Theodore Roosevelt*, 13: 521–522.

98. Theodore Roosevelt, "How Not to Help Our Poorer Brother, January, 1897," in *American Ideals/The Strenuous Life/Realizable Ideals: The Works of Theodore Roosevelt*, 13: 165.

99. Theodore Roosevelt, "The Negro Problem, February 13, 1905," in *American Problems: The Works of Theodore Roosevelt*, 16: 348.

100. Joel Williamson, *The Crucible of Race: Black-White Relations in the American South since Emancipation* (New York: Oxford University Press, 1984), 341, 345–353.

101. Patricia O'Toole, *When Trumpets Call: Theodore Roosevelt after the White House* (New York: Simon & Schuster, 2005), 73.

102. Theodore Roosevelt, "Biological Analogies in History, June 7, 1910," in *Literary Essays: The Works of Theodore Roosevelt*, 12: 58.

103. Robert Friedenberg, *Theodore Roosevelt and the Rhetoric of Militant Decency* (New York: Greenwood Press, 1990), 20–23; Hofstadter, *The American Political Tradition*, 208–209.

104. Roosevelt, "Americanism," in *America and the World War/Fear God and Take Your Own Part: The Works of Theodore Roosevelt*, 18: 392–93, 402.

105. King, *Making Americans*, 90.

106. Mary Stuckey, *Defining Americans: The Presidency and National Identity* (Lawrence: University Press of Kansas, 2004), 187–188.

107. Dalton, *Theodore Roosevelt: A Strenuous Life*, 462.

108. Theodore Roosevelt, "The Children of the Crucible, 1917," in *The Foes of Our Own Household/The Great Adventure/Letters to his Children: The Works of Theodore Roosevelt*, 19: 34.

109. Theodore Roosevelt, "The Square Deal in Americanism, 1918," in *The Foes of Our Own Household/The Great Adventure/Letters to his Children: The Works of Theodore Roosevelt*, 19: 301; Theodore Roosevelt, "Nine-Tenths of Wisdom is Being Wise in Time, June 14, 1917," in *The Foes of Our Own Household/The Great Adventure/Letters to his Children: The Works of Theodore Roosevelt*, 19: 34.

110. Theodore Roosevelt, "Speech of Col. Theodore Roosevelt at the New York Republican State Convention, Saratoga, N. Y., July 18, 1918," in *The Theodore Roosevelt Collection*, Harvard College Library, TRC-SP-1 (12), Speeches, 1918, 1. Use is by permission of the Houghton Library, Harvard University.

111. Richard Slotkin, "Dreams and Genocide: The American Myth of Regeneration through Violence," *Journal of Popular Culture* 5 (1971): 38.

112. David Leeming, *Myth: A Biography of Belief* (Oxford: Oxford University Press, 2002), 7.

113. Bercovitch, *The American Jeremiad*, 113–114.

114. Sacvan Bercovitch, *The Rites of Assent: Transformations in the Symbolic Construction of America* (New York: Routledge, 1993), 6, 41.

115. Sacvan Bercovitch, *The Puritan Origins of the American Self* (New Haven: Yale University Press, 1975), 136.

116. Richard Slotkin, *Regeneration through Violence: The Mythology of the American Frontier, 1600–1860* (Norman: University of Oklahoma Press, 1973); Richard Slotkin, *The Fatal Environment: The Myth of the Frontier in the Age of Industrialization, 1800–1890* (New York: Atheneum, 1985); Slotkin, *Gunfighter Nation*.

117. Slotkin, *Gunfighter Nation*, 10–11.

118. Slotkin, *The Fatal Environment*, 19.

119. Jim Cullen, *The American Dream: A Short History of an Idea That Shaped a Nation* (Oxford: Oxford University Press, 2003), 11–12.

120. Slotkin, *The Fatal Environment*, 24.

121. Jenni Calder, *There Must Be a Lone Ranger: The American West in Film and in Reality* (New York: Taplinger, 1974), 1.

122. Janice H. Rushing, "Mythic Evolution of 'The New Frontier' in Mass Mediated Rhetoric," *Critical Studies in Mass Communication* 3 (1986): 270, 272.

123. David H. Murdoch, *The American West: The Invention of a Myth* (Reno: University of Nevada Press, 2001), 44–53.

124. See Slotkin, *Gunfighter Nation;* Henry N. Smith, *Virgin Land: The American West as Symbol and Myth* (Cambridge: Harvard University Press, 1978).

125. Murdoch, *The American West*, 27–28.

126. Rushing, "Mythic Evolution," 265, 272.

127. See John S. Lawrence and Robert Jewett, *The Myth of the American Superhero* (Grand Rapids: William B. Eerdmans Publishing Co., 2002).

128. Slotkin, *Gunfighter Nation*, 12.

129. Slotkin, *The Fatal Environment*, 531–532.

130. Slotkin, *Gunfighter Nation*, 13.

131. Slotkin, *Gunfighter Nation*, 33–37.

132. Theodore Roosevelt, *Ranch Life and the Hunting Trail*, in *Hunting Trips of a Ranchman/Ranch Life and the Hunting Trail: The Works of Theodore Roosevelt*, 1: 351, 366.

133. Theodore Roosevelt, "Address at the Hungarian Club Dinner, New York City, February 14, 1905," in *Presidential Address and State Papers: The Works of Theodore Roosevelt*, 6: 240.

134. Stuckey refers to this as "celebratory othering." See *Defining Americans*, 4–6.

Chapter 2

1. Vanessa B. Beasley, *You, the People: American National Identity in Presidential Rhetoric* (College Station: Texas A&M University Press, 2004), 74–78.

2. Beasley, *You, the People*, 80.

3. Mary E. Stuckey, *Defining Americans: The Presidency and National Identity* (Lawrence: University Press of Kansas, 2004), 161.

4. Stuckey, *Defining Americans*, 188.

5. Edmund Morris, *Theodore Rex* (New York: Random House, 2001), 37.

6. Theodore Roosevelt, "How Not to Help Our Poorer Brother, January, 1897," in *American Ideals/The Strenuous Life/Realizable Ideal: The Works of Theodore Roosevelt*, National ed. (New York: Charles Scribner's Sons, 1926), 13: 164; Theodore Roosevelt, "True Americanism, April, 1894," in *American Ideals/The Strenuous Life/Realizable Ideal*, 13: 22.

7. G. Wallace Chessman, *Theodore Roosevelt and the Politics of Power*, ed. Oscar Handlin (Boston: Little, Brown, 1969), 27.

8. According to Samuel P. Huntington, stories of America's origin privileged "settlers" who came to "create a new community," and dismissed "immigrants" who simply moved "from one society to a different society." See *Who Are We? The Challenges to America's National Identity* (New York: Simon & Schuster, 2004), 38–43.

9. Richard Slotkin, *Gunfighter Nation: The Myth of the Frontier in Twentieth-Century America* (New York: Atheneum, 1992), 61.

10. Marion T. Bennett, *American Immigration Policies: A History* (Washington, D.C.: Public Affairs Press, 1963), 12–14.

11. Keith Fitzgerald, *The Face of the Nation: Immigration, the State, and the National Identity* (Stanford: Stanford University Press, 1996), 98–99.

12. Bennett, *American Immigration Policies*, 13; Fitzgerald, *The Face of the Nation*, 112.

13. Fitzgerald, *The Face of the Nation*, 97.

14. Fitzgerald, *The Face of the Nation*, 107.

15. Kitty Calavita, *U.S. Immigration Law and the Control of Labor: 1820–1924* (London: Academic Press, 1994), 41.

16. William S. Bernard, *American Immigration Policy—A Reappraisal* (Port Washington, NY: Kennikat, 1940), 9.

17. Slotkin, *Gunfighter Nation*, 31.

18. Bennett, *American Immigration Policies*, 17–18, 37; Roger Daniels, *Not Like Us: Immigrants and Minorities in America, 1890–1924* (Chicago: Ivan R. Dee, 1997), 73–74.

19. Paul McBride, *Culture Clash: Immigrants and Reformers, 1880–1920* (San Francisco: R and E Research Associates, 1975), 5.

20. Calavita, *U.S. Immigration Law*, 104. See also Richard Hofstadter, *Social Darwinism in American Thought* (New York: Braziller, 1959).

21. Lawrence G. Brown, *Immigration: Cultural Conflicts and Social Adjustments* (New York: Arno Press and the New York Times, 1994), 222–224; Edith Abbott, *Immigration: Select Documents and Case Records* (New York: Arno Press and the New York Times, 1969), 192–198.

22. H. W. Brands, *T. R.: The Last Romantic* (New York: BasicBooks, 1997), 762–763.

23. Matthew Frye Jacobson, *Whiteness of a Different Color: European Immigrants and the Alchemy of Race* (Cambridge: Harvard University Press, 1998), 22–23.

24. David R. Roediger, *The Wages of Whiteness: Race and the Making of the American Working Class,* Revised ed. (New York: Verso, 2003), 21.

25. Jacobson, *Whiteness of a Different Color,* 40.

26. Noel Ignatiev, *How the Irish Became White* (New York: Routledge, 1995), 41, 129–130.

27. Thomas A. Guglielmo, *White on Arrival: Italians, Race, Color, and Power in Chicago, 1890–1945* (Oxford: Oxford University Press, 2003), 7, 36.

28. Guglielmo, *White on Arrival,* 168–169.

29. David R. Roediger, *Working toward Whiteness: How America's Immigrants Became White—The Strange Journey from Ellis Island to the Suburbs* (New York: Basic Books, 2005), 62.

30. Ian F. Haney López, *White by Law: The Legal Construction of Race* (New York: New York University Press, 1996), 27–28.

31. Jacobson, *Whiteness of a Different Color,* 31–36.

32. Haney López, *White by Law,* 65–66.

33. Thomas G. Dyer, *Theodore Roosevelt and the Idea of Race* (Baton Rouge: Louisiana State University Press, 1980), 167.

34. Theodore Roosevelt, *The Winning of the West: An Account of the Exploration and Settlement of Our Country from the Alleghanies to the Pacific* in *The Works of Theodore Roosevelt,* National ed. (New York: Charles Scribner's Sons, 1926), 8: 88–89.

35. Sarah Watts, *Rough Rider in the White House: Theodore Roosevelt and the Politics of Desire* (Chicago: University of Chicago Press, 2003), 173–174.

36. Joseph Campbell, *The Power of Myth with Bill Moyers,* ed. Betty S. Flowers (New York: Anchor Books, 1991), 151–206.

37. James O. Robertson, *American Myth, American Reality* (New York: Hill & Wang, 1980), 135–136.

38. Joseph Campbell, *The Hero with a Thousand Faces* (1949; Princeton: Princeton University Press, 1973), 30.

39. Campbell, *The Hero with a Thousand Faces,* 39.

40. Roosevelt, *The Winning of the West,* 8: 7–18.

41. Campbell, *The Hero with a Thousand Faces,* 97–109.

42. Roosevelt, *The Winning of the West,* 8: 87–88.

43. Roosevelt, *The Winning of the West,* 8: 90, 94, 227.

44. Roosevelt, *The Winning of the West,* 8: 100–101.

45. Campbell, *The Hero with a Thousand Faces,* 79.

46. Roosevelt, *The Winning of the West,* 8: 28, 64, 116; Roosevelt, *The Winning of the West,* 9: 140.

47. Roosevelt, *The Winning of the West,* 8: 117–118.

48. Roosevelt, *The Winning of the West,* 8: 35, 99–100.

49. Janice H. Rushing, "Mythic Evolution of 'The New Frontier' in Mass Mediated Rhetoric," *Critical Studies in Mass Communication* 3 (1986): 272.

50. Roosevelt, *The Winning of the West,* 9: 64, 68–69, 78.

51. Roosevelt, *The Winning of the West,* 9: 75.

52. Theodore Roosevelt, *Thomas Hart Benton,* in *Thomas Hart Benton/ Gouverneur Morris: The Works of Theodore Roosevelt,* 12: 103.

53. Roosevelt, *The Winning of the West,* 8: 84–88, 148, 124–125, 278–279, 290–292, 382–383.

54. Janice Rushing, "Evolution of 'The New Frontier' in *Alien* and *Aliens:* Patriarchal Co-optation of the Feminine Archetype," *Quarterly Journal of Speech* 75 (1989): 1.

55. Roosevelt, *The Winning of the West,* 8: 93, 139–140.

56. Roosevelt, *The Winning of the West,* 9: 76–77.

57. Roosevelt, *The Winning of the West,* 8: 391, 546; Roosevelt, *The Winning of the West,* 9: 70–71.

58. The implications of Roosevelt's rhetoric regarding Native Americans will be explored in more detail in chapter 3.

59. Roosevelt, *The Winning of the West,* 8: 14.

60. Slotkin, *Gunfighter Nation,* 40.

61. Roosevelt, *The Winning of the West,* 8: 70–71.

62. Slotkin, *Gunfighter Nation,* 39.

63. Roosevelt, *The Winning of the West,* 9: 58, 274–275.

64. Roosevelt, *The Winning of the West,* 8: 105.

65. Roosevelt, *The Winning of the West,* 9: 454.

66. Roosevelt, *The Winning of the West,* 9: 454.

67. Campbell, *The Hero with a Thousand Faces,* 193.

68. Desmond King, *Making Americans: Immigration, Race, and the Origins of the Diverse Democracy* (Cambridge: Harvard University Press, 2000), 50–52; Roger Daniels, *Coming to America: A History of Immigration and Ethnicity in American Life* (Princeton: HarperCollins, 1990), 121.

69. Roosevelt, *The Winning of the West,* 9: 36.

70. Roosevelt, *The Winning of the West,* 8: 84–87.

71. Roosevelt, *The Winning of the West,* 8: 52, 77; Roosevelt, *The Winning of the West,* 9: 546.

72. Roosevelt, *The Winning of the West,* 8: 569–570.

73. Roosevelt, *The Winning of the West,* 9: 105.

74. Roosevelt, *The Winning of the West,* 8: 33, 35–37.

75. Roosevelt, *The Winning of the West,* 8: 8.

76. Roosevelt, *The Winning of the West,* 8: 17–18.

77. Roosevelt, *The Winning of the West,* 8: 17.

78. Janice H. Rushing, "The Rhetoric of the American Western Myth," *Communication Monographs* 50 (1983): 16.

79. Roosevelt, *The Winning of the West,* 8: 73.

80. Roosevelt, *The Winning of the West,* 9: 198–199.

81. Roosevelt, *The Winning of the West,* 9: 11–12.

82. Roosevelt, *The Winning of the West,* 8: 151–152.

83. Roosevelt, *The Winning of the West,* 8: 93, 407; Roosevelt, *The Winning of the West,* 9: 451.

84. Roosevelt, *The Winning of the West,* 8: 89.

85. McBride, *Culture Clash,* 3–4.

Chapter 3

1. Richard Drinnon, *Facing West: The Metaphysics of Indian-Hating and Empire Building* (Norman: University of Oklahoma Press, 1997), 51.

2. Thomas F. Gossett, *Race: The History of an Idea in America,* New ed. (New York: Oxford University Press, 1997), 20–21.

3. Colin G. Calloway, *New Worlds for All: Indians, Europeans, and the Remaking of Early America* (Baltimore: Johns Hopkins University Press, 1997), 9–11.

4. Colin G. Calloway, ed., *The World Turned Upside Down: Indian Voices from Early America* (Boston: Bedford/St. Martin's Press, 1994), 5.

5. Calloway, *New Worlds for All,* 197.

6. Drinnon, *Facing West,* 86–87, 103–116; Calloway, *New Worlds for All,* 38–39; Brian W. Dippie, *The Vanishing American: White Attitudes and U.S. Indian Policy* (Lawrence: University Press of Kansas, 1982), 34–35, 68–69, 111–121.

7. Richard Slotkin, *Gunfighter Nation: The Myth of the Frontier in Twentieth-Century America* (New York: Atheneum, 1992), 12–14.

8. Calloway, *New Worlds for All,* 110–111; Dippie, *The Vanishing American,* 18–19, 97–98.

9. Roosevelt quoted in Thomas G. Dyer, *Theodore Roosevelt and the Idea of Race* (Baton Rouge: Louisiana State University Press, 1980), 86.

10. Gary Gerstle, *American Crucible: Race and Nation in the Twentieth Century* (Princeton: Princeton University Press, 2001), 20–22.

11. Dyer, *Theodore Roosevelt and the Idea of Race,* 70, 88.

12. Lewis L. Gould, *The Presidency of Theodore Roosevelt* (Lawrence: University Press of Kansas, 1991), 209.

13. Frederick E. Hoxie, *A Final Promise: The Campaign to Assimilate the Indians, 1880–1920* (Cambridge: Cambridge University Press, 1984), 105.

14. Dippie, *The Vanishing American,* 183–185.

15. David W. Adams, *Education for Extinction: American Indians and the Boarding School Experience, 1875–1928* (Lawrence: University Press of Kansas, 1995), 6.

16. John C. Mohawk, "Indian and Democracy: No One Ever Told Us," in *Exiled in the Land of the Free: Democracy, Indian Nations, and the U.S. Constitution,* ed. Oren Lyons, John Mohawk, Vine Deloria Jr., Laurence Hauptman, Howard Berman, Donald Grinde Jr., Curtis Berkey, and Robert Venables (Santa Fe: Clear Light Publishers, 1992), 47–48.

17. Calloway, *New Worlds for All,* 93–95.

18. Stephen Cornell, *The Return of the Native: American Indian Political Resurgence* (New York: Oxford University Press, 1988), 15–16.

19. Calloway, *New Worlds,* 129–131.

20. Cornell, *The Return of the Native,* 15–24, 34.

21. Cornell, *The Return of the Native,* 25–33.

22. Henry E. Fritz, *The Movement for Indian Assimilation, 1860–1890* (Philadelphia: University of Pennsylvania Press, 1963), 109.

23. Drinnon, *Facing West,* xxvi.

24. Cornell, *The Return of the Native,* 12.

25. Cornell, *The Return of the Native,* 12.

26. Cornell, *The Return of the Native,* 40.

27. Drinnon, *Facing West,* 86, 96.

28. Dippie, *The Vanishing American,* 5.

29. Duane Champagne, ed., *Chronology of Native North American History: From Pre-Columbian Times to the Present* (Detroit: Gale Research Inc., 1994), 148.

30. Cornell, *The Return of the Native,* 48–50.

31. Dippie, *The Vanishing American,* 9.

32. Dippie, *The Vanishing American,* 8; Champagne, *Chronology of Native North American History,* 131.

33. U.S. Commission on Human Rights, "A Historical Context for Evaluation," in *Native Americans and Public Policy,* ed. Fremont J. Lyden and Lyman H. Legters (Pittsburgh: University of Pittsburgh Press, 1992), 16–17; "Indian Removal: 1814–1858," at http://www.pbs.org/wgbh/aia/part4/4p2959.html.

34. Colin G. Calloway, ed., *Our Hearts Fell to the Ground: Plains Indian Views of How the West Was Lost* (Boston: Bedford Books of St. Martin's Press, 1996), 102–103.

35. Champagne, *Chronology of Native North American History,* 193–194; Helen H. Jackson, *A Century of Dishonor: A Sketch of the United States Government's Dealings with Some of the Indian Tribes* (1885; Norman: University of Oklahoma Press, 1995), 131–133.

36. Calloway, *The World Turned Upside Down,* 155.

37. Champagne, *Chronology of Native North American History,* 170, 181–182.

38. James O. Robertson, *American Myth, American Reality* (New York: Hill & Wang, 1980), 108.

39. Slotkin, *Gunfighter Nation,* 11–12.

40. John M. Coward, *The Newspaper Indian: Native American Identity in the Press, 1820–90* (Urbana: University of Illinois Press, 1999), 31.

41. Raymond W. Stedman, *Shadows of the Indian: Stereotypes in American Culture* (Norman: University of Oklahoma Press, 1982), 75–76.

42. Drinnon, *Facing West,* 120.

43. Stedman, *Shadows of the Indian,* 79–82.

44. Philip J. Deloria, *Playing Indian* (New Haven: Yale University Press, 1998), 44.

45. Drinnon, *Facing West,* 41.

46. Adams, *Education for Extinction,* 27.

47. Dippie, *The Vanishing American,* 71–75.

48. Cornell, *The Return of the Native,* 12.

49. Cornell, *The Return of the Native,* 56–57.

50. Adams, *Education for Extinction,* 100–101.

51. Adams, *Education for Extinction,* 97–121.

52. Adams, *Education for Extinction,* 22.

53. Adams, *Education for Extinction,* 167–170.

54. Coward, *The Newspaper Indian,* 221.

55. Calloway, *Our Hearts Fell to the Ground,* 18.

56. Cornell, *The Return of the Native,* 62.

57. Richard Morris and Philip Wander, "Native American Rhetoric: Dancing in the Shadows of the Ghost Dance," *Quarterly Journal of Speech* 76 (1990): 168.

58. Brian W. Dippie, *Custer's Last Stand: The Anatomy of an American Myth* (Lincoln: University of Nebraska Press, 1976), 105.

59. Dee Brown, *Bury My Heart at Wounded Knee: An Indian History of the American West* (New York: Holt, Rinehart & Winston, 1970), 431–444.

60. Shari M. Huhndorf, *Going Native: Indians in the American Cultural Imagination* (Ithaca: Cornell University Press, 2001), 21.

61. Robert W. Rydell, *All the World's a Fair: Visions of Empire at American International Expositions, 1876–1916* (Chicago: University of Chicago Press, 1984), 95.

62. Robertson, *American Myth,* 109.

63. Stedman, *Shadows of the Indian,* 21–25.

64. Coward, *The Newspaper Indian,* 8.

65. See Deloria, *Playing Indian;* Huhndorf, *Going Native.*

66. Coward, *The Newspaper Indian,* 8–9.

67. Hoxie, *A Final Promise*, 106.

68. Theodore Roosevelt, *Theodore Roosevelt: An Autobiography* (1913; New York: Charles Scribner's Sons, 1929), 112–113.

69. Janice Rushing, "Mythic Evolution of 'The New Frontier' in Mass Mediated Rhetoric," *Critical Studies in Mass Communication* 3 (1986): 272.

70. Slotkin, *Gunfighter Nation*, 11–13.

71. Robertson, *American Myth*, 108.

72. Deloria, *Playing Indian*, 104.

73. Coward, *The Newspaper Indian*, 72.

74. Theodore Roosevelt, *The Winning of the West: An Account of the Exploration and Settlement of our Country from the Alleghanies to the Pacific*, in *The Works of Theodore Roosevelt*, National ed. (New York: Charles Scribner's Sons, 1926), 8: 68.

75. Roosevelt, *The Winning of the West*, 8: 69, 277.

76. Roosevelt, *The Winning of the West*, 8: 75.

77. Roosevelt, *The Winning of the West*, 8: 14.

78. Roosevelt, *The Winning of the West*, 8: 14.

79. Roosevelt, *The Winning of the West*, 8: 64–68.

80. Theodore Roosevelt, *Thomas Hart Benton/Gouverneur Morris*, in *The Works of Theodore Roosevelt*, 7: 136.

81. Roosevelt, *The Winning of the West*, 9: 321.

82. Roosevelt, *Thomas Hart Benton*, 7: 136.

83. Theodore Roosevelt, *Ranch Life and the Hunting Trail* in *Hunting Trips of a Ranchman/Ranch Life and the Hunting Trail: The Works of Theodore Roosevelt*, 1: 374–375.

84. Roosevelt, *Ranch Life and the Hunting Trail*, 1: 374–375.

85. Dippie, *The Vanishing American*, 25.

86. Roosevelt, *The Winning of the West*, 8: 167.

87. Roosevelt, *The Winning of the West*, 8: 167–168.

88. Richard Slotkin, *The Fatal Environment: The Myth of the Frontier in the Age of Industrialization, 1800–1890* (Norman: University of Oklahoma Press, 1994), 39–41.

89. Roosevelt, *The Winning of the West*, 8: 73.

90. Theodore Roosevelt, *Outdoor Pastimes of an American Hunter, II/A Book-Lover's Holidays in the Open*, in *The Works of Theodore Roosevelt*, 3: 233.

91. Dippie, *The Vanishing American*, 34–36; Desmond King, *Making Americans: Immigration, Race, and the Origins of the Diverse Democracy* (Cambridge: Harvard University Press, 2000), 72.

92. Cornell, *The Return of the Native*, 43.

93. Coward, *The Newspaper Indian*, 46.

94. Theodore Roosevelt, "Civil-Service Reform: A Report of Stewardship, February 21, 1893," *Campaigns and Controversies: The Works of Theodore Roosevelt*, 14: 160–161.

95. Gould, *The Presidency of Theodore Roosevelt*, 208; Hoxie, *A Final Promise*,

103; Edmund Morris, *The Rise of Theodore Roosevelt* (New York: The Modern Library, 1979), 466–467.

96. See, for example, Roosevelt, "Civil-Service Reform," in *Campaigns and Controversies,* 14: 160.

97. Jackson, *A Century of Dishonor,* 338.

98. Theodore Roosevelt, "Fourth Annual Message, December 6, 1904," in *State Papers as Governor and President, 1899–1909,* in *The Works of Theodore Roosevelt,* 15: 240.

99. Theodore Roosevelt, "Remarks of President Roosevelt to the Tulsa (Oklahoma) Commercial Club, The White House, April 17, 1908," *The Theodore Roosevelt Collection,* Harvard College Library, TRC-SP-1 (4), Speeches, 1904–1909, 65. Use is by permission of the Houghton Library, Harvard University.

100. Theodore Roosevelt, *Report of Hon. Theodore Roosevelt made to the United States Civil Service Commission, Upon a Visit to Certain Indian Reservations and Indian Schools in South Dakota, Nebraska, and Kansas (1893),* in *The Theodore Roosevelt Collection,* Harvard College Library, TRC-SP-1 (2), Speeches 1891–1899: 14–15. Use is by permission of the Houghton Library, Harvard University.

101. Theodore Roosevelt, "First Annual Message, December 3, 1901," in *State Papers as Governor and President,* 15: 129.

102. Roosevelt, "Fourth Annual Message, December 6, 1904," in *State Papers as Governor and President,* 15: 239–240.

103. Calloway, *Our Hearts Fell to the Ground,* 17–19.

104. Roosevelt, "First Annual Message," in *State Papers as Governor and President,* 15: 130.

105. Dippie, *The Vanishing American,* 184.

106. Theodore Roosevelt, "Second Annual Message, December 2, 1902," in *State Papers as Governor and President,* 15: 164.

107. Theodore Roosevelt, "The Issues of 1900, September 15, 1900," in *Campaigns and Controversies.* 14: 371.

108. Joseph Campbell, *The Hero with a Thousand Faces* (1949; Princeton: Princeton University Press, 1973), 42, 155, 177.

109. Gerstle, *American Crucible,* 22.

110. Roosevelt, *Report of Hon. Theodore Roosevelt, The Roosevelt Collection,* 8.

111. Theodore Roosevelt, *Ranch Life and the Hunting Trail,* in *Hunting Trips of a Ranchman/Ranch Life and the Hunting Trail,* 1: 352.

112. Roosevelt, *Ranch Life and the Hunting Trail,* 1: 377.

113. Roosevelt, "Second Annual Message," in *State Papers as Governor and President,* 15: 163.

114. Adams, *Education for Extinction,* 209–238.

115. Calloway, *Our Hearts Fell to the Ground,* 19–20.

116. Joel Williamson, *The Crucible of Race: Black-White Relations in the American South since Emancipation* (New York: Oxford University Press, 1984), 32.

117. Dippie, *The Vanishing American,* 82.

Chapter 4

1. Mia Bay, *The White Image in the Black Mind: African-American Ideas about White People, 1830–1925* (New York: Oxford University Press, 2000), 188.

2. Thomas Dyer, *Theodore Roosevelt and the Idea of Race* (Baton Rouge: Louisiana State University Press, 1980), 91–92, 100, 102; August Meier, *Negro Thought in America, 1880–1915: Racial Ideologies in the Age of Booker T. Washington* (Ann Arbor: University of Michigan Press, 1964), 164; H. W. Brands, *T. R.: The Last Romantic* (New York: Basic Books, 1997), 496; Kathleen Dalton, *Theodore Roosevelt: A Strenuous Life* (New York: Alfred A. Knopf, 2002), 183; Lee D. Baker, *From Savage to Negro: Anthropology and the Construction of Race, 1896–1954* (Berkeley: University of California Press, 1998), 84–86; Patricia O'Toole, *When Trumpets Call: Theodore Roosevelt after the White House* (New York: Simon & Schuster, 2005), 194.

3. See Dalton, *Theodore Roosevelt: A Strenuous Life*, 183; Lewis L. Gould, *The Presidency of Theodore Roosevelt* (Lawrence: University Press of Kansas, 1991), 23, 119–121.

4. See Dyer, *Theodore Roosevelt and the Idea of Race*, 102, 105; Brands, *T. R.: The Last Romantic*, 588; Edmund Morris, *Theodore Rex* (New York: Random House, 2001), 258–259, 424–425.

5. Dyer, *Theodore Roosevelt and the Idea of Race*, 89, 92.

6. Brands, *T. R.: The Last Romantic*, 496, 499–500.

7. Gary Gerstle, *American Crucible: Race and Nation in the Twentieth Century* (Princeton: Princeton University Press, 2001), 22–23, 46, 62, 65.

8. Gerstle, *American Crucible*, 63–64.

9. Daniel J. Tichenor, *Dividing Lines: The Politics of Immigration Control in America* (Princeton: Princeton University Press, 2002), 3–5; Brian W. Dippie, *The Vanishing American: White Attitudes and U.S. Indian Policy* (Lawrence: University Press of Kansas, 1982), 200.

10. U.S. Census Bureau, Historical Census Statistics on Population Totals By Race, 1790 to 1990, and By Hispanic Origin, United States—Race and Hispanic Origin: 1790 to 1990, http://www.census.gov/population/documentation/twps0056/tab01.pdf.

11. Gerstle, *American Crucible*, 62.

12. Gerstle, *American Crucible*, 17.

13. Morris, *Theodore Rex*, 172, 465.

14. Gerstle, *American Crucible*, 46.

15. Bay, *The White Image in the Black Mind*, 144.

16. James O. Robertson, *American Myth, American Reality* (New York: Hill & Wang, 1980), 93.

17. Robertson, *American Myth*, 100.

18. Thomas F. Gossett, *Race: The History of an Idea in America* (New York: Oxford University Press, 1997), 261–262.

19. Bay, *The White Image in the Black Mind*, 147.

20. John Kisch and Edward Mapp, *A Separate Cinema: Fifty Years of Black-Cast Posters* (New York: Noonday Press, 1992), xiv; Donald Bogle, *Toms, Coons, Mulattoes, Mammies, and Bucks: An Interpretive History of Blacks in American Films*, 3rd ed. (New York: Continuum, 1994), 3–4.

21. Kisch and Mapp, *A Separate Cinema*, xiv.

22. Cited in Gossett, *Race*, 263.

23. Bay, *The White Image in the Black Mind*, 190.

24. Matthew P. Guterl, *The Color of Race in America, 1900–1940* (Cambridge: Harvard University Press, 2001), 33.

25. Marouf A. Hasian Jr., *The Rhetoric of Eugenics in Anglo-American Thought* (Athens: University of Georgia Press, 1996), 57.

26. Robertson, *American Myth*, 97.

27. Guterl, *The Color of Race in America*, 104; and Gunnar Myrdal, *An American Dilemma: The Negro Problem and Modern Democracy* (1944; New Brunswick: Transaction Publishers, 2002), 1: 88.

28. Sean D. Cashman, *American in the Age of the Titans: The Progressive Era and World War I* (New York: New York University Press, 1988), 158–159; Gossett, *Race*, 255–257.

29. Joel Williamson, *A Rage for Order: Black/White Relations in the American South since Emancipation* (New York: Oxford University Press, 1986), 175–176.

30. Roger Daniels, *Not Like Us: Immigrants and Minorities in America, 1890–1924* (Chicago: Ivan R. Dee, 1997), 37.

31. Herbert Shapiro, *White Violence and Black Response: From Reconstruction to Montgomery* (Amherst: University of Massachusetts Press, 1988), 30.

32. Daniels, *Not Like Us*, 37; Gossett, *Race*, 269.

33. Shapiro, *White Violence and Black Response*, 31.

34. Williamson, *A Rage for Order*, 190.

35. Robertson, *American Myth*, 104.

36. Louis R. Harlan, *Booker T. Washington: The Wizard of Tuskegee, 1901–1915* (New York: Oxford University Press, 1986).

37. Meier, *Negro Thought in America*, 98–99.

38. Robertson, *American Myth*, 104.

39. See Meier, *Negro Thought in America*, 194; Guterl, *The Color of Race in America*, 100; and Williamson, *A Rage for Order*, 65.

40. W. E. Burghardt Du Bois, "The Talented Tenth," in *The Negro Problem: A Series of Articles by Representative American Negroes of To-Day*, Booker T. Washington, W. E. B. Du Bois, et al. (1903; New York: Arno Press and the New York Times, 1969), 33, 75.

41. John D. Weaver, *The Brownsville Raid* (College Station: Texas A&M University Press, 1992), 267.

42. Dyer, *Theodore Roosevelt and the Idea of Race*, 3–5.

43. Gerstle, *American Crucible*, 17.

44. Dyer, *Theodore Roosevelt and the Idea of Race*, 89.

45. Gerstle, *American Crucible,* 43, 64.

46. Dyer, *Theodore Roosevelt and the Idea of Race,* 91–92, 100.

47. Joseph L. Gardner, *Departing Glory: Theodore Roosevelt as ex-President* (New York: Charles Scribner's Sons, 1973), 80.

48. Theodore Roosevelt, *Theodore Roosevelt: An Autobiography* (1913; New York: Charles Scribner's Sons, 1929), 54.

49. Leroy G. Dorsey, "The Frontier Myth in Presidential Rhetoric: Theodore Roosevelt's Campaign for Conservation," *Western Journal of Communication* 59 (1995): 1–19; Leroy G. Dorsey and Rachel M. Harlow, "'We Want Americans Pure and Simple': Theodore Roosevelt and the Myth of Americanism," *Rhetoric & Public Affairs* 6 (2003): 55–78; Richard Slotkin, *Gunfighter Nation: The Myth of the Frontier in Twentieth-Century America* (New York: Atheneum, 1992), 29–62.

50. Ernest G. Bormann, "Symbolic Convergence Theory: A Communication Formulation," *Journal of Communication* 35 (1985): 130.

51. Gossett, *Race,* 3; Robertson, *American Myth,* 97.

52. Matthew F. Jacobson, *Whiteness of a Different Color: European Immigrants and the Alchemy of Race* (Cambridge: Harvard University Press, 1998), 22.

53. Gossett, *Race,* 244.

54. Robertson, *American Myth* 94.

55. Williamson, *A Rage for Order,* 44.

56. Gerstle, *American Crucible,* 36–37.

57. Theodore Roosevelt, *The Rough Riders* (1899; New York: Signet/The New American Library, 1961), 94–96.

58. Dorsey and Harlow, "We Want Americans Pure and Simple," 55–78.

59. Theodore Roosevelt, *Outdoor Pastimes of an American Hunter II/A Book Lover's Holidays in the Open: The Works of Theodore Roosevelt,* National ed. (New York: Charles Scribner's Sons, 1926), 3: 144–145.

60. Theodore Roosevelt, "The Strenuous Life, April 10, 1899," in *American Ideals/ The Strenuous Life/Realizable Ideals: The Works of Theodore Roosevelt,* 13: 319–320.

61. Theodore Roosevelt, *The Winning of the West: An Account of the Exploration and Settlement of our Country from the Alleghanies to the Pacific,* in *The Works of Theodore Roosevelt,* 8: 150–151.

62. Theodore Roosevelt, "The Duties of American Citizenship, January 26, 1893," in *American Ideals/The Strenuous Life/Realizable Ideals: The Works of Theodore Roosevelt,* 13: 281, 284, 286.

63. Theodore Roosevelt, "The Law of Civilization and Decay, January 1897," in *American Ideals/The Strenuous Life/Realizable Ideals: The Works of Theodore Roosevelt,* 13: 240.

64. Roosevelt, "The Duties of American Citizenship," in *American Ideals/The Strenuous Life/Realizable Ideals: The Works of Theodore Roosevelt,* 13: 281–282, 296.

65. Williamson, *A Rage for Order,* 225–226.

66. Dyer, *Theodore Roosevelt and the Idea of Race,* 97.

67. Williamson, *A Rage for Order,* 227.

68. Edmund Morris, *The Rise of Theodore Roosevelt* (New York: The Modern Library, 1979), 254.

69. Theodore Roosevelt, "The Nomination for Temporary Chairman of the Republican Convention, June 3, 1884," in *Campaigns and Controversies: The Works of Theodore Roosevelt*, 14: 38.

70. Brands, *T. R.: The Last Romantic*, 221–226.

71. Theodore Roosevelt, "An Object-Lesson in Civil-Service Reform," in *Campaigns and Controversies: The Works of Theodore Roosevelt*, 14: 120.

72. Theodore Roosevelt, "Civil-Service Reform: A Report of Stewardship, February 21, 1893," in *Campaigns and Controversies: The Works of Theodore Roosevelt*, 14: 162, 165.

73. Baker, *From Savage to Negro*, 84; Gould, *The Presidency of Theodore Roosevelt*, 22.

74. James W. Ceaser, Glen E. Thurow, Jeffrey Tulis, and Joseph M. Bessette, "The Rise of the Rhetorical Presidency," *Presidential Studies Quarterly* 2 (1981): 163. Recent scholarship reveals that several presidents before the twentieth century likewise embraced the rhetorical nature of the presidency. See also Leroy G. Dorsey, ed., *The Presidency and Rhetorical Leadership* (College Station: Texas A&M University Press, 2002).

75. For examples of Roosevelt's rhetorical presidency, see Dorsey, "The Frontier Myth in Presidential Rhetoric: Theodore Roosevelt's Campaign for Conservation," 1–19; Leroy G. Dorsey, "Sailing into the 'Wondrous Now': The Myth of the American Navy's World Cruise," *Quarterly Journal of Speech* 83 (1997): 447–465.

76. Roosevelt, *The Winning of the West*, 9: 219, 449.

77. Theodore Roosevelt, "The Monroe Doctrine, March 1896," in *American Ideals/The Strenuous Life/Realizable Ideals: The Works of Theodore Roosevelt*, 13: 179.

78. David L. Lewis, *W. E. B. Du Bois: Biography of a Race* (New York: Henry Holt and Company, 1993), 165.

79. Theodore Roosevelt, "The Education of the Negro, October 24, 1905," in *American Problems: The Works of Theodore Roosevelt*, 16: 351–352, 355.

80. Booker T. Washington, "Cotton States Exposition Address," in *American Rhetorical Discourse*, 3rd ed., ed. Ronald F. Reid and James F. Klumpp (Long Grove: Waveland Press, Inc., 2005), 505–508.

81. Theodore Roosevelt, "Sixth Annual Message, December 3, 1906," in *State Papers as Governor and President, 1899–1909: The Works of Theodore Roosevelt*, 15: 354.

82. Bay, *The White Image in the Black Mind*, 77.

83. Gossett, *Race*, 253–286.

84. Gerstle, *American Crucible*, 28.

85. Theodore Roosevelt, "The Square Deal, April 5, 1905," in *The Roosevelt Policy: Speeches, Letters and State Papers, relating to Corporate Wealth and Closely Allied Topics*, ed. William Griffith (1919; Kraus Reprint Co., 1971), 1: 252–253.

86. Theodore Roosevelt, "At the Lincoln Monument, Springfield, Ill., June 4,

1903," in *Presidential Address and State Papers of Theodore Roosevelt*, 4 vols. (Kraus Reprint Co., 1970), 2: 446.

87. Theodore Roosevelt, "Report of the Eleventh Annual Convention of the National Negro Business League held in New York City, N.Y., August 17, 18 and 19, 1910, Nashville, Tenn., A. M. E. Sunday School Union 1911," in *The Theodore Roosevelt Collection*, Houghton Library, Harvard University, TRC-SP-1 (5), Speeches, 1910 January–September, 187–188, 192. Use is by permission of the Houghton Library, Harvard University.

88. See Shapiro, *White Violence and Black Response.*

89. Roosevelt, "Sixth Annual Message," in *State Papers as Governor and President: The Works of Theodore Roosevelt*, 15: 352–353.

90. Williamson, *A Rage for Order,* 353.

91. Williamson, *A Rage for Order,* 352–353.

92. Washington, "Cotton States Exposition Address," in *American Rhetorical Discourse,* 507.

93. Bay, *The White Image in the Black Mind,* 103; Shapiro, *White Violence and Black Response,* 33–34.

94. Williamson, *A Rage for Order,* 306–308.

95. Richard Hofstadter, *The American Political Tradition and the Men Who Made It* (New York: Vintage Books, 1954), 208.

96. Morris, *Theodore Rex,* 258; and Gould, *The Presidency of Theodore Roosevelt,* 118.

97. Theodore Roosevelt, "To Winfield Taylor Durbin, Oyster Bay, August 6, 1903," in *The Letters of Theodore Roosevelt*, ed. Elting E. Morison, John M. Blum, and Alfred Chandler (Cambridge: Harvard University Press, 1951–1954), 3: 540–543.

98. Shapiro, *White Violence and Black Response,* 96–103.

99. Roosevelt, "Sixth Annual Message," in *State Papers as Governor and President: The Works of Theodore Roosevelt*, 15: 353, 355.

100. Dyer, *Theodore Roosevelt and the Idea of Race,* 122.

101. Dyer, *Theodore Roosevelt and the Idea of Race,* 112–114.

102. Morris, *Theodore Rex,* 258.

103. Roosevelt, *The Winning of the West: The Works of Theodore Roosevelt*, 8: 107, 362.

104. Roosevelt, "Sixth Annual Message," in *State Papers as Governor and President: The Works of Theodore Roosevelt*, 15: 354.

105. Roosevelt, "The Education of the Negro," in *American Problems: The Works of Theodore Roosevelt*, 16: 353.

106. Williamson, *A Rage for Order,* 345–346.

107. Theodore Roosevelt, "At City Park, Little Rock, Ark., October 25, 1905," in *Presidential Address and State Papers of Theodore Roosevelt*, 4: 535–536.

108. Roosevelt, "Sixth Annual Message," in *State Papers as Governor and President: The Works of Theodore Roosevelt*, 15: 352–353.

109. For a complete account of the Brownsville incident, see Weaver, *The Brownsville Raid.*

110. Gould, *The Presidency of Theodore Roosevelt,* 240.

111. Quoted in Joseph B. Foraker, *Notes of a Busy Life* (Cincinnati: Stewart & Kidd Company, 1917), 235–236.

112. *Congressional Record-Senate,* 59th Cong., 2nd sess., December 19, 1906, 550.

113. *Congressional Record-Senate,* 59th Cong., 2nd sess., December 19, 1906, 550.

114. Morris, *Theodore Rex,* 511.

115. *Congressional Record-Senate,* 60th Cong., 2nd sess., December 14, 1908, 186.

116. Weaver, *The Brownsville Raid,* 278; *The Handbook of Texas Online,* http://www.tsha.utexas.edu/handbook/online/articles/view/BB/pkb6.html.

117. Shapiro, *White Violence and Black Response,* 115–117.

118. Theodore Roosevelt, "Murder is not Debatable," in *Foes of Our Own Household/The Great Adventure/Letters to His Children: The Works of Theodore Roosevelt,* 19: 167, 170.

119. Theodore Roosevelt, "Remarks of Theodore Roosevelt at Meeting held under the auspices of the Circle for Negro War Relief, Carnegie Hall, Saturday Evening, November 2nd, 1918," in *The Theodore Roosevelt Collection,* Houghton Library, Harvard University, TRC-SP-1 (12), Speeches, 1918, 10. Use is by permission of the Houghton Library, Harvard University.

Chapter 5

1. Theodore Roosevelt, "Letter to Edmund Robert Otto Von Mach, November 7, 1914," in *The Letters of Theodore Roosevelt,* ed. Elting E. Morison (Cambridge, Harvard University Press, 1954), 8: 834.

2. Theodore Roosevelt, "Americanism, October 12, 1915," in *America and the World War/Fear God and Take Your Own Part: The Works of Theodore Roosevelt,* National ed. (New York: Charles Scribner's Sons, 1926), 18: 392–393. Hereafter referred to as *America/Fear God.*

3. David R. Roediger, *The Wages of Whiteness: Race and the Making of the American Working Class,* revised ed. (New York: Verso, 2003), 144–145.

4. Kenneth L. Karst, *Belonging to America: Equal Citizenship and the Constitution* (New Haven: Yale University Press, 1989), 88.

5. Leonard Dinnerstein, Roger L. Nichols, and David M. Reimers, *Natives and Strangers: A Multicultural History of Americans* (Oxford: Oxford University Press, 1996), 70.

6. Matthew F. Jacobson, *Whiteness of a Different Color: European Immigrants and the Alchemy of Race* (Cambridge: Harvard University Press, 1998), 46–47.

7. Stephen Cornell and Douglas Hartmann, *Ethnicity and Race: Making Identities in a Changing World* (Thousand Oaks, CA: Pine Forge Press, 1998), 121–128.

8. La Vern J. Rippley, *The German-American* (Boston: Twayne Publishers, 1976), 32–33.

9. Richard O'Connor, *The German Americans: An Informal History* (Boston: Little, Brown and Co., 1968), 129, 154.

10. Rippley, *The German-American*, 39.

11. Mary Jane Corry, "The Role of German Singing Societies in Nineteenth-Century America," in *Germans in America: Aspects of German-American Relations in the Nineteenth Century*, ed. E. Allen McCormick (New York: Brooklyn College/Columbia University Press, 1983), 155.

12. Joseph Wandel, *The German Dimension of American History* (Chicago: Nelson-Hall, 1979), 126–128.

13. Albert Faust, *The German Element in the United States: With Special Reference to its Political, Moral, Social, and Educational Influence* (New York: The Steuben Society of America, 1927), 2: 201–202, 221, 226, 228–229, 708.

14. Carl Wittke, *The German-Language Press in America* (Lexington: University of Kentucky Press, 1957), 6.

15. Faust, *The German Element in the United States*, 366. For the allegiance of German newspapers, see Wittke, *The German-Language Press in America*, 127.

16. Don H. Tolzmann, *The German-American Experience* (New York: Humanity Books, 2000), 398–399.

17. Faust, *The German Element in the United States*, 129, 137, 146–148.

18. Charles T. Johnson, *Culture at Twilight: The National German-American Alliance, 1901–1918* (New York: Peter Lang, 1999), 3, 13.

19. Gary Gerstle, *American Crucible: Race and Nation in the Twentieth Century* (Princeton: Princeton University Press, 2001), 19.

20. Thomas Dyer, *Theodore Roosevelt and the Idea of Race* (Baton Rouge: Louisiana State University Press, 1980), 57–58.

21. Theodore Roosevelt, "Americans of German Origin," in *American Problems: The Works of Theodore Roosevelt*, 16: 36.

22. Theodore Roosevelt, *The Winning of the West—An Account of the Exploration and Settlement of Our Country from the Alleghanies to the Pacific: The Works of Theodore Roosevelt*, 8: 88.

23. Roosevelt, *The Winning of the West: The Works of Theodore Roosevelt*, 8: 88; Theodore Roosevelt, "The Ancient Irish Sagas, December 16, 1911," in *Literary Essays: The Works of Theodore Roosevelt*, 12: 136–137.

24. Theodore Roosevelt, *New York: The Works of Theodore Roosevelt*, 10: 513–514.

25. Theodore Roosevelt, "The World Movement, May 12, 1910," in *Literary Essays: The Works of Theodore Roosevelt*, 12: 62–63.

26. Theodore Roosevelt, "The Prohibitory Liquor Traffic Bill, January 24, 1884," in *Campaigns and Controversies: The Works of Theodore Roosevelt*, 14: 31.

27. Roosevelt, *America/Fear God*, 18: 215, 279.

28. Theodore Roosevelt, "The Nomination for the Presidency, June 22, 1916," in *Social Justice and Popular Rule: The Works of Theodore Roosevelt*, 17: 420.

29. Roosevelt, *The Winning of the West: The Works of Theodore Roosevelt*, 8: 4–5.

30. Theodore Roosevelt, "The Ethnology of the Police, June, 1897," in *Cam-*

paigns and Controversies: The Works of Theodore Roosevelt, 14: 225; Theodore Roosevelt, "American Ideals in Education, November 4, 1910," in *American Problems: The Works of Theodore Roosevelt*, 16: 337; Roosevelt, "Americans of German Origin," in *American Problems: The Works of Theodore Roosevelt*, 16: 37.

31. Daniel J. Tichenor, *Dividing Lines: The Politics of Immigration Control in America* (Princeton: Princeton University Press, 2002), 50.

32. O'Connor, *The German Americans*, 314–315, 342.

33. Leonard Dinnerstein and David M. Reimers, *Ethnic Americans: A History of Immigration*, 4th ed. (New York: Columbia University Press, 1999), 55–56.

34. Cornell and Hartmann, *Ethnicity and Race*, 125–128.

35. Tolzmann, *The German-American Experience*, 235–236.

36. Johnson, *Culture at Twilight*, 1, 11–12.

37. Johnson, *Culture at Twilight*, 95, 98–99.

38. Charles J. Hexamer, *Address of Dr. C. J. Hexamer, President of the National German American Alliance, Mass Meeting at the Academy of Music, Philadelphia, PA, Tuesday, November 24, 1914* (Philadelphia: The Alliance/Graf. & Breuninger Print, 1914), microform, 3–4.

39. See Johnson, *Culture at Twilight*, 99; Carl Wittke, *German-Americans and the World War: With Special Emphasis on Ohio's German-Language Press* (Ohio: The Ohio State Archaeological and Historical Society, 1936), 31.

40. Wittke, *The German-Language Press*, 238.

41. Johnson, *Culture at Twilight*, 102–104, 111.

42. Wittke, *German-Americans and the World War*, 166–167.

43. Gerstle, *American Crucible*, 56.

44. Frederick C. Luebke, *Bonds of Loyalty: German Americans and World War I* (DeKalb: Northern Illinois University Press, 1974), 241, 248, 269–270, 280–281, 288.

45. Tolzmann, *The German-American Experience*, 283–290.

46. Roger Daniels, *Not Like Us: Immigrants and Minorities in America, 1890–1924* (Chicago: Ivan R. Dee, 1997), 97.

47. H. W. Brands, *T. R.: The Last Romantic* (New York: BasicBooks, 1997), 762.

48. Roosevelt, *New York: The Works of Theodore Roosevelt*, 10: 513.

49. Roosevelt, *New York: The Works of Theodore Roosevelt*, 10: 513.

50. Roosevelt, *New York: The Works of Theodore Roosevelt*, 10: 361.

51. Theodore Roosevelt, "True Americanism, April, 1894," in *American Ideals/ The Strenuous Life: The Works of Theodore Roosevelt*, 13: 21.

52. Theodore Roosevelt, "The Duties of American Citizenship, January 26, 1893," in *American Ideals/The Strenuous Life: The Works of Theodore Roosevelt*, 13: 295.

53. William H. Harbaugh, *The Life and Times of Theodore Roosevelt* (New York: Collier Books, 1961), 439, 449.

54. Dyer, *Theodore Roosevelt and the Idea of Race*, 133.

55. Brands, *T. R.: The Last Romantic*, 762.

56. Theodore Roosevelt, "The Children of the Crucible," in *The Foes of our Own Household/The Great Adventure/Letters to His Children: The Works of Theodore Roosevelt*, 19: 39. Hereafter referred to as *Foes/Great/Letters*.

57. James Robertson, *American Myth, American Reality* (New York: Hill & Wang, 1980), 327.

58. Richard Slotkin, *The Fatal Environment: The Myth of the Frontier in the Age of Industrialization, 1800–1890* (Norman: University of Oklahoma Press, 1994), 53.

59. Robert L. Ivie, "Images of Savagery in American Justifications for War," *Communication Monographs* 47 (1980): 283; Robert L. Ivie, "The Metaphor of Force in Prowar Discourse: The Case of 1812," *Quarterly Journal of Speech* 68 (1982): 241.

60. Slotkin, *The Fatal Environment*, 62.

61. Slotkin, *Gunfighter Nation*, 12, 14.

62. Joseph Campbell, *Myths to Live By* (New York: Penguin Books, 1972), 198.

63. Sacvan Bercovitch, *The Puritan Origins of the American Self* (New Haven: Yale University Press, 1975), 136. Italics mine.

64. Campbell, *Myths to Live By*, 198; Robertson, *American Myth*, 325; Slotkin, *Gunfighter Nation*, 11.

65. Theodore Roosevelt, "The Duty of Self-Defense and of Good Conduct Towards Others," in *America/Fear God*, 18: 3.

66. Theodore Roosevelt, "Fear God and Take Your Own Part," in *Fear God and Take Your Own Part* (New York: George H. Doran Company, 1916), 42–43. Hereafter referred to as *Fear God*.

67. Slotkin, *The Fatal Environment*, 54–55.

68. Roosevelt, "Murder on the High Seas, May 9, 1915," *Fear God*, 351–352.

69. Richard Slotkin, *Regeneration Through Violence: The Mythology of the American Frontier, 1600–1860* (Norman: University of Oklahoma Press, 1973), 21.

70. Theodore Roosevelt, "Armenian Outrages, November 24, 1915," *Fear God*, 380–381.

71. Roosevelt, "A Sword for Defense," in *Fear God*, 79.

72. Roosevelt, "Preparedness against War," in *Fear God*, 174.

73. Roosevelt, "Armenian Outrages," in *Fear God*, 133.

74. Richard Drinnon, *Facing West: The Metaphysics of Indian-Hating and Empire Building* (Norman: University of Oklahoma Press, 1997), 120.

75. Theodore Roosevelt, "The Ghost Dance of the Shadow Huns, October 1, 1917," in *Roosevelt in the Kansas City Star: War-Time Editorials by Theodore Roosevelt* (Boston: Houghton Mifflin Company, 1921), 7.

76. Theodore Roosevelt, "The German Horror," in *Foes/Great/Letters*, 19: 326.

77. Richard J. Barnet, *The Rockets' Red Glare: When America Goes to War, The Presidents and the People* (New York: Simon & Schuster, 1990), 145.

78. Theodore Roosevelt, "Colonel Roosevelt's Speech to be delivered at Boston, Mass, May 2nd, 1918, Under the auspices of the Chamber of Commerce and the Pilgrim Publicity Association," in the *Theodore Roosevelt Collection*, Harvard College

Library, TRC-SP-1 (12), Speeches 1918: 3. Use is by permission of the Houghton Library, Harvard University.

79. Roosevelt, "Fear God and Take Your Own Part," *Fear God*, 22–23.

80. Theodore Roosevelt, "International Duty and Hyphenated Americanism," in *Fear God*, 138–139.

81. Theodore Roosevelt, "Pillar-Of-Salt Citizenship, October 12, 1917," in *Kansas City Star*, 16.

82. Roosevelt, "International Duty and Hyphenated Americanism," in *Fear God*, 279, 281.

83. Theodore Roosevelt, "The Nomination for the Presidency, June 22, 1916," in *Social Justice and Popular Rule: The Works of Theodore Roosevelt*, 17: 420–421.

84. Roosevelt, "Fear God and Take Your Own Part," in *Fear God*, 19.

85. Theodore Roosevelt, "Uncle Sam's Only Friend is Uncle Sam," in *Fear God*, 211–212.

86. Roosevelt, "The Children of the Crucible," in *Foes/Great/Letters*, 19: 41.

87. O'Connor, *The German Americans*, 412–413; Tolzmann, *The German-American Experience*, 284.

88. Theodore Roosevelt, "Fear God and Take Your Own Part," in *Fear God*, 18–19.

89. Theodore Roosevelt, "America First—A Phrase or a Fact?," in *Fear God*, 116.

90. Theodore Roosevelt, "To My Fellow Americans of German Blood, April 16, 1918," in *Kansas City Star*, 136.

91. Thomas F. Gossett, *Race: The History of an Idea in America* (New York: Oxford University Press, 1997), 287–309.

92. Gail Bederman, *Manliness and Civilization: A Cultural History of Gender and Race in the United States, 1880–1917* (Chicago: University of Chicago Press, 1995), 185–186.

93. T. J. Jackson Lears, *No Place of Grace: Antimodernism and the Transformation of American Culture, 1880–1920* (New York: Pantheon Books, 1981), 51.

94. Clifford Putney, *Muscular Christianity: Manhood and Sports in Protestant America, 1880–1920* (Cambridge: Harvard University Press, 2001), 11.

95. Tolzmann, *The German-American Experience*, 287–288.

96. Roosevelt, "To My Fellow Americans of German Blood," in *Kansas City Star*, 137; Theodore Roosevelt, "A Square Deal for All Americans, April 27, 1918," in *Kansas City Star*, 143; Roosevelt, "The Children of the Crucible," in *Foes/Great/Letters*, 19: 34.

97. Theodore Roosevelt, "The Worst Enemies of Certain Loyal Americans, March 10, 1918," in *Kansas City Star*, 113–114.

98. Roosevelt, "Fear God and Take Your Own Part," in *Fear God*, 25–26, 28, 57.

99. Roosevelt, "Fear God and Take Your Own Part," in *Fear God*, 15, 17.

100. Theodore Roosevelt, "Summing Up," in *America/Fear God*, 18: 185.

101. Roosevelt, "Fear God and Take Your Own Part," in *Fear God*, 57–58.

102. Roosevelt, "The Square Deal in Americanism," in *Foes/Great/Letters*, 19: 312.

103. Tolzmann, *The German-American Experience*, 21.

104. Brands, *T. R.: The Last Romantic*, 762.

Conclusion

1. Gary Gerstle, *American Crucible: Race and Nation in the Twentieth Century* (Princeton: Princeton University Press, 2001), 80.

2. Gerstle, *American Crucible*, 6–9.

3. Claude Lévi-Strauss, *Myth and Meaning: Cracking the Code of Culture* (New York: Schocken Books, 1978), 20.

4. Roland Barthes, *Mythologies*, translated by Annette Lavers (New York: Noonday Press, 1957), 143.

5. David J. Tichenor, *Dividing Lines: The Politics of Immigration Control in America* (Princeton: Princeton University Press, 2002), 3–5.

6. Virgil J. Vogel, *This Country Was Ours: A Documentary History of the American Indian* (New York: Harper & Row, 1972), 194–195; Joan M. King and Elliot McIntire, "The Impact of the Indian Gaming Regulatory Act on Tribes in the U.S.," in *Tourism and Gaming on American Indian Lands*, ed. Alan A. Lew and George A. Van Otten (New York: Cognizant Communication Corporation, 1998), 48–55.

7. Lawrence H. Fuchs, *The American Kaleidoscope: Race, Ethnicity, and the Civic Culture* (Hanover: Wesleyan University Press, 1990), 166–168, 176.

8. Ginger Thompson, "Mexico President Urges U.S. to Act Soon on Migrants," *New York Times*, September 16, 2001, www.nytimes.com; *The Week*, "How They See Us: Blind to the Contributions of Mexicans," May 27, 2005, 14.

9. *CNN*, "L.A. Braces for Protest, as Bush Addresses 'Emotional Debate,'" March 25, 2006, http://www.cnn.com.

10. Evan Thomas, "Cracking the Terror Code," *Newsweek*, October 15, 2001, 42–46.

11. James O. Robertson, *American Myth, American Reality* (New York: Hill & Wang, 1980), 108.

12. Arian Campo-Flores, "America's Divide," *Newsweek*, April 10, 2006, 31–32.

13. *CNN*, "Bush Backs Border Fence," May 18, 2006, http://www.cnn.com.

14. Associated Press, "Sessions: 'The Senate Should be Ashamed of Itself,'" *CNN*, May 19, 2006, http://www.cnn.com.

15. George W. Bush, "President Bush Addresses the Nation on Immigration Reform, May 15, 2006," http://www.whitehouse.gov.

16. "Hearing of the Senate Judiciary Committee on the Nomination of Clarence Thomas to the Supreme Court," October 11, 1991, Electronic Text Center, University of Virginia Library, http://www.etext.virginia.edu.

17. See Hamil R. Harris, "Marchers Decry N.Y. Police Shooting," *Washington Post*, February 16, 1999, Final Edition: B03; Lynne Duke, "Juror Says Weak Case Made Diallo Verdicts Inevitable," *Washington Post*, February 28, 2000, http://www.washingtonpost.com.

18. Associated Press, "Race a Factor in Diallo Case, Clinton Says," *Washington Post,* March 5, 2000, http://www.washingtonpost.com.

19. *CNN,* "Closing Arguments Today in Texas Dragging-Death Trial," February 22, 1999, http://www.cnn.com.

20. Ellis Cose, "A Real Racial Tipping Point," *Newsweek,* February 27, 2006, 40.

21. For examples of the Frontier Myth in presidential discourse and popular media, see Richard Slotkin, *Gunfighter Nation: The Myth of the Frontier in Twentieth-Century America* (New York: Atheneum, 1992).

22. See http://www.census.gov.

23. See http://www.crocodilehunter.com; Keat Murray, "Surviving Survivor: Reading Mark Burnett's Field Guide and De-naturalizing Social Darwinism as Entertainment," *Journal of American Culture* 24 (2001): 43–54; http://www.cbs.com/primetime/amazing_race5/.

24. See Jim Cullen, *The American Dream: A Short History of an Idea that Shaped a Nation* (Oxford: Oxford University Press, 2003), 15, 120–131; Kurt Ritter and David Henry, *Ronald Reagan: The Great Communicator* (New York: Greenwood Press, 1992), 15; and G. Thomas Goodnight, "Ronald Reagan and the American Dream: A Study in the Rhetoric Out of Time," in *The Presidency and Rhetorical Leadership,* ed. Leroy G. Dorsey (College Station: Texas A&M University Press, 2002), 200–230.

25. See Cullen, *The American Dream;* Dan Rather, *The American Dream: Stories from the Heart of Our Nation* (New York: HarperCollins, 2002).

26. James T. Adams, *The Epic of America* (1931; Boston: Little, Brown, and Company, 1946), 415.

27. Jennifer Hochschild, *Facing Up to the American Dream: Race, Class, and the Soul of the Nation* (Princeton: Princeton University Press, 1995), 25, 250.

28. Michael Kinsley, "Mobility vs. Nobility," *Washington Post,* June 5, 2005, http://www.washingtonpost.com/wp-dyn/content/article/2005/06/03/AR2005060301464.html; Alan Reynolds, "Class Struggle?," *Wall Street Journal,* May 18, 2005, http://www.opinionjournal.com/editorial/feature.html?id=110006704.

29. Slotkin, *Gunfighter Nation,* 492.

30. Jonathan Alter, "The Other America," *Newsweek,* September 19, 2005, 42–48.

31. Quoted in Michael Isikoff, "With Friends Like These . . .," *Newsweek,* April 18, 2005, 44.

32. Mark Fitzgerald, "Black and White and Red All Over," *Editor & Publisher,* January 1, 2004, www.editorandpublisher.com.

33. Brett D. Fromson, *Hitting the Jackpot: The Inside Story of the Richest Indian Tribe in History* (New York: Atlantic Monthly Press, 2003), 222–223.

34. Quoted in Gene Wade, Linda Hoyman, Jimmy Hercheck, Alan Hoon, and Tim Kenyon, "What Do You Think?", *Atlanta Journal-Constitution,* December 8, 2004, Wednesday Home Edition, Gwinnett News Section, JJ4.

35. Arian Campo-Flores and Howard Fineman, "A Latin Power Surge," *Newsweek,* May 30, 2005, 25–26. Italics mine.

36. Linda Chavez, "Hispanics and the American Dream," *The Freeman,* a pub-

lication of The Foundation for Economic Education, Inc., November 1996, Vol. 25, No. 11, http://www.libertyhaven.com/countriesandregions/latinamerica/hispanics.shtml.

37. *Associated Press*, "Fox: Comment about Blacks Misinterpreted," May 17, 2005, *CNN*, http://www.cnn.com/2005/WORLD/americas/05/17/fox.blacks.ap/index.html.

38. Bush, "President Bush Addresses the Nation on Immigration Reform," http://www.whitehouse.gov.

Bibliographic Essay

~

The scholarly literature on Theodore Roosevelt, rhetoric, myth, immigration, race, Native Americans, African Americans, and German-Americans is extensive, to say the least. The majority of the citations listed here represent recent scholarship on these subjects and are limited to those works where several of these subjects intersect or that provide examples used in this book.

Theodore Roosevelt

Theodore Roosevelt was one of the most prolific politicians and public advocates in American history, writing numerous popular and scholarly articles, books, speeches, and letters. He covers his boyhood through his presidency in *An Autobiography* (New York: Charles Scribner's Sons, 1929). Many of his writings are collected in *The Works of Theodore Roosevelt*, National ed., 20 vols. (New York: Charles Scriber's Sons, 1926). *The Works* contain such books as *The Rough Riders,* which covers his exploits in the Spanish-American War; *Ranch Life and the Hunting Trail,* which recounts his life in Dakota Territory; and *Fear God and Take Your Own Part,* which collects newspaper and magazine articles he wrote during the early days of the Great War. His newspaper articles published during the last years of the Great War appear in *Roosevelt in the* Kansas City Star: *War-Time Editorials by Theodore Roosevelt* (Boston: Houghton Mifflin Company, 1921). His presidential addresses are also contained in *The Works* and are collected in several other sources, such as *Presidential Addresses and State Papers,* Homeward Bound ed., 7 vols. (New York: The Review of Reviews Company, 1910), and *Presidential Address and State Papers of Theodore Roosevelt,* 4 vols. (New York: Krause Reprint Co., 1970). In addition, his presidential addresses pertaining to the dangers and benefits of corporate power are contained in *The Roosevelt Policy: Speeches, Letters and State Papers, Relating to Corporate Wealth and Closely Allied Topics,* ed. William Griffith, 2 vols. (New York: Krause Reprint Co., 1971). Many of Roosevelt's letters to friends, family, and colleagues can be found in *The Letters of Theodore Roosevelt,* ed. Elting E. Morison, 8 vols. (Cambridge: Harvard University Press, 1951). For Roosevelt's personal papers, photographs, speeches, and other ephemera, one can visit the *Theodore Roosevelt Collection* in Harvard College Library/Houghton Library at Harvard University, and the *Theodore Roosevelt Papers* at the Library of Congress, Washington, D.C.

Historical scholarship about Roosevelt is vast, and Roosevelt has become even more popular in recent years. Two early biographies eloquently capture the triumphs and turmoil of Roosevelt's life: Henry F. Pringle, *Theodore Roosevelt: A Biography* (New York: Harcourt, Brace and Co., 1931); and William H. Harbaugh, *The Life and Times of Theodore Roosevelt* (New York: Collier Books, 1963). Pringle's book won a Pulitzer Prize. Another work by G. Wallace Chessman, *Theodore Roosevelt and the Politics of Power,* ed. Oscar Handlin (Boston: Little, Brown, 1969), covers the major national and international issues President Roosevelt faced. Lewis L. Gould, *The Presidency of Theodore Roosevelt* (Lawrence: University Press of Kansas, 1991), presents a comprehensive account of Roosevelt's challenges as a chief executive. H. W. Brands, *T. R.: The Last Romantic* (New York: Basic Books, 1997), provides a compelling narrative account of Roosevelt's colorful life. Nathan Miller, *Theodore Roosevelt: A Life* (New York: William Morrow and Co., 1992), and Kathleen Dalton, *Theodore Roosevelt: A Strenuous Life* (New York: Alfred A. Knopf, 2002), also provide good, one-volume accounts of Roosevelt's incredible lifelong career as a public advocate. Edmund Morris currently has two volumes published of his proposed trilogy. The first recounts Roosevelt's early political career and the second addresses Roosevelt's presidency, with both celebrated for their scholarship and beautiful writing: *The Rise of Theodore Roosevelt* (New York: The Modern Library, 2001), and *Theodore Rex* (New York: Random House, 2001). Several authors cover Roosevelt's post-presidential career and the adventures he sought, including Joseph L. Gardner, *Departing Glory: Theodore Roosevelt as ex-President* (New York: Charles Scribner's Sons, 1973); Patricia O'Toole, *When Trumpets Call: Theodore Roosevelt after the White House* (New York: Simon & Schuster, 2005); and Candace Miller, *The River of Doubt: Theodore Roosevelt's Darkest Journey* (New York: Doubleday, 2005).

Several noteworthy works establish Roosevelt's influence on both historical and contemporary issues. Lawrence J. Oliver, *Brander Matthews, Theodore Roosevelt, and the Politics of American Literature, 1880–1920* (Knoxville: University of Tennessee Press, 1992), explores Roosevelt's influence on Matthews, considered to be one of the most "prominent and influential American men of letters" at the turn of the twentieth century (xi). George E. Mowry attributes Roosevelt with defining modern culture and the progressive impulse in America in *Theodore Roosevelt and the Progressive Movement* (New York: Hill & Wang, 1946), and in *The Era of Theodore Roosevelt and the Birth of Modern America, 1900–1912* (New York: Harper & Row, 1958). Richard Hofstadter assesses Roosevelt's progressive tendencies in chapter 9 of *The American Political Tradition and the Men Who Made It* (New York: Vintage Books, 1954). J. Michael Hogan and John B. Judis, respectively, analyze Roosevelt's impact on contemporary foreign policy: *The Panama Canal in American Politics: Domestic Advocacy and the Evolution of Policy* (Carbondale: Southern Illinois University Press, 1986); and *The Folly of Empire: What George W. Bush Could Learn from Theodore Roosevelt and Woodrow Wilson* (New York: Scribner, 2004). Two articles that support Judis's argument about Roosevelt's importance to the politics of contemporary chief executives include William Marina and David T. Beito, "How Teddy Roosevelt Fathered the 'Bush Doctrine,'" *The Independent Institute,* December 9, 2004, http://www.independent.org/newsroom/article.asp?id=1435; and Jonathan Alter, "Between the Lines Online: Loud and Clear," *Newsweek,* September 20, 2002, http://web.lexis-nexis.com.

The discussion regarding the decline of American masculinity, and what Roosevelt can teach us about its restoration, can be found in Harvey C. Mansfield, *Manliness* (New Haven: Yale University Press, 2006); and in his article, "The Manliness of Theodore Roosevelt," *The New Criterion,* 23 (2005) http://www.newcriterion.com/archive/23/mar05/mansfield.htm. Sarah Watts provides a psychological analysis for Roosevelt's seeming obsession with masculinity in *Rough Rider in the White House: Theodore Roosevelt and the Politics of Desire* (Chicago: University of Chicago Press, 2003). Gail Bederman explores Roosevelt's part in the larger cultural debate about masculinity, gender, and race in chapter 5 of her work, *Manliness and Civilization: A Cultural History of Gender and Race in the United States, 1880–1917* (Chicago: University of Chicago Press, 1995).

Little attention has been paid to Roosevelt's racial attitudes, but Thomas G. Dyer, *Theodore Roosevelt and the Idea of Race* (Baton Rouge: Louisiana State University Press, 1980), presents a provocative examination of the origins and political implications of Roosevelt's feelings about nonwhites and immigrants. John D. Weaver, *The Brownsville Raid* (College Station: Texas A&M University Press, 1992), provides the definitive account of Roosevelt's actions in relation to the African American soldiers involved (or not) in an attack on a racially hostile Texas town in 1906. Roosevelt's messages to Congress on the Brownsville issue can be found in U.S. Congress, *Congressional Record-Senate,* 59th Cong., 2nd sess., December 19, 1906, Vol. 41, pt. 2; and U.S Congress, *Congressional Record-Senate,* 60th Cong., 2nd sess., December 14, 1908, Vol. 43, pt. 2. Gary Gerstle, *American Crucible: Race and Nation in the Twentieth Century* (Princeton: Princeton University Press, 2001), features Roosevelt in two chapters as a key figure for understanding America's conception of itself in both biological and ideological terms.

Although a much-studied historical figure, Roosevelt has gotten limited attention in the communication literature. Stephen E. Lucas, "'The Man with the Muck

Rake': A Reinterpretation," *Quarterly Journal of Speech* 59 (1973): 452–462, addresses how scholarship had viewed Roosevelt's attack on "yellow journalists" and his attack on corporate wealth in the same speech as a dichotomous and confusing event. Lucas argues that the attacks put both conservatives and liberals on notice to act in the public's interest and called for them to help establish a stable and morally upright society. Robert Friedenberg, *Theodore Roosevelt and the Rhetoric of Militant Decency* (New York: Greenwood Press, 1990), outlines the major themes in Roosevelt's discourse, including power, order, work, social responsibility, and character. Jon Paulson, "Theodore Roosevelt and the Rhetoric of Citizenship: On Tour in New England, 1902," *Communication Quarterly* 50 (2002): 123–134, examines the Rooseveltian construction of the "good citizen." Daniel O. Buehler, "Permanence and Change in Theodore Roosevelt's Conservation Jeremiad," *Western Journal of Communication* 62 (1998): 439–458, explores how Roosevelt employed the jeremiad to promote conservation in his 1908 speech to the Governors' Conference.

I cover Roosevelt's rhetorical fight against corporate greed in "Theodore Roosevelt and Corporate America, 1901–1909: A Reexamination," *Presidential Studies Quarterly* 25 (1995): 725–739. Roosevelt considered his popularization of conservation and the strengthening of America's navy as two of his most important accomplishments. I examine those topics, respectively, in "The Frontier Myth in Presidential Rhetoric: Theodore Roosevelt's Campaign for Conservation," *Western Journal of Communication* 59 (1995): 1–19; and "Sailing into the 'Wondrous Now': The Myth of the American Navy's World Cruise," *Quarterly Journal of Speech* 83 (1997): 447–465. I reject the belief that Roosevelt was not a true progressive and argue instead that his "rhetorical progressivism" merged morality and pragmatism; "true" progressives would dismiss that pragmatic aspect. For that analysis, see "Preaching Morality in Modern America: Theodore Roosevelt's Rhetorical Progressivism," in chapter 2 of *Rhetoric and Reform in the Progressive Era*, ed. J. Michael Hogan, Vol. 6 (East Lansing: Michigan State University Press, 2003). That volume is part of the MSU Press series, A Rhetorical History of the United States—Significant Moments in American Public Discourse. Finally, this author and Rachel M. Harlow examine Roosevelt's narrative history, *The Winning of the West*, in "'We Want Americans Pure and Simple': Theodore Roosevelt and the Myth of Americanism," *Rhetoric & Public Affairs* 6 (2003): 55–78. We argue that Roosevelt's recounting of settlers' experiences on the North American continent mythologized and popularized immigrants as foundational to national development.

General Background

The work of Alexis De Tocqueville, *Democracy in America*, and Hector St. John de Crèvecoeur, *Letters From an American Farmer*, provide insightful observations of early America's political, social, and economic foundations. They defined, in ideological and racial terms, what it meant to be an American. They also foretold how white Americans would marginalize those people considered nonwhite and otherwise alien. Both of these works are available online, respectively, at http://xroads.virginia.edu/~HYPER/DETOC/toc_indx.html, and http://xroads.virginia.edu/~HYPER/CREV/contents.html.

Several outstanding works trace the social and political thought processes that led to the creation of the American nation. These include Gordon S. Wood's two books, *The Creation of the American Republic, 1776–1787* (New York: W. W. Norton & Company, 1969), and *The Radicalism of the American Revolution* (New York: Vintage Books, 1993); see also Bernard Bailyn, *The Ideological Origins of the American Revolution* (Cambridge: The Belknap Press of Harvard University Press, 1992). Daniel J. Boorstin's assessment of emerging American nationalism can be found in his excellent trilogy—*The Americans: The Colonial Experience* (New York: Vintage Books, 1964); *The Americans: The National Experience* (New York: Vintage Books, 1965); and *The Americans: The Democratic Experience* (New York: Vintage Books, 1965).

Sacvan Bercovitch explores the foundations of Puritan thought and its legacy in America's development in *The Puritan Origins of the American Self* (New Haven: Yale University Press, 1975), and in *The Rites of Assent: Transformations in the Symbolic Construction of America* (New York: Routledge, 1993).

The frontier represents an essential concept in American development. The historian Frederick J. Turner's 1893 essay, "The Significance of the Frontier in American History," initiated the modern study of that concept. The essay can be found at http://xroads.virginia.edu/~HYPER/TURNER/. Ray A. Billington traces the impact of the frontier in political and intellectual thought in *America's Frontier Heritage* (New York: Holt, Rinehart and Winston, 1966), and *The Genesis of the Frontier Thesis: A Study in Historical Creativity* (San Marino, CA: The Huntington Library, 1971). Ronald H. Carpenter explains the rhetorical or persuasive power of frontier discourse in "Frederick Jackson Turner and the Rhetorical Impact of the Frontier Thesis," *Quarterly Journal of Speech* 63 (1977): 117–129, and in "The Rhetorical Genesis of Style in the 'Frontier Hypothesis' of Frederick Jackson Turner," *Southern Speech Communication Journal* 37 (1972): 233–248.

General histories covering the late nineteenth and early twentieth centuries include Sean Cashman, *America in the Age of the Titans: The Progressive Era and World War I* (New York: New York University Press, 1988); Arthur S. Link, *American Epoch: A History of the United States since the 1890's* (New York: Alfred A. Knopf, 1955); and Richard L. Watson Jr., *The Development of National Power: The United States, 1900–1919* (Boston: Houghton Mifflin Company, 1976). For the history of the Progressive Era, see David W. Noble, *The Progressive Mind: 1890–1917* (Minneapolis: Burgess Publishing Co., 1981); David B. Danbom, *"The World of Hope": Progressives and the Struggle for an Ethical Public Life* (Philadelphia: Temple University Press, 1987); Sean D. Cashman, *America in the Gilded Age: From the Death of Lincoln to the Rise of Theodore Roosevelt* (New York: New York University Press, 1993); and John Whiteclaw Chambers II, *The Tyranny of Change: America in the Progressive Era, 1890–1920* (1992; New Brunswick: Rutgers University Press, 2000). Richard Hofstadter recounts the popularization of Charles Darwin's ideas in *Social Darwin-*

ism in American Thought (New York: Braziller, 1959). Robert W. Rydell explores how worlds' fairs affirmed racist thought regarding nonwhites at home and abroad in the excellent *All the World's a Fair: Visions of Empire at American International Expositions, 1876–1916* (Chicago: University of Chicago Press, 1984).

Primary texts that reveal the progressive impulse in American thought can be found in Richard Hofstadter, ed., *The Progressive Movement 1900–1915* (Englewood Cliffs, NJ: Prentice-Hall, Inc., 1963).

Several works assess the economic consequences of corporate capitalism during Roosevelt's era. These include Gabriel Kolko, *The Triumph of Conservatism: A Reinterpretation of American History, 1900–1916* (New York: The Free Press of Glencoe, 1963), and his *Main Currents in Modern American History* (New York: Pantheon Books, 1976). Also, see Alan Trachtenberg, *The Incorporation of America: Culture and Society in the Gilded Age* (New York: Hill & Wang, 1982).

To understand the moral and social crisis caused by corporate materialism, see T. J. Jackson Lears, *No Place of Grace: Antimodernism and the Transformation of American Culture, 1880–1920* (New York: Pantheon Books, 1981). Roosevelt's friend Brooks Adams believed history demonstrated how the overemphasis on materialism doomed civilizations, and that modern America was next; see *The Law of Civilization and Decay: An Essay on History* (New York: Macmillan & Co., 1895). According to Clifford Putney, modern audiences saw sports as the answer to corporate and cultural malaise. For that analysis, see *Muscular Christianity: Manhood and Sports in Protestant America, 1880–1920* (Cambridge: Harvard University Press, 2001).

Information on Joseph B. Foraker, Roosevelt's Senate foe during the Brownsville Affair, can be found in his autobiography, *Notes of a Busy Life* (Cincinnati: Stewart & Kidd Company, 1917).

Richard J. Barnet provides a historical overview of the presidency during wartime in *The Rockets' Red Glare: When America Goes to War, The Presidents and the People* (New York: Simon & Schuster, 1990).

Rhetoric and Myth

Rhetoric involves persuasion. Donald C. Bryant illuminates this idea in his foundational essay, "Rhetoric: Its Functions and Its Scope," *Quarterly Journal of Speech* 39 (1953): 401–424. Moreover, rhetorical analysis assesses how a rhetor constructs a text to maximize its persuasiveness on a given occasion for a given audience. Lloyd F. Bitzer discusses the significance and problematic nature of the occasion and the audience in his germinal essay, "The Rhetorical Situation," in *Readings in Rhetorical Criticism*, ed. Carl R. Burgchardt, 3rd ed. (State College: Strata Publishing, Inc., 2005). Engaging the works of Homer, Jane Austen, Chief Justice John Marshall, and others, James B. White, *When Words Lose Their Meaning: Constitutions and Reconstitutions of Language, Character, and Community* (Chicago: University of Chicago Press, 1984), articulates the way that character, reason, value, and community are "made real in performances of language" (xi). Kenneth Burke, *A Rhetoric of Motives*

(1950; Berkeley: University of California Press, 1969), and *A Grammar of Motives* (1945; Berkeley: University of California Press, 1969), represent important critical examinations of the symbolic nature of language as the means to human motivation and human action.

Speeches from the seventeenth to the late nineteenth centuries can be found in Ronald F. Reid and James F. Klumpp, eds., *American Rhetorical Discourse*, 3rd ed. (Long Grove: Waveland Press, Inc., 2005).

Chief executives' involvement in race and immigration issues has gotten excellent attention in two rhetorical studies: Vanessa B. Beasley, *You, the People: American National Identity in Presidential Rhetoric* (College Station: Texas A&M University Press, 2004); and Mary Stuckey, *Defining Americans: The Presidency and National Identity* (Lawrence: University Press of Kansas, 2004). Both works analyze how presidents negotiate the balance between identity and nationalism. They explain how presidential policies, speeches, and other rhetorical acts create the parameters for who can be included in the national community, as well as establish the standards used to exclude people based on their color, gender, wealth, and the like.

The modern presidency constitutes a site of rhetorical performance, according to James W. Ceaser, Glen E. Thurow, Jeffrey Tulis, and Joseph M. Bessette, in "The Rise of the Rhetorical Presidency," *Presidential Studies Quarterly* 11 (1981): 158–171. Jeffrey K. Tulis, *The Rhetorical Presidency* (Princeton: Princeton University Press, 1987), affirms the rhetorical nature of the presidency. Interestingly, both works also bemoan the emergence of the rhetorical presidency and claim further that most pre-twentieth-century presidents eschewed rhetoric. Recent scholarship, such as Leroy G. Dorsey, ed., *The Presidency and Rhetorical Leadership* (College Station: Texas A&M University Press, 2002), demonstrates how early presidents did employ rhetoric as a tool for leadership.

Exemplary rhetorical analyses of individual presidents' use of rhetoric to govern an uneasy populace include Kurt Ritter and David Henry, *Ronald Reagan: The Great Communicator* (New York: Greenwood Press, 1992); David Zarefsky, *President Johnson's War on Poverty: Rhetoric and History* (Tuscaloosa: The University of Alabama Press, 1986); Davis Houck, *FDR and Fear Itself* (College Station: Texas A&M University, Press, 2002); Martin Medhurst, *Dwight D. Eisenhower: Strategic Communicator* (New York: Greenwood Press, 1993); and Garth E. Pauley, *The Modern Presidency and Civil Rights: Rhetoric on Race from Roosevelt to Nixon* (College Station: Texas A&M University Press, 2001).

Sacvan Bercovitch, *The American Jeremiad* (Madison: University of Wisconsin Press, 1978), offers a historical account of the Puritan sermon that ministers used to celebrate and to chastise their flock. Two works provide a foundational understanding of the jeremiad's rhetorical power: Ernest G. Bormann, "Fetching Good Out of Evil: A Rhetorical Use of Calamity," *Quarterly Journal of Speech* 63 (1977): 130–139; and Ronald H. Carpenter, "The Historical Jeremiad as Rhetorical Genre," in chapter 5 of *Form and Genre: Shaping Rhetorical Action,* ed. Karlyn K. Campbell and Kathleen H. Jamieson (Falls Church, VA: Speech Communication Association, 1978).

The jeremiad has become a staple in political rhetoric. According to John M. Murphy, "'A Time of Shame and Sorrow': Robert F. Kennedy and the American Jeremiad," *Quarterly Journal of Speech* 76 (1990): 401–414, politicians use jeremiads to calm audiences and to restore social order. For Kurt W. Ritter, "American Political Rhetoric and the Jeremiad Tradition: Presidential Nomination Acceptance Addresses, 1960–1976," *Central States Speech Journal* 31 (1980): 153–171, politicians also use the compelling nature of the jeremiad to win elections. Richard L. Johannesen, "Ronald Reagan's Economic Jeremiad," *Central States Speech Journal* 37 (1986): 79–89, concludes that presidents can use the jeremiad to foster acceptance of economic policy.

Benedict Anderson's excellent *Imagined Communities: Reflections on the Origin and Spread of Nationalism*, 12th ed. (New York: Verso, 2003), provides a historical examination of the processes by which a community comes to "imagine" itself a nation with citizens willing to die for it. Several significant rhetorical analyses mine that same ground. Maurice Charland, "Constitutive Rhetoric: The case of the "Peuple Québécois," *Quarterly Journal of Speech* 73 (1987): 133–150, uses Kenneth Burke's principal of identification to explain how the "Peuple Québécois" were called into existence as political subjects. M. Lane Bruner, *Strategies of Remembrance: The Rhetorical Dimensions of National Identity Construction* (Columbia: University of South Carolina Press, 2002), explores the relationship between public speech and national identity, using case studies involving Russia, West Germany, and Quebec to understand how rhetoric helps to obfuscate historical memories while shaping public memories. *Rhetoric and Community: Studies in Unity and Fragmentation*, ed. J. Michael Hogan (Columbia: University of South Carolina Press, 1998), illuminates how rhetoric defines, divides, marginalizes, and polarizes the nation in regards to issues of race, gender, patriotism, and science.

Marouf A. Hasian Jr., *The Rhetoric of Eugenics in Anglo-American Thought* (Athens: University of Georgia Press, 1996), examines the way in which rhetors infuse the language and ideas of eugenics in democratic discourse, and how early twentieth-century immigrants, nonwhites, and other marginalized groups contested their resulting depiction as being inferior to whites. Of particular note is Hasian's recognition that myths help to explain the persuasive appeal of eugenics.

A myth represents a powerful rhetorical form. They also have a multitude of interpretations. Joseph Campbell's groundbreaking books, along with Mireca Eliade, *Myth and Reality* (New York: Harper & Row, 1963), identify myths as narrative gateways for humans to gain religious and spiritual insight. Campbell's work includes *Myths to Live By* (New York: Penguin Books, 1972), *The Hero with a Thousand Faces* (Princeton: Princeton University Press, 1973), and *The Power of Myth with Bill Moyers*, ed. Betty S. Flowers (New York: Anchor Books, 1991).

Carl Jung, *The Basic Writings of C. G. Jung*, Violet S. De Laszlo, ed., Reprint Edition (New York: Modern Library, 1993), notes that myths are not supernatural in nature—simply put, they reflect the fears and the fantasies of the human mind. Roland Barthes, *Mythologies*, trans. Annette Lavers (New York: Noonday Press, 1972), identifies myths as shared meanings of cultural artifacts, meanings that affirm existing power relationships while appearing to make those relationships seem natural. Claude Lévi-Strauss takes a structural approach to analyzing myths, arguing that myths from around the world all seem similar because myth itself is a universal language: *Myth and Meaning: Cracking the Code of Culture* (New York: Schocken Books, 1978), and *Mythologiques,* trans. John and Doreen Weightman, 4 vols. (Chicago: University of Chicago Press, 1990).

Elizabeth M. Baeten analyzes the theories of myth offered by Barthes, Eliade, and others in *The Magic Mirror: Myths Abiding Power* (New York: State University of New York Press, 1996).

For examples of myths from various cultures around the world, see David Leeming, *The World of Myth* (New York: Oxford University Press, 1990), and his *Myth: A Biography of Belief* (Oxford: Oxford University Press, 2002).

Rhetorical scholar Ernest G. Bormann discusses the narrative elements of myths in "Symbolic Convergence Theory: A Communication Formulation," *Journal of Communication* 35 (1985): 128–138.

Richard Slotkin's magnificent three-volume work on the Frontier Myth traces that centuries-old concept in popular media. Please see his *Gunfighter Nation: The Myth of the Frontier in Twentieth-Century America* (New York: Atheneum, 1992); *Regeneration through Violence: The Mythology of the American Frontier, 1600–1860* (Norman: University of Oklahoma Press, 1973); and *The Fatal Environment: The Myth of the Frontier in the Age of Industrialization, 1800–1890* (New York: Atheneum, 1985). Janice H. Rushing also brings insightful analyses to understanding the rhetorical dimensions of the Frontier Myth in popular media: "Mythic Evolution of 'The New Frontier' in Mass Mediated Rhetoric," *Critical Studies in Mass Communication* 3 (1986): 265–296; "The Rhetoric of the American Western Myth," *Communication Monographs* 50 (1983): 14–32; "Evolution of 'The New Frontier' in *Alien* and *Aliens:* Patriarchal Co-optation of the Feminine Archetype," *Quarterly Journal of Speech* 75 (1989): 1–24; and *Projecting the Shadow: The Cyborg Hero in American Film* (Chicago: University of Chicago Press, 1995)—coauthored with Thomas Frentz.

Slotkin's essay, "Dreams and Genocide: The American Myth of Regeneration through Violence," *The Journal of Popular Culture* 5 (1971): 38–59, discusses the mythic nature of Native American "savages." Mary E. Stuckey and John M. Murphy, "By Any Other Name: Rhetorical Colonialism in North America," *American Indian Culture and Research Journal* 25 (2001): 73–98, also examine Native Americans' identity as "savages" in early American rhetoric.

Savagery as a rhetorical/mythic concept used to justify acts of war is explored in Robert Ivie's, "Images of Savagery in American Justifications for War," *Communication Monographs* 47 (1980): 279–294, and "The Metaphor of Force in Prowar Discourse: The Case of 1812," *Quarterly Journal of Speech* 68 (1982): 240–253.

The Wild West as a manifestation of the Frontier Myth is discussed by Jenni Calder, *There Must be a Lone Ranger: The American West in Film and in Reality* (New York: Taplinger, 1974); David H. Murdoch, *The American West: The Invention of a Myth* (Reno: University of Nevada Press, 2001); and Henry N. Smith, *Vir-*

gin Land: The American West as Symbol and Myth (Cambridge: Harvard University Press, 1978).

The Crocodile Hunter, Survivor, and *The Amazing Race* are several popular television shows that articulate a contemporary version of the Frontier Myth, one that focuses on the economic aspects of conquering target wildernesses. Please see http://www.crocodilehunter.com; Keat Murray, "Surviving *Survivor:* Reading Mark Burnett's Field Guide and De-naturalizing Social Darwinism as Entertainment," *The Journal of American Culture* 24 (2001): 43–54; and http://www.cbs.com/primetime/amazing_race5/.

The American Dream represents an evolved version of the Frontier Myth. James T. Adams first popularized the term—American Dream—in *The Epic of America* (Boston: Little, Brown, and Company, 1946). Other insightful treatises on the American Dream include Jim Cullen, *The American Dream: A Short History of an Idea That Shaped a Nation* (Oxford: Oxford University Press, 2003); G. Thomas Goodnight, "Ronald Reagan and the American Dream: A Study in the Rhetoric Out of Time," in chapter 9 of *The Presidency and Rhetorical Leadership;* and Jennifer Hochschild, *Facing Up to the American Dream: Race, Class, and the Soul of the Nation* (Princeton: Princeton University Press, 1995). The stories from people who believe they have experienced the American Dream are collected by Studs Terkel, *American Dreams: Lost and Found* (New York: New Press, 1999); and by Dan Rather, *The American Dream: Stories from the Heart of Our Nation* (New York: HarperCollins, 2002).

Contemporary media, such as Michael Kinsley, "Mobility vs. Nobility," *Washington Post,* June 5, 2005, http://www.washingtonpost.com/wp-dyn/content/article/2005/06/03/AR2005060301464.html, declare that the mythic Dream is dying. Other recent media, such as Alan Reynolds, "Class Struggle?" *Wall Street Journal,* May 18, 2005, http://www.opinionjournal.com/editorial/feature.html?id=110006704, claim that the Dream is thriving. According to Linda Chavez, "Hispanics and the American Dream," *The LibertyHaven Foundation,* November 1996, http://www.libertyhaven.com/countriesandregions/latinamerica/hispanics.shtml, Hispanics are faring better with the Dream than other nonwhite groups.

For discussions of other, uniquely American myths, see James O. Robertson, *American Myth, American Reality* (New York: Hill & Wang, 1980); Richard T. Hughes, *Myths America Lives By* (Urbana: University of Illinois Press, 2004); Brian W. Dippie, *Custer's Last Stand: The Anatomy of an American Myth* (Lincoln: University of Nebraska Press, 1976); and John S. Lawrence and Robert Jewett, *The Myth of the American Superhero* (Grand Rapids: William B. Eerdmans Publishing Co., 2002).

Race and Immigration

The U.S. Census Bureau provides the statistical data regarding immigration rates in "Historical Census Statistics on Population Totals By Race, 1790 to 1990, and By Hispanic Origin, United States—Race and Hispanic Origin: 1790 to 1990," http://www.census.gov/population/documentation/twps0056/tab01.pdf.

For comprehensive histories of immigration trends, see Roger Daniels, *Coming to America: A History of Immigration and Ethnicity in American Life* (New York: HarperPerennial, 1990); Leonard Dinnerstein, Roger L. Nichols, and David M. Reimers, *Natives and Strangers: A Multicultural History of Americans* (New York: Oxford University Press, 1996); Leonard Dinnerstein and David M. Reimers, *Ethnic Americans: A History of Immigration*, 4th ed. (New York: Columbia University Press, 1999); and Ronald Takaki, *A Different Mirror: A History of Multicultural America* (New York: Little, Brown and Company, 1993).

Other works focus on one of the most volatile periods in immigration history, the late nineteenth and early twentieth centuries. For those that recount the social, economic, and political dynamics of that time, see Roger Daniels, *Not Like Us: Immigrants and Minorities in America, 1890–1924* (Chicago: Ivan R. Dee, 1997); John Higham, *Strangers in the Land: Patterns of American Nativism, 1860–1925* (New Brunswick: Rutgers University Press, 1988); and Paul McBride, *Culture Clash: Immigrants and Reformers, 1880–1920* (San Francisco: R and E Research Associates, 1975).

Primary documents reflecting the development of immigration policies are contained in Edith Abbott, *Immigration: Select Documents and Case Records* (New York: Arno Press and the New York Times, 1969).

Several studies provide the historical development of immigration control and reform. Daniel J. Tichenor and Keith Fitzgerald offer thorough and sweeping treatments in their respective books, *Dividing Lines: The Politics of Immigration Control in America* (Princeton: Princeton University Press, 2002); and *The Face of the Nation: Immigration, the State, and the National Identity* (Stanford: Stanford University Press, 1996). Desmond King, *Making Americans: Immigration, Race, and the Origins of the Diverse Democracy* (Cambridge: Harvard University Press, 2000), offers another insightful study that discusses how the definition of "whiteness" influenced immigration policies. Other works include Marion T. Bennett, *American Immigration Policies: A History* (Washington, D.C.: Public Affairs Press, 1963); Kitty Calavita, *U.S. Immigration Law and the Control of Labor: 1820–1924* (London: Academic Press, 1994); William S. Bernard, *American Immigration Policy—A Reappraisal* (Port Washington, NY: Kennikat, 1940); and Lawrence G. Brown, *Immigration: Cultural Conflicts and Social Adjustments* (New York: Arno Press and the New York Times, 1994).

Whiteness represents a contested yet powerful term, one that Anglo-Saxon Americans have used to determine which immigrant group qualifies to become an American. For example, see David R. Roediger, *Working toward Whiteness: How America's Immigrants Became White—The Strange Journey from Ellis Island to the Suburbs* (New York: Basic Books, 2005). How Irish and Italian immigrants, respectively, earned their whiteness is explored in Noel Ignatiev, *How the Irish Became White* (New York: Routledge, 1995); and Thomas A. Guglielmo, *White on Arrival: Italians, Race, Color, and Power in Chicago, 1890–1945* (Oxford: Oxford University Press, 2003). Matthew F. Jacobson, *Whiteness of a Different Color: European*

Immigrants and the Alchemy of Race (Cambridge: Harvard University Press, 1998), also provides an excellent analysis of the history and social implications of "whiteness" from the eighteenth century through the civil rights movement. For early-twentieth-century primary documents describing how immigrants could become white, see Winthrop Talbot, ed., *Americanization: Principles of Americanism/Essentials of Americanization/Technic of Race-Assimilation* (New York: H. W. Wilson Company, 1917).

White immigrants became a part of the legendary "melting pot," a national belief that whites from other parts of the world could be "mixed" together to form an American. The term became popular in the early twentieth century thanks to Israel Zangwill's play, *The Melting Pot: A Drama in Four Acts,* in *The Works of Israel Zangwill: The Melting Pot/Plaster Saints,* Edition De Luxe, vol. 12 (New York: AMS Press, 1969). The political and social consequences of the term "melting pot" are explored in Philip Gleason's works, "The Melting Pot: Symbol of Fusion or Confusion?" *American Quarterly* 16 (1964): 20–46, and in *Speaking of Diversity: Language and Ethnicity in Twentieth-Century America* (Baltimore: Johns Hopkins University Press, 1992). For other analyses of this term, see Charles Hirschman, "America's Melting Pot Reconsidered," *Annual Review of Sociology* 9 (1983): 397–423; and Neil L. Shumsky, "Zangwill's 'The Melting Pot': Ethnic Tensions on Stage," *American Quarterly* 27 (1975): 29–41.

Several exemplary works discuss the historical and social construction of nonwhite races. Thomas F. Gossett explores the evolution of race theory from the fourteenth through the twentieth centuries in *Race: The History of an Idea in America,* New Edition (New York: Oxford University Press, 1997). Two provocative books focus on the origin of racial belief from the seventeenth through the nineteenth centuries: Reginald Horsman, *Race and Manifest Destiny: The Origins of American Racial Anglo-Saxonism* (Cambridge: Harvard University Press, 1981); and Ronald Takaki, *Iron Cages: Race and Culture in Nineteenth-Century America* (Seattle: University of Washington Press, 1979). Matthew P. Guterl, *The Color of Race in America, 1900–1940* (Cambridge: Harvard University Press, 2001), examines the lives of four prominent nonwhites of the early twentieth century to illuminate how whites and blacks struggled to control their racial identities.

David Roediger discusses the connection between working-class racism and racial stereotypes in *The Wages of Whiteness: Race and the Making of the American Working Class,* Revised Edition (New York: Verso, 2003). Other scholarship addresses how race has influenced the legal and constitutional meaning of citizenship, including Ian F. Haney López, *White by Law: The Legal Construction of Race* (New York: New York University Press, 1996); Kenneth L. Karst, *Belonging to America: Equal Citizenship and the Constitution* (New Haven: Yale University Press, 1989); and Rogers M. Smith's excellent history of race and U.S. citizenship laws, *Civic Ideals: Conflicting Visions of Citizenship in U.S. History* (New Haven: Yale University Press, 1997).

For historical scholarship on the presidency and race, see Russell L. Riley, *The Presidency and the Politics of Racial Inequality: Nation-Keeping from 1831 to 1965* (New York: Columbia University Press, 1999); and Kenneth O' Reilly, *Nixon's Piano: Presidents and Racial Politics from Washington to Clinton* (New York: Free Press, 1995). Roosevelt gets little coverage in either book.

For examinations of the complex relationship between American character and racial/ethnic diversity, see Lawrence H. Fuch's exemplary historical study, *The American Kaleidoscope: Race, Ethnicity, and the Civic Culture* (Hanover: Wesleyan University Press, 1990). Stephen Cornell and Douglas Hartmann bring a sociological perspective to American identity in *Ethnicity and Race: Making Identities in a Changing World* (Thousand Oaks: Pine Forge Press, 1998). In *Concepts of Ethnicity* (Cambridge: Harvard University Press, 1982), William Petersen, Michael Novak, and Philip Gleason illuminate the unique characteristics of racial/ethnic groups and their impact on the multicultural nature of America.

Several books question the acceptance of multiculturalism as a standard for national identity. Arthur M. Schlesinger Jr., *The Disuniting of America: Reflections on a Multicultural Society* (New York: Norton & Company, 1998), takes issue with "radical multiculturalism" being used as a response to racism, arguing that the former threatens the ideals upon which the country was founded. More controversial in their conclusions regarding the threat of multiculturalism to an intact American culture are Samuel P. Huntington, *Who Are We? The Challenges to America's National Identity* (New York: Simon & Schuster, 2004); and Patrick J. Buchanan, *The Death of the West: How Dying Populations and Immigrant Invasions Imperil Our Country and Civilization* (New York: St. Martin's Press, 2002).

Political correctness as a consequence of multiculturalism is explored by Richard Feldstein, *Political Correctness: A Response from the Cultural Left* (Minneapolis: University of Minnesota Press, 1997); Marilyn Friedman and Jan Narveson, *Political Correctness: For and Against* (Lanham: Rowman & Littlefield Publishers, 1995); and M. E. Banning, "The Limits of PC Discourse: Linking Language Use to Social Practice," *Pedagogy* 4 (2004): 191–214.

Immediately after September 11, 2001, the media warned of the dangers of uncontrolled multiculturalism, particularly in relation to suspected Islamic terrorists living in the country: see, for example, Evan Thomas, "Cracking the Terror Code," *Newsweek*, October 15, 2001, 42–46; and Ginger Thompson, "Mexico President Urges U.S. to Act Soon on Migrants," *New York Times*, September 16, 2001, www.nytimes.com.

Recent periodicals note that many Americans believe Hispanic culture is growing more powerful and threatens to take over the social identity of America. For examples, see Arian Campo-Flores and Howard Fineman, "A Latin Power Surge," *Newsweek*, May 30, 2005, 25–31; *The Week*, "How They See Us: Blind to the Contributions of Mexicans," May 27, 2005, 14; Massimo Calabresi, "Deal or No Deal?," *Newsweek*, April 10, 2006, http://www.cnn.com; Arian Campo-Flores, "America's

Divide," *Newsweek,* April 10, 2006, 28–38; *CNN,* "Estimated Number of Illegal Immigrants in U.S.," May 11, 2006, http://www.cnn.com; Gregory Rodriguez, "Why We're the New Irish," *Newsweek,* May 30, 2005, 35; Dan Whitcomb, "LA Immigration Activists Mobilize for Washington," *Washington Post,* May 9, 2006, http://www.washingtonpost.com; Fareed Zakaria, "To Become an American," *Newsweek,* April 10, 2006, 39; Peter D. Salins, "Assimilation Nation," *New York Times,* May 11, 2006, http://www.nytimes.com; Ruben Navarrette Jr., "No Such Thing as a Good Immigrant," *San Diego Union-Tribune,* March 29, 2006, http://www.signonsandiego.com; and Gene Wade, Linda Hoyman, Jimmy Hercheck, Alan Hoon, and Tim Kenyon, "What Do You Think?", *Atlanta Journal-Constitution,* December 8, 2004, Wednesday Home Edition, Gwinnett News Section.

The media identifies several themes in the 2006 "culture war" over illegal immigrants and reform measures. Some sources argue that illegal immigrants negatively affect the economy: *The Week,* "A GOP Split over Immigration," April 7, 2006, 2; David Streitfeld, "A Job Americans Won't Do, Even at $34 an Hour," *Los Angeles Times,* May 18, 2006, http://www.latimes.com; and Teresa Watanabe and Joe Mathews, "Unions Helped to Organize 'Day Without Immigrants,'" *Los Angeles Times,* May 3, 2006, http://www.latimes.com. According to other sources, illegal immigrants highlight the fear of continued terrorist threats: Frank Ahrens, "For Mexicans and Americans, A Nudge to 'Think Together,'" *Washington Post,* May 7, 2006, http://www.washingtonpost.com; and Holly Bailey "A Border War," *Newsweek,* April 3, 2006, 22–25.

For media coverage of the pro-immigration responses to immigration reform in 2006, including information on "A Day Without Immigrants," see Darryl Fears and N. C. Aizenman, "Immigrant Groups Split on Boycott," *Washington Post,* April 14, 2006, http://www.washingtonpost.com; Gary Polakovic, "Marchers Raise Voice in County," *Los Angeles Times,* May 2, 2006, http://www.latimes.com; Dudley Althaus and Cynthia Leonor Garza, "Dreams of Many Ride on Boycott," *Houston Chronicle,* May 1, 2006, http://www.chron.com; Darryl Fears and Krissah Williams, "Boycott Gives Voice to Illegal Workers," *Washington Post,* May 2, 2006, http://www.washingtonpost.com; Erin Texeira, "Some Immigrants Reluctant to Boycott," *Dallas Morning News,* April 30, 2006, http://www.dallasnews.com; Darryl Fears, "After Protests, Backlash Grows," *Washington Post,* May 3, 2006, http://www.washingtonpost.com; Leslie Sanchez, "Boycott? More Like Bullying," *Los Angeles Times,* May 4, 2006, http://www.latimes.com; Erin A. Kaplan, "What Was Lost in the Crowd," *Los Angeles Times,* May 3, 2006, http://www.latimes.com; and *Associated Press,* "Sessions: 'The Senate Should be Ashamed of Itself,'" *CNN,* May 19, 2006, http://www.cnn.com.

For information on the controversy surrounding the Spanish-language version of the national anthem, see Laura Wides-Munoz, "'Star-Spangled Banner' in Spanish Draws Protest," *Houston Chronicle,* April 28, 2006, http://www.chron.com; Ana Veciana-Suarez, "Anthem Debate Hits Sour Notes," *Houston Chronicle,* May 10, 2006, http://www.chron.com; *Associated Press,* "Bush: Sing 'Star-Spangled Banner' in English," *CNN,* April 28, 2006, http://www.cnn.com; Ralph E. Shaffer and Walter P. Coombs, "Our Discordant Anthem," *Los Angeles Times,* May 2, 2006, http://www.latimes.com.

President George W. Bush's May 2006 nationally televised address outlines his proposal for immigration reform: "President Bush Addresses the Nation on Immigration Reform, May 15, 2006," http://www.whitehouse.gov. Responses to Bush's ideas can be found at CNN's website, http://www.cnn.com, including "L.A. Braces for Protest, as Bush Addresses 'Emotional Debate,'" March 25, 2006; and "Bush Backs Border Fence," May 18, 2006.

Finally, several authors and activists discuss the tension between American identity and their nonwhite identities during a four-part discussion on *National Public Radio* in January 2005. "Racial Identity in Multi-Ethnic America" can be heard at http://www.npr.org/templates/story/story.php?storyId=4257450.

Native Americans

At the end of the nineteenth century, one of the most influential books to chronicle the mistreatment of American Indians was Helen H. Jackson's *A Century of Dishonor: A Sketch of the United States Government's Dealings with Some of the Indian Tribes* (1881; Norman: University of Oklahoma Press, 1995). Jackson's book guided public opinion against the political machinations destroying Indian cultures. For books that reacquainted readers of the late twentieth century with the calculated abuses that American Indians faced, see Dee Brown, *Bury My Heart at Wounded Knee: An Indian History of the American West* (New York: Holt, Rinehart & Winston, 1970); and Virgil J. Vogel, *This Country Was Ours: A Documentary History of the American Indian* (New York: Harper & Row, 1972).

Colin G. Calloway's thought-provoking book, *New Worlds for All: Indians, Europeans, and the Remaking of Early America* (Baltimore: Johns Hopkins University Press, 1997), discusses Indians' histories and their relationships with European settlers. Calloway's edited collections provide accounts by Native Americans of how they interpreted "civilization" being forced upon them: *Our Hearts Fell to the Ground: Plains Indian Views of How the West was Lost* (Boston: Bedford Books of St. Martin's Press, 1996); and *The World Turned Upside Down: Indian Voices from Early America* (Boston: Bedford/St. Martin's Press, 1994).

The political, cultural, and pedagogical attempts by the government to assimilate Indians at the end of the nineteenth century are discussed by Brian W. Dippie, *The Vanishing American: White Attitudes and U.S. Indian Policy* (Lawrence: University Press of Kansas, 1982); Henry E. Fritz, *The Movement for Indian Assimilation, 1860–1890* (Philadelphia: University of Pennsylvania Press, 1963); and Frederick E. Hoxie, *A Final Promise: The Campaign to Assimilate the Indians, 1880–1920* (Cambridge: Cambridge University Press, 1984). On public policies involving Native Americans in the latter part of the twentieth century, see Fremont J. Lyden and

Lyman H. Legters, eds., *Native Americans and Public Policy* (Pittsburgh: University of Pittsburgh Press, 1992); and Oren Lyons, John Mohawk, Vine Deloria Jr., Laurence Hauptman, Howard Berman, Donald Grinde Jr., Curtis Berkey, and Robert Venables, eds., *Exiled in the Land of the Free: Democracy, Indian Nations, and the U.S. Constitution* (Santa Fe: Clear Light Publishers, 1992).

The harsh treatment of American Indians while on reservations, particularly in the reservation schools, is recounted in two important books: David W. Adams, *Education for Extinction: American Indians and the Boarding School Experience, 1875–1928* (Lawrence: University Press of Kansas, 1995); and Richard H. Pratt, *Battlefield and Classroom: Four Decades with the American Indian, 1867–1904*, ed. Robert M. Utley (1904; Norman: University of Oklahoma Press, 2003). Pratt, an army officer, developed the famous Carlisle Indian School. Richard Morris and Philip Wander, "Native American Rhetoric: Dancing in the Shadows of the Ghost Dance," *Quarterly Journal of Speech* 76 (1990): 164–191, provide a rhetorical analysis of the "ghost dance," a controversial religious ritual some Indians practiced while being held on reservations.

Several works examine the construction of American Indians' image in the popular imagination. John M. Coward, *The Newspaper Indian: Native American Identity in the Press, 1820–90* (Urbana: University of Illinois Press, 1999), describes how Indians became a symbolic marker by which whites could judge their own progress. Raymond W. Stedman, *Shadows of the Indian: Stereotypes in American Culture* (Norman: University of Oklahoma Press, 1982), illuminates how films, novels, and sports' mascots cemented the images of the "noble savage" and the "bloodthirsty savage" in the public's mind. Richard Drinnon, *Facing West: The Metaphysics of Indian-Hating and Empire Building* (Norman: University of Oklahoma Press, 1997), links racism and colonialism to document the national pastime of hating Indians, and how that hatred became the justification for the conquest of the North American continent and for American imperialism. Shari M. Huhndorf, *Going Native: Indians in the American Cultural Imagination* (Ithaca: Cornell University Press, 2001), and Philip J. Deloria, *Playing Indian* (New Haven: Yale University Press, 1998), discuss whites' attempts to define a romanticized version of what it means to be "Native," and to use that construction to exclude Native Americans from national society. Jackson Miller's "'Indians,' 'Braves,' and 'Redskins': A Performative Struggle for Control of an Image," *Quarterly Journal of Speech* 85 (1999): 188–202, examines how baseball team owners and fans negotiate with American Indians who claim that baseball team mascots negatively depict Native Americans.

For a chronological account of Indians' cultures from their earliest days to the present, see Duane Champagne, ed., *Chronology of Native North American History: From Pre-Columbian Times to the Present* (Detroit: Gale Research Inc., 1994).

For analyses of how Native Americans construct their own images and how they have increased their political power in modern times, see Joane Nagel, *American Indian Ethnic Renewal: Red Power and the Resurgence of Identity and Culture* (New York: Oxford University Press, 1997); and Stephen Cornell, *The Return of the*

Native: American Indian Political Resurgence (New York: Oxford University Press, 1988).

Contemporary accounts of Indians as prosperous entrepreneurs include Brett D. Fromson, *Hitting the Jackpot: The Inside Story of the Richest Indian Tribe in History* (New York: Atlantic Monthly Press, 2003); Joan M. King and Elliot McIntire, "The Impact of the Indian Gaming Regulatory Act on Tribes in the U.S.," in chapter 3 of *Tourism and Gaming on American Indian Lands,* ed. Alan A. Lew and George A. Van Otten (New York: Cognizant Communication Corporation, 1998); Mark Fitzgerald, "Black and White and Red All Over," *Editor & Publisher,* January 1, 2004, www.editorandpublisher.com; and Michael Isikoff, "With Friends Like These . . . ," *Newsweek,* April 18, 2005, 44. However, according to John J. Miller, "Keeping Indians Down on the Reservation," *The Week,* February 10, 2006, 12, most Indians are far from being financially independent.

African Americans

Gunnar Myrdal's two-volume work, *An American Dilemma: The Negro Problem and Modern Democracy* (New Brunswick: Transaction Publishers, 2002), represents the germinal examination of virtually all aspects of African American life as it had been impacted by slavery and racism. Myrdal's work, originally published in 1944, was instrumental in the Supreme Court's 1954 anti-segregation decision.

The lives of two nineteenth-century leaders of the African American community are covered, respectively, in Louis R. Harlan, *Booker T. Washington: The Wizard of Tuskegee, 1901–1915* (New York: Oxford University Press, 1986); and David L. Lewis, *W. E. B. Du Bois: Biography of a Race* (New York: Henry Holt and Company, 1993). One of Du Bois's most famous speeches, "The Talented Tenth," which called for the most gifted blacks to receive the best education in order to lead their community, can be found in chapter 2 of *The Negro Problem: A Series of Articles by Representative American Negroes of To-Day,* Contributions by Booker T. Washington, W. E. B. Du Bois, Paul L. Dunbar, Charles W. Chesnutt, and others (New York: Arno Press and the *New York Times,* 1969).

Blacks' negative stereotypes in popular culture are discussed by Donald Bogle, *Toms, Coons, Mulattoes, Mammies, and Bucks: An Interpretive History of Blacks in American Films,* 3rd ed. (New York: Continuum, 1994); and John Kisch and Edward Mapp, *A Separate Cinema: Fifty Years of Black-Cast Posters* (New York: Noonday Press, 1992).

Two important works outlining the grudging economic and social relationship between blacks and whites in the South are C. Vann Woodward's *The Strange Career of Jim Crow* (1955; Oxford: Oxford University Press, 2001); and W. J. Cash, *The Mind of the South* (1941; New York: Vintage, 1991). Other scholarship presents a revisionist interpretation to Woodward and Cash, one that does not discount those earlier works, but argues that whites viewed blacks as more expendable after the Civil War, particularly since whites of all economic levels united to establish a "pure" community. For example, see Joel Williamson's treatises, *The Crucible of Race: Black-White Relations in the American South since Emancipation* (New York: Oxford University Press, 1984), and *A Rage for Order: Black/White Relations in the American South since Emancipation* (New York: Oxford University Press, 1986).

Other books cover various aspects of African American history and intellectual thought. August Meier, *Negro Thought in America, 1880–1915: Racial Ideologies in the Age of Booker T. Washington* (Ann Arbor: University of Michigan Press, 1964), and Mia Bay, *The White Image in the Black Mind: African-American Ideas about White People, 1830–1925* (New York: Oxford University Press, 2000), discuss the complexity of thought regarding how blacks saw their captors, both before and after slavery. Lee D. Baker, *From Savage to Negro: Anthropology and the Construction of Race, 1896–1954* (Berkeley: University of California Press, 1998), explores the development of racial categories for blacks through scientific, legal, and popular means. Herbert Shapiro, *White Violence and Black Response: From Reconstruction to Montgomery* (Amherst: University of Massachusetts Press, 1988), details the organized plans of violence against blacks in South Carolina from the late nineteenth century to the civil rights era.

Recent media report on African Americans' place in contemporary society. Ellis Cose, "A Real Racial Tipping Point" *Newsweek,* February 27, 2006, 40, identifies the political and corporate success that some blacks enjoy. Other articles focus on the racism that continues to stymie blacks' advancement. Jonathan Alter, "The Other America," *Newsweek,* September 19, 2005, 42–48, reports on the plight of African Americans following Hurricane Katrina. The *Associated Press,* "Fox: Comment about Blacks Misinterpreted," May 17, 2005, http://www.cnn.com/2005/WORLD/americas/05/17/fox.blacks.ap/index.html, reports on Mexican president Vicente Fox's comment that Mexican immigrants were willing to prove themselves by taking the jobs "that even blacks won't do." *The Week,* "Bennett: The Meaning of a Racial Comment," October 14, 2005, 21, summarizes the furor caused by William Bennett's remark about aborting African American babies as a means to decrease crime. Coverage of the shooting incident involving four white New York City police officers killing an unarmed and innocent West African man in 1999 includes Hamil R. Harris, "Marchers Decry N.Y. Police Shooting," *Washington Post,* February 19, 1999, Final Edition, http://www.washingtonpost.com; Lynne Duke, "Juror Says Weak Case Made Diallo Verdicts Inevitable," *Washington Post,* February 28, 2000, http://www.washingtonpost.com; and *Washington Post,* "Race a Factor in Diallo Case, Clinton Says," March 5, 2000, http://www.washingtonpost.com. Clarence Thomas's infamous remark about lynching can be found in "Hearing of the Senate Judiciary Committee on the Nomination of Clarence Thomas to the Supreme Court," October 11, 1991, *Electronic Text Center,* University of Virginia Library, http://www.etext.virginia.edu. Finally, coverage by CNN of James Byrd's dragging death can be found at http://www.cnn.com; for example, see "Closing Arguments Today in Texas Dragging-Death Trial," February 22, 1999.

Several studies examine the history and influence of German immigration to America. La Vern J. Rippley, *The German-American* (Boston: Twayne Publishers, 1976), covers the pre-Revolutionary period to the post–Civil War era. Other works address German-American history through post–World War One, including Richard O'Connor, *The German Americans: An Informal History* (Boston: Little, Brown and Co., 1968); and Albert Faust, *The German Element in the United States: With Special Reference to its Political, Moral, Social, and Educational Influence*, 2 Vols. (New York: The Steuben Society of America, 1927). Joseph Wandel, *The German Dimension of American History* (Chicago: Nelson-Hall, 1979), discusses German influence through World War Two. The more recent work by Don H. Tolzman, *The German-American Experience* (New York: Humanity Books, 2000), examines various facets of German culture through the 1990s. Mary Jane Corry's "The Role of German Singing Societies in Nineteenth-Century America," in *Germans in America: Aspects of German-American Relations in the Nineteenth Century,* ed. E. Allen McCormick (New York: Brooklyn College/Columbia University Press, 1983), recounts how Germans aided America in becoming a "musical mecca." In fact, this volume contains essays on various political, social, economic, and literary aspects of German influence in America. Finally, Colin G. Calloway, Gerd Gemünden, and Susanne Zantop, eds., *Germans and Indians: Fantasies, Encounters, Projections* (Lincoln: University of Nebraska Press, 2002), examine the historical and cultural interactions between German immigrants and Native Americans.

Several studies focus primarily on German-Americans' "fall from grace" during World War I. Charles T. Johnson, *Culture at Twilight: The National German-American Alliance, 1901–1918* (New York: Peter Lang, 1999), chronicles how the NGAA sought to preserve an intact German culture in America. Frederick C. Luebke, *Bonds of Loyalty: German Americans and World War I* (DeKalb: Northern Illinois University Press, 1974), and Clifton J. Child, *The German-Americans in Politics 1914–1917* (Madison: University of Wisconsin Press), provide accounts of the rampant xenophobia, and the attending violence, which German-Americans faced. Carl Wittke offers insightful analyses of the decline of the German-American press during the Great War: *German-Americans and the World War: With Special Emphasis on Ohio's German-Language Press* (Ohio: The Ohio State Archaeological and Historical Society, 1936), and *The German-Language Press in America* (Lexington: University of Kentucky Press, 1957).

Speeches and articles by prominent supporters and critics of German-Americans during World War I can be found in *Pamphlets in American History: European War,* Microfiche/Microfilm. For supporters, see Richard Bartholdt, "The Attitude of American Citizens of German Blood in the European War, February 19, 1915, in the House of Representatives," Microfiche (Washington, D.C.: Government Printing Office, 1915); William H. Harm, "A Big American Speech by a Big American of

German Birth, 1917," Microfiche (Pender, NB: Pender Republic, 1917); and Charles J. Hexamer, "Address of Dr. C. J. Hexamer, President of the National German American Alliance, Mass Meeting at the Academy of Music, Philadelphia, PA, Tuesday, November 24, 1914," Microfilm (Philadelphia: The Alliance/Graf. & Breuninger Print, 1914). For condemnations of German-Americans, see Frances A. Kellor, "Neighborhood Americanization: A Discussion of the Alien in a New Country and of the Native American in his Home Country, February 8, 1918," Microfiche (New York: Colony Club, 1918); and Frank H. Simonds, "Act and Act Quickly," Microfiche (New York: Conference Committee on National Preparedness, 1917).

Bibliography

Abbott, Edith. *Immigration: Select Documents and Case Records.* New York: Arno Press and the New York Times, 1969.

Adams, Brooks. *The Law of Civilization and Decay: An Essay on History.* New York: Macmillan & Co., 1895.

Adams, David W. *Education for Extinction: American Indians and the Boarding School Experience, 1875–1928.* Lawrence: University Press of Kansas, 1995.

Adams, James T. *The Epic of America.* Boston: Little, Brown, and Company, 1946.

Ahrens, Frank. "For Mexicans and Americans, A Nudge to " 'Think Together.' " *Washington Post,* May 7, 2006, http://www.washingtonpost.com.

Alter, Jonathan. "Between the Lines Online: Loud and Clear." *Newsweek,* September 20, 2002. http://web.lexis-nexis.com.

———. "The Other America." *Newsweek,* September 19, 2005, 42–48.

Althaus, Dudley, and Cynthia Leonor Garza. "Dreams of Many Ride on Boycott." *Houston Chronicle, May 1, 2006,* http://www.chron.com

Anderson, Benedict. *Imagined Communities: Reflections on the Origin and Spread of Nationalism.* 12th ed. New York: Verso, 2003.

Associated Press. "Bush: Sing 'Star-Spangled Banner' in English." *CNN,* April 28, 2006, http://www.cnn.com.

———. "Fox: Comment about Blacks Misinterpreted." *CNN,* May 17, 2005, http://www.cnn.com.

————. "Sessions: 'The Senate Should be Ashamed of Itself.' " *CNN*, May 19, 2006, http://www.cnn.com.

Bailey, Holly. "A Border War." *Newsweek,* April 3, 2006, 22–25.

Bailyn, Bernard. *The Ideological Origins of the American Revolution.* Cambridge: The Belknap Press of Harvard University Press, 1992.

Baker, Lee D. *From Savage to Negro: Anthropology and the Construction of Race, 1896–1954.* Berkeley: University of California Press, 1998.

Ballot Box Bunny. I. Freleng, Director. Warner Brothers. 1951.

Banning, M. E. "The Limits of PC Discourse: Linking Language Use to Social Practice." *Pedagogy* 4 (2004): 191–214.

Barnet, Richard J. *The Rockets' Red Glare: When America Goes to War, The Presidents and the People.* New York: Simon and Schuster, 1990.

Barthes, Roland. *Mythologies.* Translated by Annette Lavers. New York: Noonday Press, 1972.

Bay, Mia. *The White Image in the Black Mind: African-American Ideas about White People, 1830–1925.* New York: Oxford University Press, 2000.

Beasley, Vanessa B. *You, the People: American National Identity in Presidential Rhetoric.* College Station: Texas A&M University Press, 2004.

Bederman, Gail. *Manliness and Civilization: A Cultural History of Gender and Race in the United States, 1880–1917.* Chicago: University of Chicago Press, 1995.

Bennett, Marion T. *American Immigration Policies: A History.* Washington, DC: Public Affairs Press, 1963.

Bercovitch, Sacvan. *The American Jeremiad.* Madison: University of Wisconsin Press, 1978.

————. *The Puritan Origins of the American Self.* New Haven: Yale University Press, 1975.

————. *The Rites of Assent: Transformations in the Symbolic Construction of America.* New York: Routledge, 1993.

Bernard, William S. *American Immigration Policy—A Reappraisal.* Port Washington, NY: Kennikat, 1940.

Billington, Ray A. *America's Frontier Heritage.* New York: Holt, Rinehart and Winston, 1966.

————. *The Genesis of the Frontier Thesis: A Study in Historical Creativity.* San Marino, CA: Huntington Library, 1971.

Bitzer, Lloyd F. "The Rhetorical Situation." In *Readings in Rhetorical Criticism.* 3rd ed. Edited by Carl R. Burgchardt. State College: Strata Publishing, Inc., 2005.

Bogle, Donald. *Toms, Coons, Mulattoes, Mammies, and Bucks: An Interpretive History of Blacks in American Films.* 3rd ed. New York: Continuum, 1994.

Boorstin, Daniel J. *The Americans: The National Experience.* New York: Vintage Books, 1965.

Bormann, Ernest G. "Fetching Good Out of Evil: A Rhetorical Use of Calamity." *Quarterly Journal of Speech* 63 (1977): 130–139.

———. "Symbolic Convergence Theory: A Communication Formulation." *Journal of Communication* 35 (1985): 128–138.

Brands, H. W. *T. R.: The Last Romantic.* New York: Basic Books, 1997.

Brown, Dee. *Bury My Heart at Wounded Knee: An Indian History of the American West.* New York: Holt, Rinehart & Winston, 1970.

Brown, Lawrence G. *Immigration: Cultural Conflicts and Social Adjustments.* New York: Arno Press and The New York Times, 1994.

Bruner, M. Lane. *Strategies of Remembrance: The Rhetorical Dimensions of National Identity Construction.* Columbia: University of South Carolina Press, 2002.

Bryant, Donald C. "Rhetoric: Its Functions and Its Scope." *Quarterly Journal of Speech* 39 (1953): 401–424.

Buchanan, Patrick J. *The Death of the West: How Dying Populations and Immigrant Invasions Imperil Our Country and Civilization.* New York: St. Martin's Press, 2002.

Burke, Kenneth. *A Rhetoric of Motives.* Berkeley: University of California Press, 1969.

Bush, George W. "President Bush Addresses the Nation on Immigration Reform, May 15, 2006." http://www.whitehouse.gov.

Calabresi, Massimo. "Deal or No Deal?" *Newsweek,* April 10, 2006. http://www.cnn.com/2006/POLITICS/04/10/immigration.tm/index.html.

Calavita, Kitty. *U.S. Immigration Law and the Control of Labor: 1820–1924.* London: Academic Press, 1994.

Calder, Jenni. *There Must Be a Lone Ranger: The American West in Film and in Reality.* New York: Taplinger, 1974.

Calloway, Colin G. *New Worlds for All: Indians, Europeans, and the Remaking of Early America.* Baltimore: Johns Hopkins University Press, 1997.

———, ed. *Our Hearts Fell to the Ground: Plains Indian Views of How the West Was Lost.* Boston: Bedford Books/St. Martin's Press, 1996.

———, ed. *The World Turned Upside Down: Indian Voices from Early America.* Boston: Bedford Books/St. Martin's Press, 1994.

Campbell, Joseph. *Myths to Live By.* New York: Penguin Books, 1972.

———. *The Hero with a Thousand Faces.* Princeton: Princeton University Press, 1973.

———. *The Power of Myth with Bill Moyers.* Edited by Betty S. Flowers. New York: Anchor Books, 1991.

Campo-Flores, Arian. "America's Divide." *Newsweek,* April 10, 2006, 28–38.

Campo-Flores, Arian, and Howard Fineman. "A Latin Power Surge." *Newsweek,* May 30, 2005, 25–31.

Carpenter, Ronald H. "Frederick Jackson Turner and the Rhetorical Impact of the Frontier Thesis." *Quarterly Journal of Speech* 63 (1977): 117–129.

———. "The Historical Jeremiad as Rhetorical Genre." In *Form and Genre: Shaping Rhetorical Action.* Edited by Karlyn K. Campbell and Kathleen H. Jamieson. Falls Church, VA: Speech Communication Association, 1978.

. "The Rhetorical Genesis of Style in the 'Frontier Hypothesis of Frederick Jackson Turner.'" *Southern Speech Communication Journal* 37 (1972): 233–248.

Cashman, Sean. *American in the Age of the Titans: The Progressive Era and World War I.* New York: New York University Press, 1988.

Ceaser, James W., Glen E. Thurow, Jeffrey Tulis, and Joseph M. Bessette. "The Rise of the Rhetorical Presidency." *Presidential Studies Quarterly* 11 (1981): 158–171.

Champagne, Duane, ed. *Chronology of Native North American History: From Pre-Columbian Times to the Present.* Detroit: Gale Research, Inc., 1994.

Chavez, Linda. "Hispanics and the American Dream." *The Liberty Haven Foundation*, November 1996. http://www.libertyhaven.com/countriesandregions/latinamerica/hispanics.shtml.

Chessman, G. Wallace. *Theodore Roosevelt and the Politics of Power.* Edited by Oscar Handlin. Boston: Little, Brown, and Company, 1969.

CNN. "Bush Backs Border Fence." May 18, 2006. http://www.cnn.com.

. "Closing Arguments Today in Texas Dragging-Death Trial." February 22, 1999. http://www.cnn.com.

. "Estimated Number of Illegal Immigrants in U.S." May 11, 2006. http://www.cnn.com.

. "L.A. Braces for Protest, as Bush Addresses 'Emotional Debate.'" March 25, 2006. http://www.cnn.com.

Cornell, Stephen. *The Return of the Native: American Indian Political Resurgence.* New York: Oxford University Press, 1988.

Cornell, Stephen, and Douglas Hartmann. *Ethnicity and Race: Making Identities in a Changing World.* Thousand Oaks: Pine Forge Press, 1998.

Corry, Mary Jane. "The Role of German Singing Societies in Nineteenth-Century America." In *Germans in America: Aspects of German-American Relations in the Nineteenth Century.* Edited by E. Allen McCormick. New York: Brooklyn College/Columbia University Press, 1983.

Cose, Ellis. "A Real Racial Tipping Point." *Newsweek*, February 27, 2006, 40.

Coward, John M. *The Newspaper Indian: Native American Identity in the Press, 1820–90.* Urbana: University of Illinois Press, 1999.

Cullen, Jim. *The American Dream: A Short History of an Idea that Shaped a Nation.* Oxford: Oxford University Press, 2003.

Dalton, Kathleen. *Theodore Roosevelt: A Strenuous Life.* New York: Alfred A. Knopf, 2002.

Daniels, Roger. *Coming to America: A History of Immigration and Ethnicity in American Life.* New York: HarperPerennial, 1990.

. *Not Like Us: Immigrants and Minorities in America, 1890–1924.* Chicago: Ivan R. Dee, 1997.

Deloria, Philip J. *Playing Indian.* New Haven: Yale University Press, 1998.

Dinnerstein, Leonard, and David M. Reimers. *Ethnic Americans: A History of Immigration.* 4th ed. New York: Columbia University Press, 1999.

Dinnerstein, Leonard, Roger L. Nichols, and David M. Reimers. *Natives and Strang-*

ers: *A Multicultural History of Americans.* New York: Oxford University Press, 1996.

Dippie, Brian W. *Custer's Last Stand: The Anatomy of an American Myth.* Lincoln: University of Nebraska Press, 1976.

———. *The Vanishing American: White Attitudes and U.S. Indian Policy.* Lawrence: University Press of Kansas, 1982.

Dorsey, Leroy G. "Preaching Morality in Modern America: Theodore Roosevelt's Rhetorical Progressivism." Chap. 2 in *Rhetoric and Reform in the Progressive Era.* Vol. 6. Edited by J. Michael Hogan. *A Rhetorical History of the United States: Significant Moments in American Public Discourse.* East Lansing: Michigan State University Press, 2003.

———. "Sailing into the 'Wondrous Now': The Myth of the American Navy's World Cruise." *Quarterly Journal of Speech* 83 (1997): 447–465.

———. "The Frontier Myth in Presidential Rhetoric: Theodore Roosevelt's Campaign for Conservation." *Western Journal of Communication* 59 (1995): 1–19.

———. "Theodore Roosevelt and Corporate America, 1901–1909: A Reexamination." *Presidential Studies Quarterly* 25 (1995): 725–739.

———, ed. *The Presidency and Rhetorical Leadership.* College Station: Texas A&M University Press, 2002.

Dorsey, Leroy G., and Rachel M. Harlow. "'We Want Americans Pure and Simple': Theodore Roosevelt and the Myth of Americanism." *Rhetoric & Public Affairs* 6 (2003): 55–78.

Drinnon, Richard. *Facing West: The Metaphysics of Indian-Hating and Empire Building.* Norman: University of Oklahoma Press, 1997.

Du Bois, W. E. Burghardt. "The Talented Tenth." Chap. 2 in *The Negro Problem: A Series of Articles by Representative American Negroes of To-Day.* Contributions by Booker T. Washington, W. E. B. Du Bois, Paul L. Dunbar, Charles W. Chesnutt, and others. New York: Arno Press and the New York Times, 1969.

Duke, Lynne. "Juror Says Weak Case Made Diallo Verdicts Inevitable." *Washington Post,* February 28, 2000, http://www.washingtonpost.com.

Dyer, Thomas G. *Theodore Roosevelt and the Idea of Race.* Baton Rouge: Louisiana State University Press, 1980.

Eliade, Mircea. *Myth and Reality.* New York: Harper & Row, 1963.

Electronic Text Center. "Hearing of the Senate Judiciary Committee on the Nomination of Clarence Thomas to the Supreme Court, October 11, 1991." University of Virginia Library. http://www.etext.virginia.edu.

Faust, Albert. *The German Element in the United States: With Special Reference to its Political, Moral, Social, and Educational Influence.* Vol. 2. New York: The Steuben Society of America, 1927.

Fears, Darryl. "After Protests, Backlash Grows." *Washington Post,* May 3, 2006, http://www.washingtonpost.com.

Fears, Darryl, and Krissah Williams. "Boycott Gives Voice to Illegal Workers." *Washington Post,* May 2, 2006, http://www.washingtonpost.com.

Fears, Darryl, and N. C. Aizenman. "Immigrant Groups Split on Boycott." *Washington Post,* April 14, 2006, http://www.washingtonpost.com.

Feldstein, Richard. *Political Correctness: A Response from the Cultural Left.* Minneapolis: University of Minnesota Press, 1997.

Fitzgerald, Keith. *The Face of the Nation: Immigration, the State, and the National Identity.* Stanford: Stanford University Press, 1996.

Fitzgerald, Mark. "Black and White and Red All Over." *Editor & Publisher,* January 1, 2004, www.editorandpublisher.com.

Foraker, Joseph B. *Notes of a Busy Life.* Cincinnati: Stewart & Kidd Company, 1917.

Friedenberg, Robert. *Theodore Roosevelt and the Rhetoric of Militant Decency.* New York: Greenwood Press, 1990.

Friedman, Marilyn, and Jan Narveson. *Political Correctness: For and Against.* Lanham: Rowman & Littlefield Publishers, 1995.

Fritz, Henry E. *The Movement for Indian Assimilation, 1860–1890.* Philadelphia: University of Pennsylvania Press, 1963.

Fromson, Brett D. *Hitting the Jackpot: The Inside Story of the Richest Indian Tribe in History.* New York: Atlantic Monthly Press, 2003.

Fuchs, Lawrence H. *The American Kaleidoscope: Race, Ethnicity, and the Civic Culture.* Hanover: Wesleyan University Press, 1990.

Gardner, Joseph L. *Departing Glory: Theodore Roosevelt as ex-President.* New York: Charles Scribner's Sons, 1973.

Gerstle, Gary. *American Crucible: Race and Nation in the Twentieth Century.* Princeton: Princeton University Press, 2001.

Gleason, Philip. *Speaking of Diversity: Language and Ethnicity in Twentieth-Century America.* Baltimore: Johns Hopkins University Press, 1992.

———. "The Melting Pot: Symbol of Fusion or Confusion?" *American Quarterly* 16 (1964): 20–46.

Goodnight, G. Thomas. "Ronald Reagan and the American Dream: A Study in the Rhetoric Out of Time." Chap. 9 in *The Presidency and Rhetorical Leadership.* Edited by Leroy G. Dorsey. College Station: Texas A&M University Press, 2002.

Gossett, Thomas F. *Race: The History of an Idea in America.* New ed. New York: Oxford University Press, 1997.

Gould, Lewis L. *The Presidency of Theodore Roosevelt.* Lawrence: University Press of Kansas, 1991.

Griffith, William, ed. *The Roosevelt Policy: Speeches, Letters and State Papers, relating to Corporate Wealth and Closely Allied Topics.* 2 vols. New York: Krause Reprint Co., 1971.

Guglielmo, Thomas A. *White on Arrival: Italians, Race, Color, and Power in Chicago, 1890–1945.* Oxford: Oxford University Press, 2003.

Guterl, Matthew P. *The Color of Race in America, 1900–1940.* Cambridge: Harvard University Press, 2001.

Harbaugh, William H. *The Life and Times of Theodore Roosevelt.* New York: Collier Books, 1963.

Harlan, Louis R. *Booker T. Washington: The Wizard of Tuskegee, 1901–1915.* New York: Oxford University Press, 1986.

Harris, Hamil R. "Marchers Decry N.Y. Police Shooting." *Washington Post,* February 16, 1999, Final Edition, B.03.

Hasian Jr., Marouf A. *The Rhetoric of Eugenics in Anglo-American Thought.* Athens: University of Georgia Press, 1996.

Hexamer, Charles J. "Address of Dr. C. J. Hexamer, President of the National German American Alliance, Mass Meeting at the Academy of Music, Philadelphia, PA, Tuesday, November 24, 1914." In *Pamphlets in American History: European War.* Microfilm. Philadelphia: The Alliance/Graf. & Breuninger Print, 1914.

Higham, John. *Strangers in the Land: Patterns of American Nativism, 1860–1925.* New Brunswick: Rutgers University Press, 1988.

Hirschman, Charles. "America's Melting Pot Reconsidered." *Annual Review of Sociology* 9 (1983): 397–423.

Hochschild, Jennifer. *Facing Up to the American Dream: Race, Class, and the Soul of the Nation.* Princeton: Princeton University Press, 1995.

Hofstadter, Richard. *Social Darwinism in American Thought.* New York: Braziller, 1959.

———. *The American Political Tradition and the Men Who Made It.* New York: Vintage Books, 1954.

Hogan, J. Michael. *The Panama Canal in American Politics: Domestic Advocacy and the Evolution of Policy.* Carbondale: Southern Illinois University Press, 1986.

Horsman, Reginald. *Race and Manifest Destiny: The Origins of American Racial Anglo-Saxonism.* Cambridge: Harvard University Press, 1981.

Hoxie, Frederick E. *A Final Promise: The Campaign to Assimilate the Indians, 1880–1920.* Cambridge: Cambridge University Press, 1984.

http://www.cbs.com/primetime/amazing_race5/.

http://www.crocodilehunter.com.

Hughes, Richard T. *Myths America Lives By.* Urbana: University of Illinois Press, 2004.

Huhndorf, Shari M. *Going Native: Indians in the American Cultural Imagination.* Ithaca: Cornell University Press, 2001.

Huntington, Samuel P. *Who Are We? The Challenges to America's National Identity.* New York: Simon & Schuster, 2004.

Ignatiev, Noel. *How the Irish Became White.* New York: Routledge, 1995.

Isikoff, Michael. "With Friends Like These. . . ." *Newsweek,* April 18, 2005, 44.

Ivie, Robert L. "Images of Savagery in American Justifications for War." *Communication Monographs* 47 (1980): 279–294.

———. "The Metaphor of Force in Prowar Discourse: The Case of 1812." *Quarterly Journal of Speech* 68 (1982): 240–253.

Jackson, Helen H. *A Century of Dishonor: A Sketch of the United States Government's Dealings with Some of the Indian Tribes.* Norman: University of Oklahoma Press, 1995.

Jacobson, Matthew F. *Whiteness of a Different Color: European Immigrants and the Alchemy of Race*. Cambridge: Harvard University Press, 1998.

Johannesen, Richard L. "Ronald Reagan's Economic Jeremiad." *Central States Speech Journal* 37 (1986): 79–89.

Johnson, Charles T. *Culture at Twilight: The National German-American Alliance, 1901–1918*. New York: Peter Lang, 1999.

Judis, John B. *The Folly of Empire: What George W. Bush Could Learn from Theodore Roosevelt and Woodrow Wilson*. New York: Scribner, 2004.

Kaplan, Erin A. "What Was Lost in the Crowd." *Los Angeles Times*, May 3, 2006, http://www.latimes.com.

Karst, Kenneth L. *Belonging to America: Equal Citizenship and the Constitution*. New Haven: Yale University Press, 1989.

King, Desmond. *Making Americans: Immigration, Race, and the Origins of the Diverse Democracy*. Cambridge: Harvard University Press, 2000.

King, Joan M., and Elliot McIntire. "The Impact of the Indian Gaming Regulatory Act on Tribes in the U.S." Chap. 3 in *Tourism and Gaming on American Indian Lands*. Edited by Alan A. Lew and George A. Van Otten. New York: Cognizant Communication Corporation, 1998.

Kinsley, Michael. "Mobility vs. Nobility." *Washington Post*, June 5, 2005, http://www.washingtonpost.com/wp-dyn/content/article/2005/06/03/AR2005060301464.html.

Kisch, John, and Edward Mapp. *A Separate Cinema: Fifty Years of Black-Cast Posters*. New York: Noonday Press, 1992.

Kolko, Gabriel. *Main Currents in Modern American History*. New York: Pantheon Books, 1976.

———. *The Triumph of Conservatism: A Reinterpretation of American History, 1900–1916*. New York: Free Press of Glencoe, 1963.

Lawrence, John S., and Robert Jewett. *The Myth of the American Superhero*. Grand Rapids: William B. Eerdmans Publishing Co., 2002.

Lears, T. J. Jackson. *No Place of Grace: Antimodernism and the Transformation of American Culture, 1880–1920*. New York: Pantheon Books, 1981.

Leeming, David. *Myth: A Biography of Belief*. Oxford: Oxford University Press, 2002.

Lévi-Strauss, Claude. *Myth and Meaning: Cracking the Code of Culture*. New York: Schocken Books, 1978.

Lewis, David L. *W. E. B. Du Bois: Biography of a Race*. New York: Henry Holt and Company, 1993.

López, Ian F. Haney. *White by Law: The Legal Construction of Race*. New York: New York University Press, 1996.

Lucas, Stephen E. "'The Man with the Muck Rake': A Reinterpretation." *Quarterly Journal of Speech* 59 (1973): 452–462.

Luebke, Frederick C. *Bonds of Loyalty: German Americans and World War I*. DeKalb: Northern Illinois University Press, 1974.

McBride, Paul. *Culture Clash: Immigrants and Reformers, 1880–1920*. San Francisco: R and E Research Associates, 1975.

Mansfield, Harvey. "The Manliness of Theodore Roosevelt." *New Criterion* 23 (2005): http://www.newcriterion.com/archive/23/mar05/mansfield.htm.

Marina, William, and David T. Beito. "How Teddy Roosevelt Fathered the 'Bush Doctrine.'" *The Independent Institute,* December 9, 2004, http://www.independent. org/newsroom/article.asp?id=1435.

Meier, August. *Negro Thought in America, 1880–1915: Racial Ideologies in the Age of Booker T. Washington.* Ann Arbor: University of Michigan Press, 1964.

Millard, Candace. *The River of Doubt: Theodore Roosevelt's Darkest Journey.* New York: Doubleday, 2005.

Miller, John J. "Keeping Indians Down on the Reservation." *The Week,* February 10, 2006, 12.

Miller, Nathan. *Theodore Roosevelt: A Life.* New York: William Morrow and Co., 1992.

Mohawk, John C. "Indian and Democracy: No One Ever Told Us." Chap. 2 in *Exiled in the Land of the Free: Democracy, Indian Nations, and the U.S. Constitution.* Edited by Oren Lyons, John Mohawk, Vine Deloria Jr., Laurence Hauptman, Howard Berman, Donald Grinde Jr., Curtis Berkey, and Robert Venables. Santa Fe: Clear Light Publishers, 1992.

Morison, Elting E., ed. *The Letters of Theodore Roosevelt.* 8 vols. Cambridge: Harvard University Press, 1951.

Morris, Edmund. *Theodore Rex.* New York: Random House, 2001.

———. *The Rise of Theodore Roosevelt.* New York: The Modern Library, 2001.

Morris, Richard, and Philip Wander. "Native American Rhetoric: Dancing in the Shadows of the Ghost Dance." *Quarterly Journal of Speech* 76 (1990): 164–191.

Mowry, George E. *Theodore Roosevelt and the Progressive Movement.* New York: Hill & Wang, 1946.

Murdoch, David H. *The American West: The Invention of a Myth.* Reno: University of Nevada Press, 2001.

Murphy, John M. "'A Time of Shame and Sorrow': Robert F. Kennedy and the American Jeremiad." *Quarterly Journal of Speech* 76 (1990): 401–414.

Murray, Keat. "Surviving *Survivor:* Reading Mark Burnett's Field Guide and Denaturalizing Social Darwinism as Entertainment." *Journal of American Culture* 24 (2001): 43–54.

Myrdal, Gunnar. *An American Dilemma: The Negro Problem and Modern Democracy.* 2 vols. New Brunswick: Transaction Publishers, 2002.

National Public Radio. "Racial Identity in Multi-Ethnic America." January 6, 2005, pt. 4, http://www.npr.org/templates/story/story.php?storyId=4271005.

Navarrette Jr., Ruben. "No Such Thing as a Good Immigrant." *San Diego Union-Tribune,* March 29, 2006. http://www.signonsandiego.com.

Noble, David W. *The Progressive Mind: 1890–1917.* Minneapolis: Burgess Publishing Co., 1981.

O'Connor, Richard. *The German Americans: An Informal History.* Boston: Little, Brown and Co., 1968.

O'Toole, Patricia. *When Trumpets Call: Theodore Roosevelt after the White House.* New York: Simon & Schuster, 2005.

Petersen, William, Michael Novak, and Philip Gleason. *Concepts of Ethnicity.* Cambridge: Harvard University Press, 1982.

Polakovic, Gary. "Marchers Raise Voice in County." *Los Angeles Times,* May 2, 2006, http://www.latimes.com.

Pringle, Henry F. *Theodore Roosevelt: A Biography.* New York: Harcourt, Brace and Co., 1931.

Putney, Clifford. *Muscular Christianity: Manhood and Sports in Protestant America, 1880–1920.* Cambridge: Harvard University Press, 2001.

Rather, Dan. *The American Dream: Stories from the Heart of Our Nation.* New York: HarperCollins, 2002.

Reid, Ronald F., and James F. Klumpp, eds. *American Rhetorical Discourse.* 3rd ed. Long Grove: Waveland Press, Inc., 2005.

Reynolds, Alan. "Class Struggle?" *Wall Street Journal,* May 18, 2005, http://www.opinionjournal.com/editorial/feature.html?id=110006704.

Rippley, La Vern J. *The German-American.* Boston: Twayne Publishers, 1976.

Ritter, Kurt W. "American Political Rhetoric and the Jeremiad Tradition: Presidential Nomination Acceptance Addresses, 1960–1976." *Central States Speech Journal* 31 (1980): 153–171.

Ritter, Kurt, and David Henry. *Ronald Reagan: The Great Communicator.* New York: Greenwood Press, 1992.

Robertson, James O. *American Myth, American Reality.* New York: Hill & Wang, 1980.

Rodriguez, Gregory. "Why We're the New Irish." *Newsweek,* May 30, 2005, 35.

Roediger, David R. *The Wages of Whiteness: Race and the Making of the American Working Class.* Revised ed. New York: Verso, 2003.

———. *Working toward Whiteness: How America's Immigrants Became White—The Strange Journey from Ellis Island to the Suburbs.* New York: Basic Books, 2005.

Roosevelt, Theodore. *An Autobiography.* New York: Charles Scribner's Sons, 1929.

———. *Fear God and Take Your Own Part.* New York: George H. Doran Company, 1916.

———. *Presidential Addresses and State Papers.* 7 vols. Homeward Bound Edition. New York: The Review of Reviews Company, 1910.

———. *Presidential Address and State Papers of Theodore Roosevelt.* 4 vols. New York: Kraus Reprint Co., 1970.

———. *Ranch Life and the Hunting Trail.* Lincoln: University of Nebraska Press, 1983.

———. *Roosevelt in the* Kansas City Star: *War-Time Editorials by Theodore Roosevelt.* Boston: Houghton Mifflin Company, 1921.

———. *The Rough Riders.* New York: Signet Classics, 1961.

———. *The Theodore Roosevelt Collection.* Speeches TRC-SP-1. Harvard College Library. Houghton Library. Harvard University.

———. *The Works of Theodore Roosevelt.* 20 vols. National ed. New York: Charles Scriber's Sons, 1926.

Rushing, Janice H. "Evolution of 'The New Frontier' in *Alien* and *Aliens:* Patriarchal Co-optation of the Feminine Archetype." *Quarterly Journal of Speech* 75 (1989): 1–24.

———. "Mythic Evolution of 'The New Frontier' in Mass Mediated Rhetoric." *Critical Studies in Mass Communication* 3 (1986): 265–296.

———. "The Rhetoric of the American Western Myth." *Communication Monographs* 50 (1983): 14–32.

Rydell, Robert W. *All the World's a Fair: Visions of Empire at American International Expositions, 1876–1916.* Chicago: University of Chicago Press, 1984.

Salins, Peter D. "Assimilation Nation." *New York Times,* May 11, 2006, http://www.nytimes.com.

Sanchez, Leslie. "Boycott? More Like Bullying." *Los Angeles Times,* May 4, 2006, http://www.latimes.com.

Shaffer, Ralph E., and Walter P. Coombs. "Our Discordant Anthem." *Los Angeles Times,* May 2, 2006, http://www.latimes.com.

Shapiro, Herbert. *White Violence and Black Response: From Reconstruction to Montgomery.* Amherst: University of Massachusetts Press, 1988.

Schlesinger Jr., Arthur M. *The Disuniting of America: Reflections on a Multicultural Society.* New York: Norton & Company, 1998.

Shumsky, Neil L. "Zangwill's 'The Melting Pot': Ethnic Tensions on Stage." *American Quarterly* 27 (1975): 29–41.

Slotkin, Richard. "Dreams and Genocide: The American Myth of Regeneration through Violence." *Journal of Popular Culture* 5 (1971): 38–59.

———. *Gunfighter Nation: The Myth of the Frontier in Twentieth-Century America.* New York: Atheneum, 1992.

———. *Regeneration through Violence: The Mythology of the American Frontier, 1600–1860.* Norman: University of Oklahoma Press, 1973.

———. *The Fatal Environment: The Myth of the Frontier in the Age of Industrialization, 1800–1890.* New York: Atheneum, 1985.

Smith, Henry N. *Virgin Land: The American West as Symbol and Myth.* Cambridge: Harvard University Press, 1978.

Smith, Rogers M. *Civic Ideals: Conflicting Visions of Citizenship in U.S. History.* New Haven: Yale University Press, 1997.

St. John de Crévecoeur, Hector. *Letters From an American Farmer.* New York: Fox, Duffield, 1904. http://xroads.virginia.edu/~HYPER/CREV/letter03.html.

Stedman, Raymond W. *Shadows of the Indian: Stereotypes in American Culture.* Norman: University of Oklahoma Press, 1982.

Streitfeld, David. "A Job Americans Won't Do, Even at $34 an Hour." *Los Angeles Times,* May 18, 2006, http://www.latimes.com.

Stuckey, Mary. *Defining Americans: The Presidency and National Identity.* Lawrence: University Press of Kansas, 2004.

Stuckey, Mary E., and John M. Murphy. "By Any Other Name: Rhetorical Colonialism in North America." *American Indian Culture and Research Journal* 25 (2001): 73–98.

Takaki, Ronald. *A Different Mirror: A History of Multicultural America*. New York: Little, Brown and Company, 1993.

———. *Iron Cages: Race and Culture in Nineteenth-Century America*. Seattle: University of Washington Press, 1979.

Talbot, Winthrop, ed. *Americanization: Principles of Americanism/Essentials of Americanization/Technic of Race-Assimilation*. New York: H. W. Wilson Company, 1917.

Texeira, Erin. "Some Immigrants Reluctant to Boycott." *Dallas Morning News,* April 30, 2006, http://www.dallasnews.com.

Thomas, Evan. "Cracking the Terror Code." *Newsweek,* October 15, 2001, 42–46.

Thompson, Ginger. "Mexico President Urges U.S. to Act Soon on Migrants." *New York Times,* September 16, 2001, www.nytimes.com.

Tichenor, Daniel J. *Dividing Lines: The Politics of Immigration Control in America*. Princeton: Princeton University Press, 2002.

Tocqueville, Alexis de. *Democracy in America*. http://xroads.virginia.edu/~HYPER/DETOC/toc_indx.html.

Tolzmann, Don H. *The German-American Experience*. New York: Humanity Books, 2000.

Trachtenberg, Alan. *The Incorporation of America: Culture and Society in the Gilded Age*. New York: Hill & Wang, 1982.

Tulis, Jeffrey K. *The Rhetorical Presidency*. Princeton: Princeton University Press, 1987.

Turner, Frederick Jackson. "The Significance of the Frontier in American History." http://xroads.virginia.edu/~HYPER/TURNER/.

U.S. Census Bureau. "Historical Census Statistics on Population Totals By Race, 1790 to 1990, and By Hispanic Origin, United States—Race and Hispanic Origin: 1790 to 1990." http://www.census.gov/population/documentation/twps0056/tab01.pdf.

U.S. Commission on Human Rights. "A Historical Context for Evaluation." Chap. 1 in *Native Americans and Public Policy*. Edited by Fremont J. Lyden and Lyman H. Legters. Pittsburgh: University of Pittsburgh Press, 1992.

U.S. Congress. *Congressional Record-Senate*. 59th Cong., 2nd sess., December 19, 1906. Vol. 41, pt. 2.

———. *Congressional Record-Senate*. 60th Cong., 2nd sess., December 14, 1908. Vol. 43., pt. 2.

Veciana-Suarez, Ana. "Anthem Debate Hits Sour Notes." *Houston Chronicle,* May 10, 2006, http://www.chron.com.

Vogel, Virgil J. *This Country Was Ours: A Documentary History of the American Indian*. New York: Harper & Row, 1972.

Wade, Gene, Linda Hoyman, Jimmy Hercheck, Alan Hoon, and Tim Kenyon. "WHAT

DO YOU THINK?" *Atlanta Journal-Constitution,* December 8, 2004, Wednesday Home Edition, Gwinnett News Section. JJ4.

Wandel, Joseph. *The German Dimension of American History.* Chicago: Nelson-Hall, 1979.

Washington Post. "Race a Factor in Diallo Case, Clinton Says." March 5, 2000, http://www.washingtonpost.com.

Watanabe, Teresa, and Joe Mathews. "Unions Helped to Organize 'Day Without Immigrants.'" *Los Angeles Times,* May 3, 2006, http://www.latimes.com.

Watson Jr., Richard L. *The Development of National Power: The United States, 1900–1919.* Boston: Houghton Mifflin Company, 1976.

Watts, Sarah. *Rough Rider in the White House: Theodore Roosevelt and the Politics of Desire.* Chicago: University of Chicago Press, 2003.

Weaver, John D. *The Brownsville Raid.* College Station: Texas A&M University Press, 1992.

The Week. "A GOP Split over Immigration." April 7, 2006, 2.

———. "Bennett: The Meaning of a Racial Comment." October 14, 2005, 21.

———. "How They See Us: Blind to the Contributions of Mexicans." May 27, 2005, 14.

Whitcomb, Dan. "LA Immigration Activists Mobilize for Washington." *Washington Post,* May 9, 2006, http://www.washingtonpost.com.

White, James B. *When Words Lose Their Meaning: Constitutions and Reconstitutions of Language, Character, and Community.* Chicago: University of Chicago Press, 1984.

Wides-Munoz, Laura. "'Star-Spangled Banner' in Spanish Draws Protest." *Houston Chronicle,* April 28, 2006, http://www.chron.com.

Williamson, Joel. *A Rage for Order: Black/White Relations in the American South since Emancipation.* New York: Oxford University Press, 1986.

———. *The Crucible of Race: Black-White Relations in the American South since Emancipation.* New York: Oxford University Press, 1984.

Wittke, Carl. *German-Americans and the World War: With Special Emphasis on Ohio's German-Language Press.* Ohio: The Ohio State Archaeological and Historical Society, 1936.

———. *The German-Language Press in America.* Lexington: University of Kentucky Press, 1957.

Wood, Gordon S. *The Creation of the American Republic, 1776–1787.* New York: W. W. Norton & Company, 1969.

———. *The Radicalism of the American Revolution.* New York: Vintage Books, 1993.

Zakaria, Fareed. "To Become an American." *Newsweek,* April 10, 2006, 39.

Zangwill, Israel. *The Melting Pot: A Drama in Four Acts.* In *The Works of Israel Zangwill: The Melting Pot/Plaster Saints.* Vol. 12. Edition De Luxe. New York: AMS Press, 1969.